International Conference on Information and Knowledge Engineering (IKE'19)

Las Vegas, Nevada, USA
29 July - 1 August 2019

Editors:

Hamid R. Arabnia
Ray Hashemi
Fernando G. Tinetti
Cheng-Ying Yang
Ashu M.G. Solo

ISBN: 978-1-7138-5244-5

Printed from e-media with permission by:

Curran Associates, Inc.
57 Morehouse Lane
Red Hook, NY 12571

Printed by Curran Associates, Inc. (2022)

For permission requests, please contact CSREA Press
at the address below.

CSREA Press
ATTN: Hamid R. Arabnia
1060 Long Creek Drive
Watkinsville, GA 30677
USA

Phone: (706) 542-3480

hra@cs.uga.edu

Additional copies of this publication are available from:

Curran Associates, Inc.
57 Morehouse Lane
Red Hook, NY 12571 USA
Phone: 845-758-0400
Fax: 845-758-2633
Email: curran@proceedings.com
Web: www.proceedings.com

Contents

SESSION: DATA MINING, TEXT MINING, PATTERN MINING, MACHINE LEARNING, PREDICTION METHODS, AND APPLICATIONS:

SESSION: DATA SCIENCE AND APPLICATIONS + MIS AND DATABASES

SESSION: INFORMATION AND KNOWLEDGE EXTRACTION AND ENGINEERING + APPLICATIONS

SESSION: INTERNATIONAL WORKSHOP ON ELECTRONICS & INFORMATION TECHNOLOGY; IWEIT-2019

SESSION: POSTER PAPERS AND EXTENDED ABSTRACTS

SESSION: LATE BREAKING PAPERS: INFORMATION EXTRACTION AND APPLICATIONS

PROCEEDINGS OF THE 2019 INTERNATIONAL CONFERENCE ON INFORMATION & KNOWLEDGE ENGINEERING

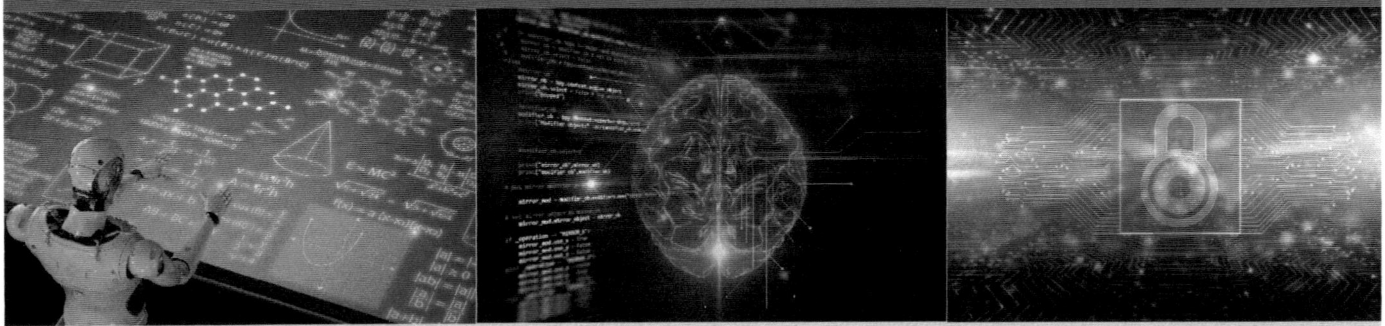

IKE'19

Editors

Hamid R. Arabnia

Ray Hashemi, Fernando G. Tinetti

Cheng-Ying Yang

Associate Editor

Ashu M. G. Solo

Publication of the 2019 World Congress in Computer Science, Computer Engineering, & Applied Computing (CSCE'19)
July 29 - August 01, 2019 | Las Vegas, Nevada, USA
https://americancse.org/events/csce2019

Foreword

It gives us great pleasure to introduce this collection of papers to be presented at the 2019 International Conference on Information & Knowledge Engineering (IKE'19), July 29 – August 1, 2019, at Luxor Hotel (a property of MGM Resorts International), Las Vegas, USA. The preliminary edition of this book (available in July 2019 for distribution on site at the conference) includes only a small subset of the accepted research articles. The final edition (available in August 2019) will include all accepted research articles. This is due to deadline extension requests received from most authors who wished to continue enhancing the write-up of their papers (by incorporating the referees' suggestions). The final edition of the proceedings will be made available at https://americancse.org/events/csce2019/proceedings .

An important mission of the World Congress in Computer Science, Computer Engineering, and Applied Computing, CSCE (a federated congress to which this conference is affiliated with) includes *"Providing a unique platform for a diverse community of constituents composed of scholars, researchers, developers, educators, and practitioners. The Congress makes concerted effort to reach out to participants affiliated with diverse entities (such as: universities, institutions, corporations, government agencies, and research centers/labs) from all over the world. The congress also attempts to connect participants from institutions that have* ***teaching*** *as their main mission with those who are affiliated with institutions that have* ***research*** *as their main mission. The congress uses a quota system to achieve its institution and geography diversity objectives."* By any definition of diversity, this congress is among the most diverse scientific meeting in USA. We are proud to report that this federated congress has authors and participants from 57 different nations representing variety of personal and scientific experiences that arise from differences in culture and values. As can be seen (see below), the program committee of this conference as well as the program committee of all other tracks of the federated congress are as diverse as its authors and participants.

The program committee would like to thank all those who submitted papers for consideration. About 58% of the submissions were from outside the United States. Each submitted paper was peer-reviewed by two experts in the field for originality, significance, clarity, impact, and soundness. In cases of contradictory recommendations, a member of the conference program committee was charged to make the final decision; often, this involved seeking help from additional referees. In addition, papers whose authors included a member of the conference program committee were evaluated using the double-blinded review process. One exception to the above evaluation process was for papers that were submitted directly to chairs/organizers of pre-approved sessions/workshops; in these cases, the chairs/organizers were responsible for the evaluation of such submissions. The overall paper acceptance rate for regular papers was 24%; 18% of the remaining papers were accepted as poster papers (at the time of this writing, we had not yet received the acceptance rate for a couple of individual tracks.)

We are very grateful to the many colleagues who offered their services in organizing the conference. In particular, we would like to thank the members of Program Committee of IKE'19, members of the congress Steering Committee, and members of the committees of federated congress tracks that have topics within the scope of IKE. Many individuals listed below, will be requested after the conference to provide their expertise and services for selecting papers for publication (extended versions) in journal special issues as well as for publication in a set of research books (to be prepared for publishers including: Springer, Elsevier, BMC journals, and others).

- *Prof. Emeritus Nizar Al-Holou (Congress Steering Committee); Professor and Chair, Electrical and Computer Engineering Department; Vice Chair, IEEE/SEM-Computer Chapter; University of Detroit Mercy, Detroit, Michigan, USA*
- *Prof. Hamid R. Arabnia (Congress Steering Committee); Graduate Program Director (PhD, MS, MAMS); The University of Georgia, USA; Editor-in-Chief, Journal of Supercomputing (Springer); Fellow, Center of Excellence in Terrorism, Resilience, Intelligence & Organized Crime Research (CENTRIC).*
- *Dr. Travis Atkison; Director, Digital Forensics and Control Systems Security Lab, Department of Computer Science, College of Engineering, The University of Alabama, Tuscaloosa, Alabama, USA*
- *Dr. Arianna D'Ulizia; Institute of Research on Population and Social Policies, National Research Council of Italy (IRPPS), Rome, Italy*

- *Prof. Emeritus Kevin Daimi (Congress Steering Committee); Director, Computer Science and Software Engineering Programs, Department of Mathematics, Computer Science and Software Engineering, University of Detroit Mercy, Detroit, Michigan, USA*
- *Prof. Zhangisina Gulnur Davletzhanovna; Vice-rector of the Science, Central-Asian University, Kazakhstan, Almaty, Republic of Kazakhstan; Vice President of International Academy of Informatization, Kazskhstan, Almaty, Republic of Kazakhstan*
- *Prof. Leonidas Deligiannidis (Congress Steering Committee); Department of Computer Information Systems, Wentworth Institute of Technology, Boston, Massachusetts, USA; Visiting Professor, MIT, USA*
- *Prof. Mary Mehrnoosh Eshaghian-Wilner (Congress Steering Committee); Professor of Engineering Practice, University of Southern California, California, USA; Adjunct Professor, Electrical Engineering, University of California Los Angeles, Los Angeles (UCLA), California, USA*
- *Prof. Ray Hashemi (Session Chair, IKE); Professor of Computer Science and Information Technology, Armstrong Atlantic State University, Savannah, Georgia, USA*
- *Prof. Dr. Abdeldjalil Khelassi; Computer Science Department, Abou beker Belkaid University of Tlemcen, Algeria; Editor-in-Chief, Medical Technologies Journal; Associate Editor, Electronic Physician Journal (EPJ) - Pub Med Central*
- *Prof. Louie Lolong Lacatan; Chairperson, Computer Engineerig Department, College of Engineering, Adamson University, Manila, Philippines; Senior Member, International Association of Computer Science and Information Technology (IACSIT), Singapore; Member, International Association of Online Engineering (IAOE), Austria*
- *Dr. Andrew Marsh (Congress Steering Committee); CEO, HoIP Telecom Ltd (Healthcare over Internet Protocol), UK; Secretary General of World Academy of BioMedical Sciences and Technologies (WABT) a UNESCO NGO, The United Nations*
- *Dr. Somya D. Mohanty; Department of CS, University of North Carolina - Greensboro, North Carolina, USA*
- *Dr. Ali Mostafaeipour; Industrial Engineering Department, Yazd University, Yazd, Iran*
- *Dr. Houssem Eddine Nouri; Informatics Applied in Management, Institut Superieur de Gestion de Tunis, University of Tunis, Tunisia*
- *Prof. Dr., Eng. Robert Ehimen Okonigene (Congress Steering Committee); Department of Electrical & Electronics Engineering, Faculty of Engineering and Technology, Ambrose Alli University, Nigeria*
- *Prof. James J. (Jong Hyuk) Park (Congress Steering Committee); Department of Computer Science and Engineering (DCSE), SeoulTech, Korea; President, FTRA, EiC, HCIS Springer, JoC, IJITCC; Head of DCSE, SeoulTech, Korea*
- *Dr. Prantosh K. Paul; Department of CIS, Raiganj University, Raiganj, West Bengal, India*
- *Dr. Xuewei Qi; Research Faculty & PI, Center for Environmental Research and Technology, University of California, Riverside, California, USA*
- *Dr. Akash Singh (Congress Steering Committee); IBM Corporation, Sacramento, California, USA; Chartered Scientist, Science Council, UK; Fellow, British Computer Society; Member, Senior IEEE, AACR, AAAS, and AAAI; IBM Corporation, USA*
- *Chiranjibi Sitaula; Head, Department of Computer Science and IT, Ambition College, Kathmandu, Nepal*
- *Ashu M. G. Solo (Publicity), Fellow of British Computer Society, Principal/R&D Engineer, Maverick Technologies America Inc.*
- *Prof. Fernando G. Tinetti (Congress Steering Committee); School of CS, Universidad Nacional de La Plata, La Plata, Argentina; also at Comision Investigaciones Cientificas de la Prov. de Bs. As., Argentina*
- *Varun Vohra; Certified Information Security Manager (CISM); Certified Information Systems Auditor (CISA); Associate Director (IT Audit), Merck, New Jersey, USA*
- *Dr. Haoxiang Harry Wang (CSCE); Cornell University, Ithaca, New York, USA; Founder and Director, GoPerception Laboratory, New York, USA*
- *Prof. Shiuh-Jeng Wang (Congress Steering Committee); Director of Information Cryptology and Construction Laboratory (ICCL) and Director of Chinese Cryptology and Information Security Association (CCISA); Department of Information Management, Central Police University, Taoyuan, Taiwan; Guest Ed., IEEE Journal on Selected Areas in Communications.*
- *Prof. Layne T. Watson (Congress Steering Committee); Fellow of IEEE; Fellow of The National Institute of Aerospace; Professor of Computer Science, Mathematics, and Aerospace and Ocean Engineering, Virginia Polytechnic Institute & State University, Blacksburg, Virginia, USA*
- *Prof. Jane You (Congress Steering Committee); Associate Head, Department of Computing, The Hong Kong Polytechnic University, Kowloon, Hong Kong*

We would like to extend our appreciation to the referees, the members of the program committees of individual sessions, tracks, and workshops; their names do not appear in this document; they are listed on the web sites of individual tracks.

As Sponsors-at-large, partners, and/or organizers each of the followings (separated by semicolons) provided help for at least one track of the Congress: Computer Science Research, Education, and Applications Press (CSREA); US Chapter of World Academy of Science; American Council on Science & Education & Federated Research Council (http://www.americancse.org/). In addition, a number of university faculty members and their staff (names appear on the cover of the set of proceedings), several publishers of computer science and computer engineering books and journals, chapters and/or task forces of computer science associations/organizations from 3 regions, and developers of high-performance machines and systems provided significant help in organizing the conference as well as providing some resources. We are grateful to them all.

We express our gratitude to keynote, invited, and individual conference/tracks and tutorial speakers - the list of speakers appears on the conference web site. We would also like to thank the followings: UCMSS (Universal Conference Management Systems & Support, California, USA) for managing all aspects of the conference; Dr. Tim Field of APC for coordinating and managing the printing of the proceedings; and the staff of Luxor Hotel (Convention department) at Las Vegas for the professional service they provided. Last but not least, we would like to thank the Co-Editors of IKE'19: Prof. Hamid R. Arabnia, Prof. Ray Hashemi, Prof. Fernando G. Tinetti, Prof. Cheng-Ying Yang, and Associate Editor, Ashu M. G. Solo.

We present the proceedings of IKE'19.

Steering Committee, 2019
http://americancse.org/

SESSION

DATA MINING, TEXT MINING, PATTERN MINING, MACHINE LEARNING, PREDICTION METHODS, AND APPLICATIONS:

Chair(s)

TBA

Improved Hiding of Business Sensitive Patterns Using Candidate-less Approach

Nishtha Agrawal and Durga Toshniwal
Department of Computer Science and Engineering, Indian Institute of Technology - Roorkee, Roorkee, Uttarakhand, India
nishtha.agarwal.28@gmail.com, durgatoshniwal@gmail.com

Abstract – *A large amount of transactional data is getting generated in present times due to traditional retail sales and e-commerce activities. Organizations may want to analyze their data collaboratively to find out trends and patterns from the global transactional data. This can lead to improved business strategies in general. However, this may also lead to revelation of some business sensitive patterns. So, to avoid this, privacy preserving frequent pattern mining is performed. Most of the existing techniques for privacy preserved frequent pattern mining rely on Apriori Principle for candidate frequent pattern generation. This is very time inefficient due to large itemset space involved. In the present work an improved technique for sensitive frequent pattern hiding has been proposed which leverages candidate-less frequent pattern mining. Extensive experiments have been performed on benchmark datasets and the results are very promising.*

Keywords: Privacy Preserving Data Mining, Frequent Pattern Mining, Sensitive Patterns, FP-Growth

1 Introduction

Frequent Pattern Mining is an important technique used by organizations in order to discover the information or useful patterns from large amount of transactional dataset for more profitable business. Along with pattern generation, there are chances that some private information also gets mined. This information is sensitive to the organization and cannot be shared with the third party. Therefore, there comes a challenge to mine the useful patterns in such a way that the sensitive/confidential information remains hidden.

Threats caused by data mining techniques can be of two types: (i) Data itself contains some private information which might be a threat and is known as *data privacy*. (ii) Some confidential information can be extracted from the knowledge mined from datasets which is known as *knowledge privacy*. Hence, Privacy Preservation Data Mining comes into the picture here. It is the field in which the confidential or sensitive information has to be hidden from the transactional datasets before releasing it to the third party for preserving its privacy.

Sensitive pattern/information comprises of some confidential or inside information of the individual or the organization such as company policies, security/identity number of an individual, bank transactions details etc., which are not meant to be shared with third party. Sensitive pattern hiding method sanitizes or hides the sensitive patterns from the knowledge extracted from the results, obtained after applying any rule or pattern mining algorithm on the transactional dataset.

As a result of collaborative data mining, privacy is quite essential. Collaborative data mining is used when two or more organizations join hands for sharing their data with each other to mine interesting patterns from other's data which may benefit the organizations. Data shared by an organization may contain sensitive pattern and if it gets misused by another party then there can be a great loss to the organization that has shared the data.

Sensitive pattern hiding methodologies are fairly divided into three primary categories: Exact approaches, border-based approaches and heuristics-based approaches. Exact and border-based approaches are complicated to implement and really time-consuming, therefore these approaches do not suit for large datasets, because as the dataset size increases the computational time also increases exponentially. On the other-hand, Heuristics-based approaches are simpler in implementation as compared to the other two methods. Heuristics-based approaches are efficient and fast as compared to the exact and border-based approaches as they take decision based on local optima. These techniques provide good approximate solution; therefore, these techniques are of major importance for data scientists.

This paper is organized in six sections. In the first section, a brief introduction about frequent pattern mining, privacy issues in pattern mining and why they should be preserved has been given. In the second section, we discuss about some state of art algorithms and the work that has been done in the same area. The third section discusses the basic terminologies going to be used. In fourth section the proposed approach will be discussed. In the fifth section, we will discuss the experiments performed and the corresponding results obtained. The sixth section will conclude the paper.

2 Related Work

Oliveira & Zaïane [4] provided a two scans solution, in which multiple itemsets get hidden in two scans of dataset only. First scan is used to create an index file, which was used to efficiently retrieve sensitive transaction for any sensitive itemset. Second scan is used to sanitize the data such that non-sensitive patterns are affected minimally. They introduced three algorithms: MaxFIA- Maximum Frequent Itemset Algorithm, MinFIA- Minimum Frequent Itemset Algorithm and IGA-Itemset Grouping Algorithm. MinFIA works as follows, first the sensitive transactions are identified; sensitive transactions are those transactions which contain any sensitive patterns. After that they are sorted according to the degree of conflict. Then from each transaction (depending upon the threshold), victim item is removed, victim item for each sensitive pattern is chosen as the one with maximum support. MaxFIA works in the same manner but instead of choosing the victim item as the one with maximum support, it is chosen as the one with minimum support. IGA works as follows: Common items in sensitive itemsets are grouped together and then victim item is the one which is having minimum support and is shared by all the itemsets of that group.

Verykios [6] proposed a confidence-based approach. According to this approach the sensitive patterns are hidden by decreasing the confidence of an association rule because this causes lesser side effects to the sanitized dataset. But this approach does not any guarantee hiding of all the sensitive patterns.

Cheng [7] introduced another heuristic approach. According to this approach, in first step for each transaction store a count of non-sensitive patterns it supports. In second step for each sensitive pattern store count of transaction it supports. Then transaction identified in the second step are sorted according to their count calculated in first step. Then to the threshold, it removes the victim itemset from the transactions. Victim item is the item in sensitive pattern which has maximum support.

Oliveira & Zaïane [5] proposed one another approach, called SWA (Sliding Window Algorithm). In this approach, first all the transactions that does not support any sensitive patterns are copied to sanitize database and then for each sensitive pattern we select the victim item with the maximum support, and then based on threshold it is removed from group of remaining transaction.

A. Amiri [8] proposed three approaches: Aggregate approach: in this approach the transaction which is removed from the dataset is chosen in the following way- the transaction which supports a smaller number of non-sensitive frequent patterns but a large number of sensitive patterns. Disaggregate approach: In this approach the item is removed from the transaction rather than whole transaction. The victim item is chosen in the same manner as in above method the transaction is chosen. Hybrid approach: in this approach, the transaction is chosen according to the aggregate approach and the item to be removed is chosen according to the disaggregate method.

The techniques used for hiding sensitive patterns in all the above discussed techniques are based on candidate-based pattern generation which takes a lot of computational time, therefore using candidate less approach for the same can drastically reduce the time.

3 Basic Terminologies

In market basket analysis, a transactional Dataset D consists of many transactions and each transaction has a unique identifier TID. Each transaction T_i contains a set of items with it. From this transactional data organizations try to find the interesting patterns i.e. Frequent Patterns. Frequent Pattern mining is a data mining technique to find frequently occurring rules or itemsets in a database. A predefined minimum support threshold is given based upon which the frequent patterns are identified. This technique discovers all those patterns in which the support values of the itemsets are greater than the given minimum threshold denoted by σ which is provided by the organization itself.

Table I shows an example of general transactional dataset.

TABLE I. DATASET D

Transaction ID	Items
T1	ABC
T2	ABCD
T3	BCE
T4	ACDE
T5	DE
T6	AB

3.1 Frequent Pattern Generation

There are two types of pattern generation techniques: a). Candidate based pattern generation (Apriori) and b). Candidate Less pattern generation (FP-Growth). The Apriori algorithm is based on the fact that if a subset S appears k times, any other subset S' that contains S will appear k times or less. So, if S doesn't pass the minimum support threshold, neither does S'. There is no need to calculate S', it is discarded a priori.

FP-Growth is an improvement of Apriori designed to eliminate some of the heavy bottlenecks in Apriori. F P-Growth [3] simplifies all the problems present in Apriori by using a structure called an FP-Tree. In an FP-Tree each node represents an item and its current count, and each branch represents a different association. In FP-Growth Algorithm, each transaction is sorted in descending order of the support of each item present in it and then each item is added to tree.

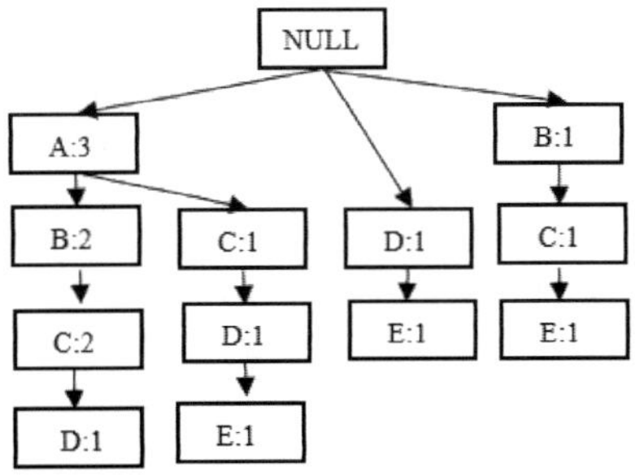

Figure 1. FP-Tree for Dataset D as shown in Table I.

For the dataset shown in Table 1, FP-Tree in figure 1 is built. Let minimum threshold i.e. σ be 2. Therefore, the frequent patterns generated from this *D* are: {ABC, ACD, CE and DE}.

3.2 Sanitization Process

The sanitizing process acts by removing a small number of items from some transactions containing sensitive itemsets such that it is no more frequent and hence preserves the privacy.

For the dataset given in Table 1, let the sensitive pattern be {AC} and σ be 2. Frequent patterns generated by this data are {ABC, ACD, CE and DE}. Out of which {ABC and ACD} contains the sensitive pattern {AC}, therefore there is requirement for preservation of privacy because patterns ABC and ACD are revealing the sensitive information. After applying the sanitization algorithm database changes from D to D′ as shown in table II.

TABLE II. DATASET D'

Transaction ID	Items
T1	BC
T2	ABCD
T3	BCE
T4	CDE
T5	DE
T6	AB

3.3 Metrics used for performance evaluation

Consider *S* as set of sensitive itemset, *OF* as set of frequent itemset in original database and *SF* as set of frequent itemset in sanitized database. Hiding Ratio is used to check the efficiency of the proposed algorithm. More is the Hiding ratio more the proposed algorithm is efficient. Equation 1 denotes the Hiding ratio:

$$Hiding\ Ratio = SF/OF \tag{1}$$

Misses Cost denotes the number of legitimate non-sensitive patterns which got hidden after the sanitization process. Lesser is the Misses cost more the proposed algorithm is efficient. Equation 2 denotes the Misses cost:

$$Misses\ Cost = OF\text{-}SF \tag{2}$$

There are two other parameters upon which the quality of solution depends *Hiding Failure* and *Pseudo Patterns.* Hiding Failure represents the set of sensitive itemsets which are still present in the updated database after the sanitization process has been applied to the original database. Pseudo Patterns represents those patterns that were not frequent in the original database but after the application of sanitization process, they are converted to the frequent itemsets in the sanitized database.

4 Proposed Solution

A FP-Tree based Sensitive Patterns Removal (FSR) approach has been proposed. The proposed approach uses the advantage of candidate-less pattern generation technique. i.e. FP Tree. Candidate-less pattern generation technique is used here because of two major reasons: first, it generates less itemset search space and second, it is very time efficient as compared to candidate-based pattern generation techniques.

In figure 2, the framework of Data sanitization process is described. Original dataset and sensitive patterns are provided as input to the algorithm. Sanitized dataset is obtained as the output of the algorithm. Data Sanitization using FP-Tree is the block where the proposed approach works.

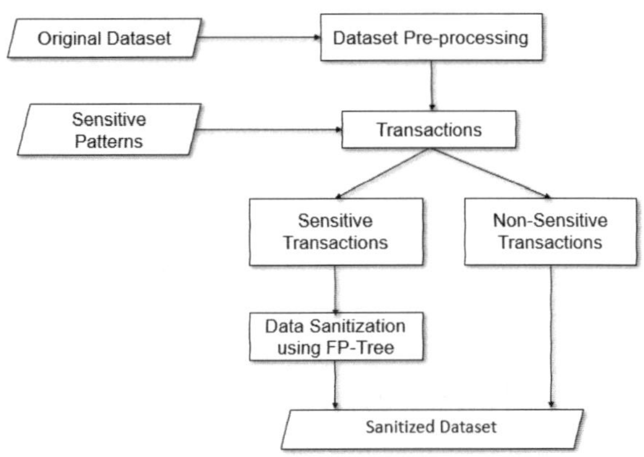

Figure 2. Framework for Dataset Sanitization.

4.1 FP-Tree based Sensitive Pattern Removal Approach (FSR)

In this approach, the transactions are divided into different sets: Sensitive Transactions and Non-Sensitive Transactions. Sensitive transactions are those transactions which contains any sensitive pattern as whole or any subset in itself. Two sets are created one with sensitive transactions which is gone for further sanitization process and the non-sensitive transactions are simply added to sanitized dataset. In the same scan the support of each item of transactional data is also calculated.

For each sensitive itemset, victim item is chosen. Victim item is the item that has to be removed from the sensitive transaction so that we can hide the sensitive pattern. Victim item for any sensitive itemset is chosen as the item with minimum support among all items of that itemset. After this we build FP-Tree [3] and while adding the sensitive transaction to the tree, we mask the victim item such that its count in the tree does not exceed minimum support, so that it does not become frequent and will not be present in any frequent pattern. After that we can call FP-Growth algorithm [3] to obtain the frequent itemset data is also calculated.

In this algorithm, a dictionary Tree Count (TC) is maintained which stores the item and their count in the tree. FP- Tree is built in the following way: First, create FP-Tree root node as 'NULL' data is also calculated. For each sensitive transaction, sort the itemset in decreasing order of their item support and add this itemset to the tree in following manner: for each item in the itemset check whether it is a victim item or not, if not then simply add it to the tree, increase the count of that node by one and update TC by one. But if it is a victim item, then check its count in TC, if it is one lower than threshold i.e. σ-1, then simply add that to tree, increase the count of that node by one and also update TC by one but if it becomes equal to σ -1, then do not increase its count in node because by increasing the count, the item will become frequent and will appear in the frequent patterns. Therefore, do not increase its count and the item becomes infrequent and does not appear in frequent patterns. After building the FP-Tree, decompose it into the sanitized dataset and also FP-Growth algorithm can be applied to obtain the frequent itemset.

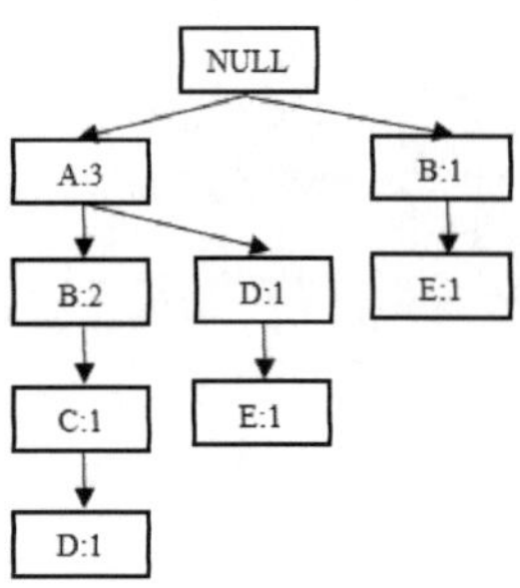

Figure 3. M odified FP-Tree for Dataset shown in Table II

Consider the dataset used in Table 1. Suppose the minimum threshold used is 2 and the sensitive pattern be {AC}. By applying the above algorithm, the modified FP-Tree is built, as shown in figure 3.

The proposed approach will have 0% hiding failure, as all the sensitive patterns gets hidden i.e., no frequent pattern will be generated from the sanitized data that would contain any sensitive pattern. And also, zero pseudo patterns will be generated i.e., patterns which were not present in original dataset will also not be generated from the sanitized dataset. But there will be some misses cost i.e., some legitimate non-sensitive patterns may get hidden after the sanitization process.

5 Experiments and Discussions

Different experiments were conducted in order to test the hiding ratio and the misses cost of data transformed by Sensitive pattern hiding algorithm. All the experiments were conducted on the Windows workstation. In order to analyse the performance of proposed approaches, comparison of proposed approaches with existing approaches has been done.

5.1 Implementation

The performance of the proposed sensitive pattern hiding algorithm (FSR) has been analyzed by comparing it with the earlier approaches (MinFIA [4] - current state of art algorithm). Three types of cases have been generated by comparing the results of proposed approach with that of current state-of-art algorithm MinFIA:

1. Comparing hiding ratio and misses cost, keeping the number of transactions and minimum support threshold constant but varying the number of sensitive patterns.

2. Comparing hiding ratio and misses cost, keeping the number of sensitive patterns and minimum support threshold constant but varying the number of transactions.

3. Comparing running time keeping the number of sensitive patterns and minimum support threshold constant but varying the number of transactions.

5.2 Dataset Used

The dataset used for the experiments was synthetically generated by the IBM Quest synthetic data generator [2], which is a standard tool for this type of dataset. Different configurations of datasets are generated for the analysis purpose varying in number of transactions and number of sensitive patterns as shown in Table III.

TABLE III. CONFIGURATION OF DATASETS USED, HERE N = NUMBER OF SENSITIVE PATTERNS, FOR EACH DATASET, DIFFERENT NUMBER OF SENSITIVE PATTERNS HAVE BEEN USED

Number of Transactions	Number of items	Min. Support	Number of sensitive patterns (N)
10,000	100	10%	{3, 10, 20, 50, 100}
20,000	100	10%	{3, 10, 20, 50, 100}
30,000	200	10%	{3, 10, 20, 50, 100}
50,000	200	10%	{10, 20, 50, 100, 200}
1,00,000	200	10%	{10, 20, 50, 100, 200}

Case 1: Comparing hiding ratio of proposed FSR algorithm with MinFIA.

Hiding Ratio (described in equation 1) has been calculated for different set of datasets. For each configuration, the results have been calculated by taking the average hiding ratio of different datasets with same configuration. Tests were performed on a synthetic dataset with 10000 number of transactions having an average length of 10 items per transaction, the total number of items was 50 and number of sensitive itemsets were n= {3,10,20,50,100}. The minimum support threshold was set to 10% of total number of transactions.

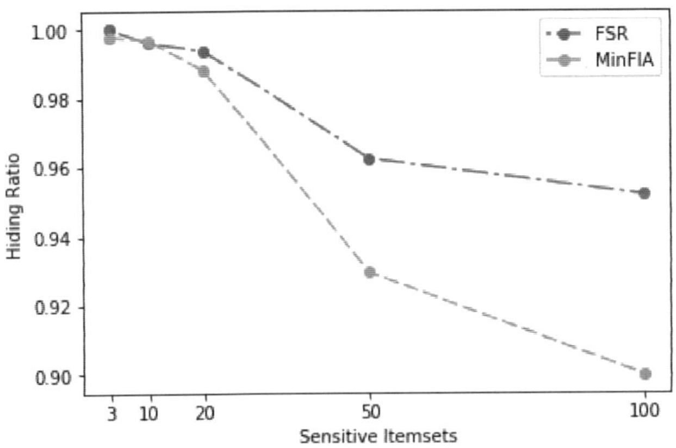

Figure 4. Hiding Ratio of Proposed FSR vs MinFIA on Synthetic Dataset with 10,000 transactions.

In Figure 4, the number of transactions are 10,000 and Figure 5, the number of transactions are 1,00,000, it has been observed that the hiding ratio of proposed FSR is compared with the current state-of-art MinFIA algorithm. In both of figures, by increasing the number of sensitive itemsets hiding ratio is decreasing but the accuracy of the results is higher in comparison to MinFIA.

In figure 6, it has been observed that different datasets with different number of transactions n, i.e, n = 10,000, 20,000, 50,000, and 100,000 and for each dataset different number of sensitive patterns have been used. For each of the configuration hidig ratio has been calculated and as we can see foe each individual 'n' i.e. dataset with 10,000 transaction hiding ratio decreases and also when the number of transaction increases, hiding ratio again is decreasing but as comapred to earlier aprroaches i.e. MinFIA hiding ratio is better in proposed FSR(as shown in figure 4 and figure 5).

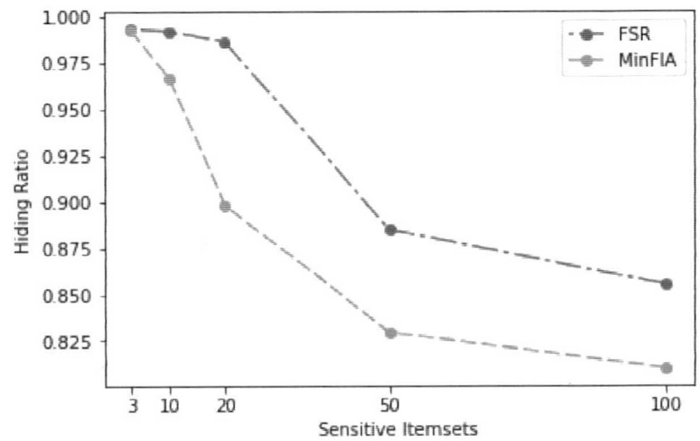

Figure 5. Hiding Ratio of Proposed FSR vs MinFIA on Synthetic Dataset with 100,000 transactions.

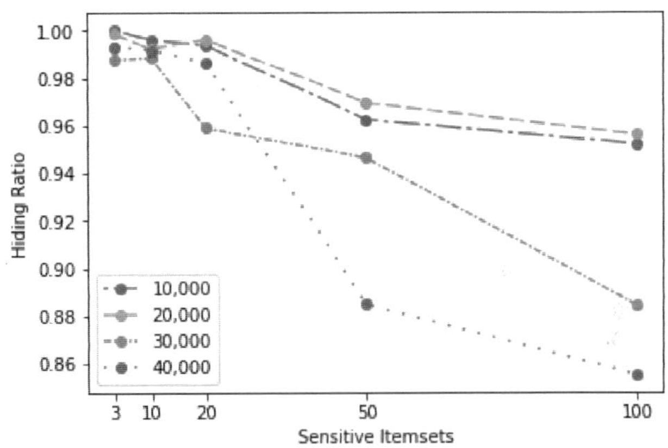

Figure 6. Hiding Ratio of Proposed FSR for different number of transactions(n), n = 10,000; 20,000; 50,000 and 100,000 transactions.

Case 2: Comparing misses cost of proposed FSR algorithm with MinFIA.

Misses Cost (described in equation 2) has been calculated for different set of datasets. For each configuration, the results have been calculated by taking the average hiding ratio of different datasets with same configuration. Tests were performed on a synthetic dataset with 10000 number of transactions having an average length of 10 items per transaction, the total number of items was 50 and number of sensitive itemsets were n= {3,10,20,50,100}. The minimum threshold was set to 10% of total number of transactions.

In Figure 7 , number of transactions are 10,000 and Figure 8 , number of transactions are 1,00,000, it has been observed that the misses cost of proposed FSR is compared with the current state-of-art MinFIA algorithm. In both of figures, by increasing the number of sensitive itemsets misses cost is inceasing but the accuracy of the results is higher in comparison to MinFIA.

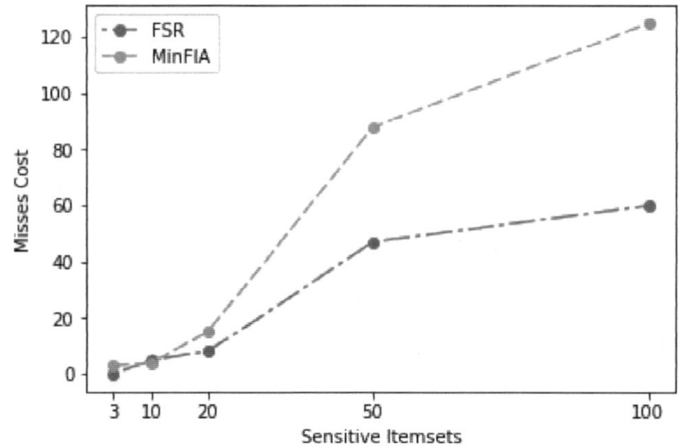

Figure 7. Misses Cost of Proposed FSR vs MinFIA on Synthetic Dataset with 10,000 transactions.

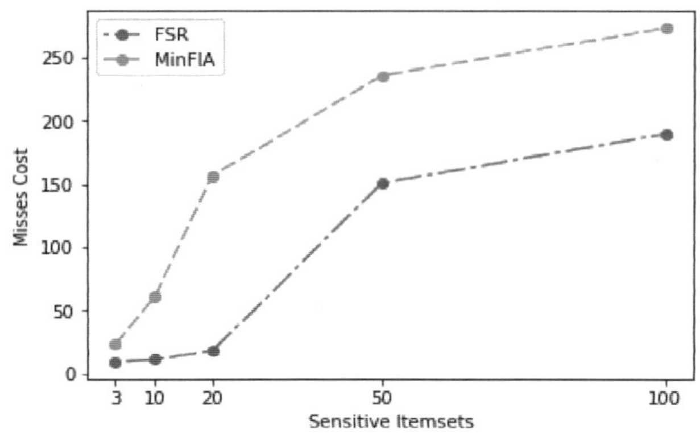

Figure 8. Misses Cost of Proposed FSR vs MinFIA on Synthetic Dataset with 100,000 transactions.

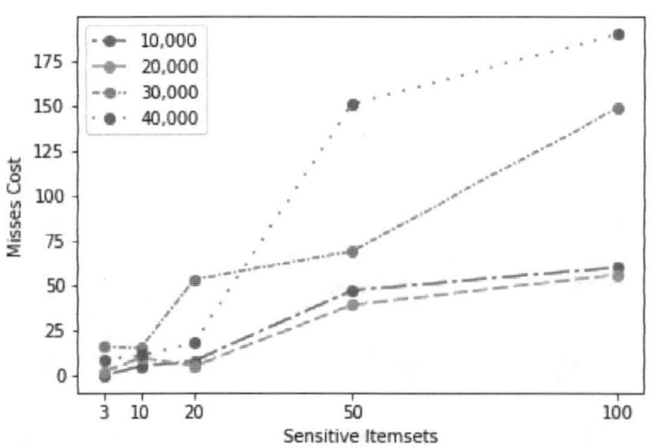

Figure 9. Misses Cost of Proposed FSR for different number of transactions(n), n = 10,000; 20,000; 50,000 and 100,000 transactions.

In figure 9, it has been observed that different datasets with different number of transactions n, i.e, n = 10,000, 20,000, 50,000, and 100,000 and for each dataset different number of sensitive patterns have been used. For each of the configuration misses cost has been calculated and as we can see for each individual 'n' i.e. dataset with 10,000 transaction misses cost decreases and also when the number of transaction increases, misses cost again is decreasing but as comapred to earlier aprroaches i.e. MinFIA hiding ratio is better in proposed FSR(as shown in figure 7 and figure 8).

Case 3: Comparing running time of proposed FSR with MinFIA keeping the number of sensitive patterns constant and minimum support threshold constant but varying the number of transactions.

In figure 10, it can be observed that time taken by proposed FSR is very less as comaprde to earlier MinFIA approach. Runtime of proposed FSR totally outcast MinFIA this is only because of the reason that FSR uses candidate-less patterns generation technique and therefore its item search space is very less as compared to MinFIA which is based on candidate generation pattern technique.

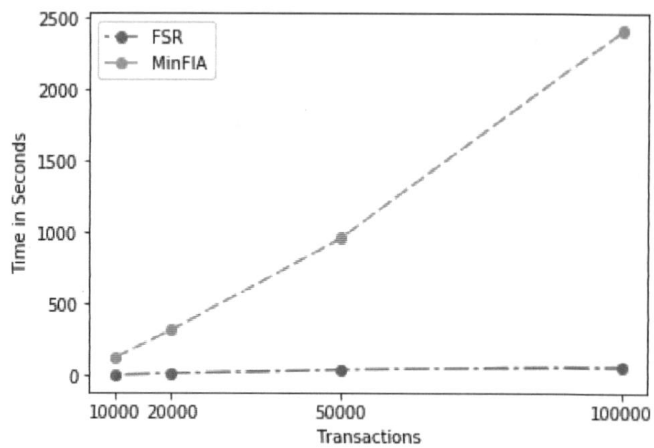

Figure 10. Running time Comparison of Proposed FSR vs MinFIA on Synthetic Dataset for different number of transactions.

In all the above graphs, we can see that the proposed FSR has better hiding ratio and less misses cost. This is because the effect of hiding victim items from k-itemset in sensitive transaction in Apriori algorithm affects or propogates to next level i.e., k+1-itemsets, which leads to more misses cost, but in FP-tree it does not affect all other frequent patterns. Each branch of the tree is independent of the other, therfore, change in any transaction or any branch of the tree does not affect others and hence the search space remains small, the misses cost is lesser and hiding ratio is higher with this approach as comapred to previous approaches.

6 Conclusions

The proposed approach makes use of candidate-less pattern generation technique for hiding the sensitive patterns which reduces the time as compared to earlier approaches and it also provides better accuracy of results as it has more hiding ratio and lesser misses cost as compared to current state-of-the-art algorithm MinFIA. The proposed approach provides better results because candidate-less pattern generation technique has lesser itemset search space as compared to candidate-based pattern generation schemes. Also, these techniques are very time efficient. Therefore, proposed approach is suitable for large datasets because it takes very less time as compared to earlier approaches. Extensive experiments have been performed on the benchmark datasets and results obtained are very promising. Along with this proposed solution, some modifications are also under progress i.e., parallelization of the proposed approach.

7 References

[1] Agrawal R., Srikant R. Privacy Preserving Data Mining. ACM SIGMOD, *International Conference on Management of data*, 2000.

[2] R. Agrawal, A. Arning, T. Bollinger, M. Mehta, J. Shafer, R. Srikant, "The Quest data mining system", *Proceedings of the 2nd International Conference on Knowledge Discovery in Databases and Data Mining*, Aug. 1996.

[3] J. Han, J. Pei, and Y. Yin. Mining frequent patterns without candidate generation. In W. Chen, J. Naughton, and P. A. Bernstein, editors, 2000 *ACM SIGMOD Intl. Conference on Management of Data*. ACM Press, May 2000.

[4] Stanley R. M. Oliveira, Osmar R. Zaıane2, Privacy Preserving Frequent Itemset Mining, *IEEE international conference on Privacy, security and data mining*, pp. 43-54, 2002.

[5] S. R. M. Oliveira, O. R. Zaïane. Protecting sensitive knowledge by data sanitization. *3rd IEEE International Conference on Data Mining (ICDM)*, pages 211– 218, 2003.

[6] V. S. Verykios, A. Elmagarmid, E. Bertino, Y. Saygin, E Dasseni, Association Rule Hiding, *IEEE Transactions on Knowledge and Data Engineering*, vol. 16, no. 4, pp. 434-447, 2004.

[7] G. Lee, C. Cheng, A. L.P Chen, Hiding Sensitive Patterns in Association Rules Mining, *28thAnnual International Computer Software and Applications Conference*, pp. 424-429, 2004.

[8] A. Amiri. Dare to share: Protecting sensitive knowledge with data sanitization. Decision Support Systems, 43(1):181–191, 2007.

[9] Charu C. Agarwal, Philip S. Yu. Privacy-Preserving Data Mining Models and Algorithms. Springer ISBN: 978-0-387-70991-8 (Print) 978-0-38770992-5 (Online)

[10] C. Lin, T. Hong, K. Yang, S. Wang, The GA-based algorithms for optimizing hiding sensitive itemsets through transaction deletion, Applied Intelligence, vol. 42, no. 2, pp. 201-230, 2015.

[11] P. Cheng, J. F. Roddick, S. C. Chu, C.W. Lin, Privacy preservation through a greedy, distortion-based rule-hiding method, Applied Intelligence, vol. 44, no. 2, pp. 295-306, 201.

Hierarchical Topic Clustering over Large Collections of Documents

Jingwen Wang **Jie Wang**
jingwen_wang@student.uml.edu wang@cs.uml.edu
Department of Computer Science, University of Massachusetts, Lowell, MA 01854, USA

Abstract— *Grouping a collection of documents according to similar topics enables readers to quickly obtain information conveyed by these documents. It also plays a critical role in the automatic generation of an overview report. For a large corpus containing thousands of (long) documents, however, each topic may further contain multiple subtopics. This motivates us to study hierarchical topic clustering over a very large collection of documents. We present HTC, a hierarchical topic clustering scheme, to discover efficiently topic relationships over a large corpus of documents with high accuracy based on a one-level topic clustering algorithm. In particular, we implement HTC based on LDA and Spectral Clustering and evaluate their performance over two large datasets. We show that HTC with LDA over summaries of documents with length ratio (summary length over document length) equal to 0.3 achieves a good trade-off between accuracy and time complexity.*

Keywords: text mining, hierarchical topic clustering, document clustering, latent dirichlet allocation, spectral clustering

1. Introduction

Partitioning a collection of text documents into multiple clusters according to similar topics is an important task in information engineering. It enables readers, for example, to quickly obtain information conveyed by these documents. Documents in the same cluster are under the same topic, while those in different clusters are under different topics. Such a partition also plays a critical role in the automatic generation of an overview report of them.

For a large corpus of documents of moderate and large sizes, however, each topic associated with a cluster may likely contain multiple subtopics. By "a large corpus" we mean a collection of several thousands of documents. Such a collection may be, for example, the output from a depository of news articles under a search of certain keywords.

Fig. 1 depicts an example of a hierarchical topic subtree over a BBC-News dataset. In this subtree, each node is a topic together with six keywords of the highest ranks associated with the underlying topic. The root is the highest ranked keywords of the corpus. The root has two subtopics: *Entertainment* and *Technology*. When words such as "series", "comedy", and "episode" under topic *Entertainment* are discovered for a substantial number of times, a subtopic of *TV Series* may be detected. Thus, hierarchically structured topic clusters provide topic-subtopic relationships contained in a corpus of documents.

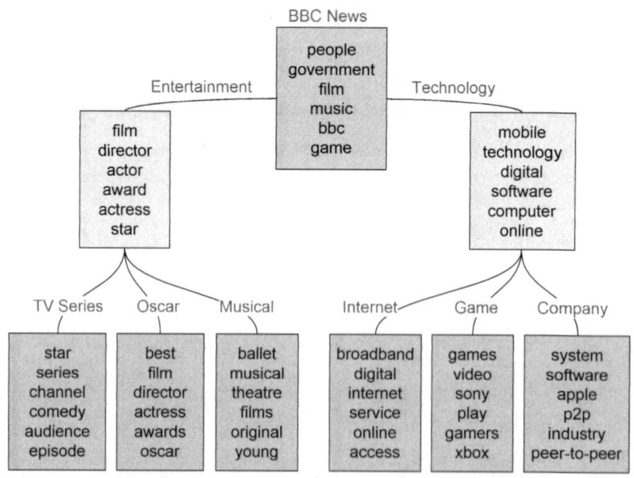

Fig. 1: A subtree of hierarchical topic clusters learned from a BBC News dataset.

We study how to obtain a hierarchical topic clustering over a large collection of documents. Our major contributions are listed below:

1) We devise HTC, a hierarchical topic clustering scheme for a large corpus of text documents based on a one-level topic clustering algorithm.
2) We implement HTC based on, respectively, Latent Dirichlet Allocation (LDA) [1] and Spectral Clustering (SC) [2] with and without generating summaries of documents. We denote by HLDA-D and HSC-D the implementations using LDA and SC, respectively, on the original documents. Likewise, HLDA-S and HSC-S denote the implementations of HTC using LDA and SC, respectively, on summaries of the original documents. We evaluate their performance over two large datasets. We show that HLDA-D offers the best clustering accuracy but also incurs the worst time complexity. We also show that the accuracy by SC-D is much worse than HLDA-S while both SC-D and SC-S are more efficient.
We show that HLDA-S on summaries with length equal to 30% of the original document length offers a good trade-off between clustering accuracy and time complexity.

The rest of this paper is organized as follows: We describe in Section 2 related work on document clustering, and in Section 3, we present HTC. In Section 4 we evaluate HLDA and HSC and conclude the paper in Section 5.

2. Related Work

Document clustering partitions documents into topic clusters with each cluster associated with a distinct topic. Methods on clustering textual data include partitional clustering, probabilistic topic modeling, and hierarchical clustering.

2.1 Partitional clustering

Partitional clustering algorithms such as K-means clustering [3], PAM [4], and CLARA [5], divide a set of documents into several disjoint clusters. Spectral Clustering (SC) [2] is a deterministic and faster partitional clustering algorithm. Like K-means and other common topic clustering algorithms, SC needs to preset the number of topics k. It uses eigenvalues of an affinity matrix to reduce dimensions. It then uses K-means to generate clusters over eigenvectors corresponding to the k smallest eigenvalues.

2.2 Probabilistic topic modeling

Probabilistic topic modeling methods include naive Bayes [6], probabilistic Latent Semantic Indexing (pLSI) [7], and LDA [1]. Among these methods, the naive Bayes model is too limited to model a large collection of documents and the pLSI topic model is overfitting prone. LDA is one of the most popular topic clustering methods. It treats each document in a corpus as a mixture of latent topics that generate words for each hidden topic with certain probabilities. As a probabilistic algorithm, LDA may produce somewhat different clusters on the same corpus of documents on a different run. It also needs to predetermine the number of topics. Other clustering methods, such as PW-LDA [8], Dirichlet multinomial mixture [9], and neural network models [10] are targeted at corpora of short documents such as abstracts of scientific papers.

2.3 Hierarchical clustering

A hierarchical clustering algorithm (HCA) groups documents into a set of clusters with a dendrogram structure. Early hierarchical clustering algorithms follow the following two approaches: *agglomerative clustering* (bottom-up) and *divisive clustering* (top-down). Fung et al [11] devised an HCA named FIHC that uses the keywords in documents to build a hierarchical topic tree. However, FIHC ignores the semantic meanings of words, leading to low clustering accuracy. More recently, Lee et al [12] presented a new HCA named OCF using common words and ontology to capture semantics. OCFI is capable of mining the meanings behind the words in documents and building a hierarchical topic tree. Zhao et al [13] devised constrained agglomerative algorithms that combine partitional clustering algorithms and agglomerative clustering algorithms to generate hierarchical clusters. Vikram and Dasgupta [14] introduced an interactive Bayesian hierarchical clustering algorithm that incorporates user interaction into hierarchical clustering. Charikar et al [15] devised two hierarchical clustering algorithms based on semi-definite programming.

3. Hierarchical Topic Clustering

Throughout this paper, we will use n, m, and K to denote, respectively, the number of documents, the number of words in the corpus, and the number of clusters. We will use D to denote a collection of n documents to be clustered, $C_1, C_2, \ldots, C_K$ the K clusters, and $n_1, n_2, \ldots, n_K$ the sizes of the corresponding clusters. HTC consists of the following two modules:

a) Preprocessing Module (PM): The PM module performs two tasks: (1) filtering and (2) single document summarization (SDS). In particular, PM first determines what language an input document is written in, eliminates irrelevant text (such as URLs) and duplicates, and extracts, for each document, the title and subtitles (if any), publication time, publication source, and the main content. PM then generates, for each document, a summary of an appropriate length. Extracting summaries is necessary for speeding up the clustering process and deemed sufficient for generating good hierarchical topic clusters. Each sentence in a document is also ranked by an SDS algorithm (e.g., using [16]) with a numeric score that can be used to compute a score of the original document.

b) Hierarchical Clustering Module (HCM): HTC is devised to capture topic structures. In particular, the HCM module partitions a corpus of documents into multilevel topic clusters and ranks the topic clusters according to their salience.

HCM is a multiple-level topic clustering algorithm and we describe a two-level topic clustering in this paper (three or more level topic clustering is similar). The input can be either the original documents or the summaries generated in the PM module. Note that clustering on the original documents and clustering on the summaries of the documents may result in different partitions (see Section 4). For simplicity, we sometimes use "documents" to mean both.

The pseudocode of HCM is given in Algorithm 1. In particular, HCM first partitions documents into K clusters, denoted by $\mathcal{C} = \{C_1, C_2, \ldots, C_K\}$, using a one-level clustering method such as LDA or SC. These are referred to as the top-level clusters. For each top-level cluster C_i, if $|C_i| > N$, where $|C_i|$ denotes the number of documents contained in C_i and N is a preset number (for example, $N = 100$), then HCM further partitions C_i into K_i sub-clusters as the second-level clusters, where $K_i = 1 + \lfloor |C_i|/N \rfloor$. If

Algorithm 1 HCM

1: $D \leftarrow$ a large corpus
2: $K \leftarrow$ the number of top-level clusters
3: $N \leftarrow$ a preset number
4: **procedure** TOP-LEVEL-CLUSTERS($\mathcal{C}1$)
5: $\quad \mathcal{C}1 \leftarrow$ generate K clusters on D
6: $Queue \leftarrow \mathcal{C}1$
7: **procedure** SECOND-LEVEL-CLUSTERS($\mathcal{C}2$)
8: $\quad$ **for each** cluster $C_i \in Queue$ **do**
9: $\quad\quad D_i \leftarrow$ documents in cluster C_i
10: $\quad\quad$ **if** $|D_i| > N$ **then**
11: $\quad\quad\quad K_i \leftarrow 1 + \lfloor |C_i|/N \rfloor$
12: $\quad\quad\quad \mathcal{C}' \leftarrow$ generate K_i clusters on D_i
13: $\quad\quad\quad$ **if** $|\mathcal{C}'|$ is 1 **then**
14: $\quad\quad\quad\quad \mathcal{C}' \leftarrow$ split D_i into K_i clusters sorted
15: $\quad\quad\quad\quad$ in descending order of document scores
16: $\quad\quad\quad$ merge $\mathcal{C}'$ to $\mathcal{C}2$
17: **if** $\exists |D_i| > N$ for $C_i \in \mathcal{C}2$ **then**
18: $\quad Queue \leftarrow \mathcal{C}2$
19: $\quad$ **go to** 7

in this new clustering, all but one cluster are empty, then this means that documents in C_i cannot be further divided into sub-topics. In this case, we sort the documents in C_i in descending order of document scores and split C_i evenly into K_i clusters (except the last one). The score of a document d, denoted by $r(d)$, is the summation of the scores of its sentences normalized by the number of its sentences, namely,

$$r(d) = \sum_{s \in d} \frac{r(s)}{|d|},$$

where s is a sentence, $r(s)$ is the score of s, and $|d|$ is the number of sentences in d.

For a second-level cluster C_{ij} of C_i, if $|C_{ij}| > N$, we may further create a third-level sub-clustering by clustering C_{ij} or simply splits C_{ij} evenly into $K_{ij} = 1 + \lfloor |C_{ij}|/N \rfloor$ clusters (except the last one), still at the second-level. Note that at each level of clustering, there may be empty clusters.

Assume that cluster C consists of n documents, denoted by d_i, where $i = 1, 2, \ldots, n$. Let p_i denote the probability that d_i belongs to cluster C. (Such a probability can be easily computed using LDA.) We define the score of cluster C using the following empirical formula:

$$S_C = \frac{1}{n^2} \sum_{j=i}^{n} 2^{p_i}.$$

4. Evaluations

We describe datasets, selections of algorithms, and parameter setting for evaluating HTC.

4.1 Datasets

We use the following two types of corpora for our evaluations:

1) A large corpus of classified documents. In particular, we use the **BBC News** dataset [17] of 2,225 classified articles stemmed from BBC News in the years of 2004 and 2005 labeled in business, entertainment, politics, sports, and technology.
2) A large corpus of unclassified documents. In particular, we use the **Factiva-Marx** dataset[1] of 5,300 unclassified articles extracted from Factiva under the search of keyword "Marxism" (provided by a public sentiment analysis project).

The statistics of these two datasets are shown in Table 1.

4.2 Selections of algorithms for evaluating HTC

In the PM module, we use the state-of-the-art Semantic WordRank SDS algorithm [16] to extract a summary for each document with the length of a summary equal to 30% of the length of the original document. This algorithm is an unsupervised extractive summarization algorithm, and runs fast. In the HCM module, we use LDA [1] and SC [2], respectively, as the underlying single-level topic clustering algorithm and compare their performance.

a) Semantic WordRank: The Semantic WordRank algorithm extracts a summary over a weighted word graph with semantic and co-occurrence edges. It solves the summarization problem as a multi-objective optimization problem:

$$\text{maximize} \sum_{i=1}^{n_d} s_i x_i \text{ and } F_d,$$
$$\text{subject to} \sum_{i=1}^{n_d} l_i x_i < L,$$
$$x_i \in \{0, 1\},$$

where d is a document consisting of n_d sentences, l_i and s_i denote the length and score of a sentence, L is the summary length, and F_d is the diversity coverage measure over d.

b) LDA: Assume that a corpus D of document summaries consists of K topics with a multinomial distribution over the set of words W. The probability of a document summary d_s of d over topic $k \in K$ is $\theta_d = \{\theta_{k|d_s)}\}$. The priors over $\Theta = \{\theta_1, \ldots, \theta_D\}$ are Dirichlet with parameter α. For each word i in document summary d_s, draw a topic index $z_i \in \{1, ..., K\}$ with probability θ_d. The probability of observed word w_i over selected topic is $\phi_{i|k}$. Finally, a Dirichlet prior with parameter β is placed on the topic $\phi_{i|k}$. That is, $\theta_{k|d_s} \sim \mathcal{D}[\alpha]$, $\phi_{w|k} \sim \mathcal{D}[\beta]$, $z_i \sim \theta_{k|d_s}$, and $w_i \sim \phi_{w|z_i}$.

[1] The Factiva-Marx dataset is available at http://www.ndorg.net.

Table 1: Statistics of the BBC-News and Factiva-Marx datasets

Dataset	# of docs	avg. # of docs / task	# of tokens	avg. # of tokens / doc	vocabulary size
Factiva-Marx	$5,300$	$5,300$	1.09×10^7	$2,100$	3.89×10^5
BBC News	$2,225$	$2,200$	8.5×10^5	380	6.56×10^4

The joint distribution of a set of m words $\boldsymbol{w}$, a set of K topics $\boldsymbol{z}$, a topic mixture Θ, and a word mixture Φ over given parameters α and β is given by

$$p(\boldsymbol{w}, \boldsymbol{z}, \Theta, \Phi|\alpha, \beta) = p(\Theta|\alpha)p(\boldsymbol{z}|\Theta)p(\boldsymbol{w}|\boldsymbol{z}, \beta)$$
$$= p(\Theta|\alpha)\prod_{i=1}^{m} p(z_i)p(w_i|z_i, \beta).$$

We use Gibbs sampling [18] to compute the posterior distribution over latent topics $\boldsymbol{z}$, topic mixture θ, and topics ϕ for Bayesian inference.

c) SC: SC constructs an undirected graph $G = (V, E)$, where each node $v_i \in V$ is a document summary, $i = 1, 2, \ldots, |D|$. Edges are connected between nodes using ε-neighborhood. Let $\boldsymbol{W}$ and $\boldsymbol{D}$ denote the corresponding weight matrix and diagonal matrix for G. Construct a Laplacian matrix $\boldsymbol{L} = \boldsymbol{D} - \boldsymbol{W}$. Fig. 2 is an example of undirected graph and its corresponding matrices. Let $\boldsymbol{u}_1, \boldsymbol{u}_2, \ldots, \boldsymbol{u}_k$ be the first k eigenvectors of Laplacian matrix $\boldsymbol{L}$. Let $\boldsymbol{U}$ be the matrix with $\boldsymbol{u}_1, \boldsymbol{u}_2, \ldots, \boldsymbol{u}_k$ being the columns. Let $\boldsymbol{y}_1, \boldsymbol{y}_2, \ldots, \boldsymbol{y}_n$ be the row vectors of $\boldsymbol{U}$. SC clusters these rows using the K-means algorithm into clusters $C_1, C_2, \ldots, C_k$. The output clusters is $A_1, A_2, \ldots, A_k$ where $A_i = \{j|y_j \in C_i\}$.

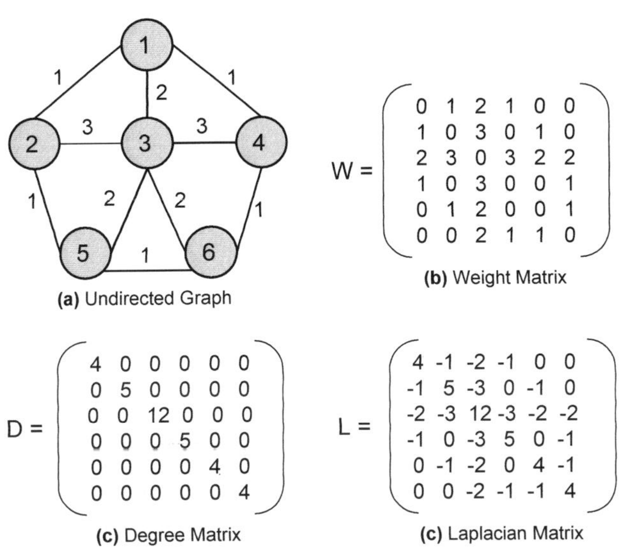

Fig. 2: An example of an undirected graph and its corresponding matrices

Our evaluations in Section 4.5 show that LDA outperforms SC on accuracy, while SC achieves better time efficiency.

4.3 Parameter settings

Let HLDA denote HTC using LDA and HSC denote HTC using SC. For each dataset, we evaluate the performance of HTC over original documents and HTC over document summaries. Moreover, we compare the efficiency and accuracy of HLDA and HSC. The parameter settings are listed below:

In the SDS submodule, we use Semantic WordRank algorithm to extract a summary with length ratio $\lambda = 0.3$ of each document. Note that the summary length ratio $\lambda \in (0, 1]$ is evaluated in Section 4.5 (see Fig. 4).

In the HCM module, to achieve a higher topic clustering accuracy, we set the number K of the top-level clusters to $K = 9$ as suggested in Section 4.6.1 (see Fig. 5). To generate the second-level clusters, we set $N = 200$ to determine if a sub-cluster should be further divided (recall that if a cluster contains more than N documents, a further division will be performed). The number of second-level clusters is automatically determined using the method mentioned in Section 3.

4.4 CSD F1-scores

We define a new CSD F1 measure based on symmetric differences of clusters. Recall that D is a corpus of text documents. Suppose that we have a gold-standard partition of D into K clusters $C = \{C_1, C_2, \ldots, C_K\}$, and a clustering algorithm generates K clusters, denoted by $A = \{A_1, A_2, \ldots, A_K\}$. We rearrange these clusters so that the symmetric difference of C_i and A_i, denoted by $\Delta(C_i, A_i)$, is minimum, where $\Delta(X, Y) = |X \cup Y| - |X \cap Y|$. That is, for all $1 \leq i \leq K$, $\Delta(C_i, A_i) = \min_{1 \leq j \leq k} \Delta(C_i, A_j)$. We define CSD F1-score for A and C as follows, where CSD stands for **C**lusters **S**ymmetric **D**ifference:

$$F_1(A, C) = \frac{1}{K}\sum_{i=1}^{K} F_1(A_i, C_i),$$
$$F_1(A_i, C_i) = \frac{2P(A_i, C_i)R(A_i, C_i)}{P(A_i, C_i) + R(A_i, C_i)},$$

with P and R being precision and recall defined by

$$P(A_i, C_i) = \frac{|A_i \cap C_i|}{|A_i|},$$
$$R(A_i, C_i) = \frac{|A_i \cap C_i|}{|C_i|}.$$

Note that $F1(A_i, C_i)$ can also be written as

$$F_1(A_i, C_i) = \frac{2|A_i \cap C_i|}{|A_i| + |C_i|}.$$

Clearly, $F1(A, C) \leq 1$ and $F1(A, C) = 1$ is the best possible.

4.5 Topic clustering evaluations

The performance of HTC relies on the quality of the underlying one-level topic clustering. We evaluate performance on both accuracy and efficiency. To obtain high accuracy while reducing time complexity, we would want to find the optimal summary length ratio λ over the length of the original document.

We use the labeled BBC-News dataset as a gold standard. Fig. 3 and Fig. 4 show the running time and CSD F1 scores for LDA and SC with summary length ratio $\lambda \in (0, 1]$. Overall, LDA clustering outperforms SC clustering in terms of CSD F1 scores, while SC is faster than LDA. The CSD F1 scores for both LDA and SC tend to increase when λ gradually increases, and the highest CSD F1 score is achieved when $\lambda = 1$. We note that the CSD F1 scores of LDA clustering increases dramatically when λ increases to 0.3. We can therefore cluster D based on summaries of this length ratio, with the benefit of reducing time complexity.

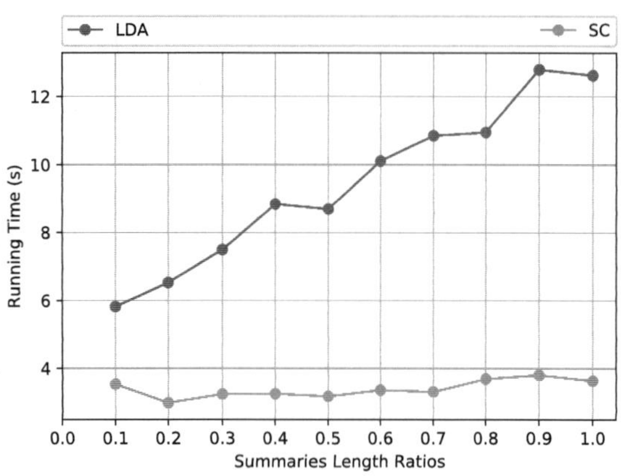

Fig. 3: Running Time of LDA and SC on BBC News.

4.6 HTC Evaluations

Let HLDA-D, HSC-D, HLDA-S, and HSC-S denote, respectively, the algorithms of applying HLDA and HSC on original documents and 0.3-summaries generated by Semantic WordRank [16].

4.6.1 Comparisons of clustering quality

Fig. 5 compares the CSD F1-scores of HLDA-D, HLDA-S, HSC-D, and HSC-S over the labeled corpus of BBC News articles for various summary length ratios. We can see that

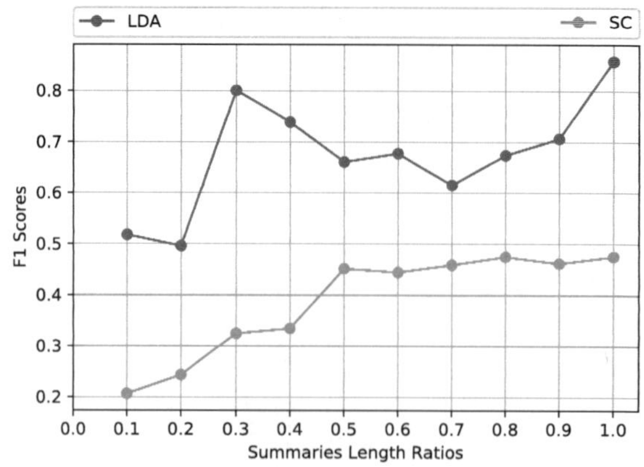

Fig. 4: CSD F1-scores of LDA and SC on BBC News.

HLDA-D is better than HLDA-S, which is better than HSC-D, and HSC-D is better than HSC-S. All of these algorithms have the highest CSD F1-scores when the number of top-level topics $K = 9$. This is in line with a common experience that the number of top-level sections should be around 10.

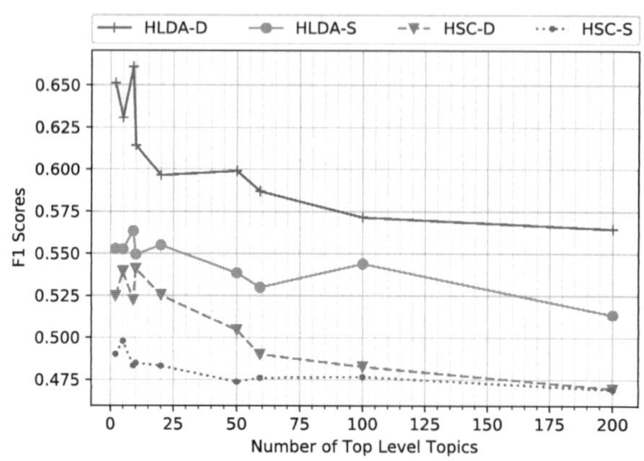

Fig. 5: CSD F1-scores on the labeled BBC News corpus

We observe that HLDA-D offers the best accuracy. Thus, we will use the clustering generated by HLDA-D as the baseline for comparing CSD F1 scores of HLDA-S, SC-D, and SC-S. Fig. 6a and Fig. 6b depict the comparison results of HLDA-S, HSC-D, and HSC-S agains HLDA-D on the two corpora of BBC News and Factiva-Marx.

4.6.2 Comparisons of clustering running time

We strive to achieve both accuracy and efficiency on multi-level topic clustering. For example, in the commissioned project of public sentiment analysis we mentioned earlier, where the Factiva-Marx dataset was provided to us for testing, we were asked to generate a 20-page overview report over several thousands of documents in a few hours. Topic clustering is a critical component of our overview

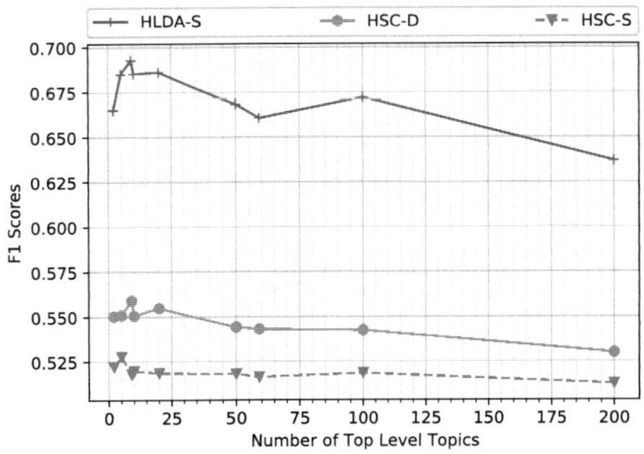

(a) CSD F1-scores on BBC News

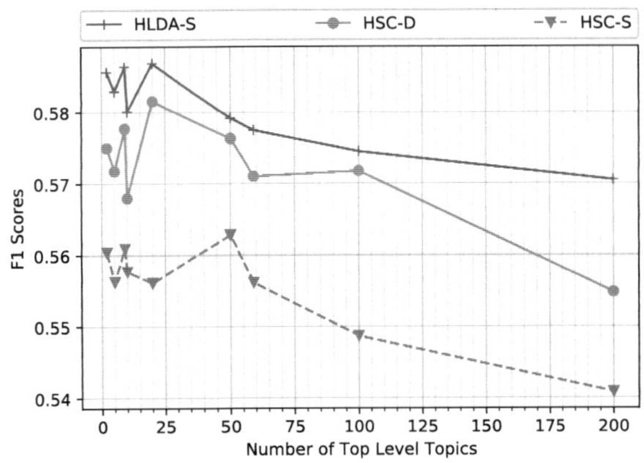

(b) CSD F1-scores on Factiva-Marx

Fig. 6: CSD F1-scores against HLDA-D

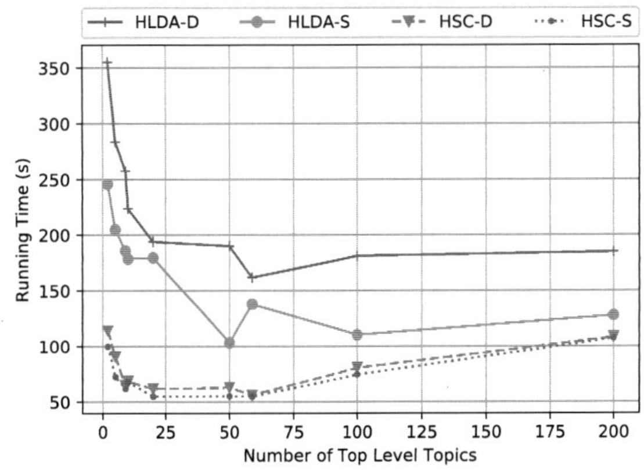

(a) Running time of clustering the BBC News corpus

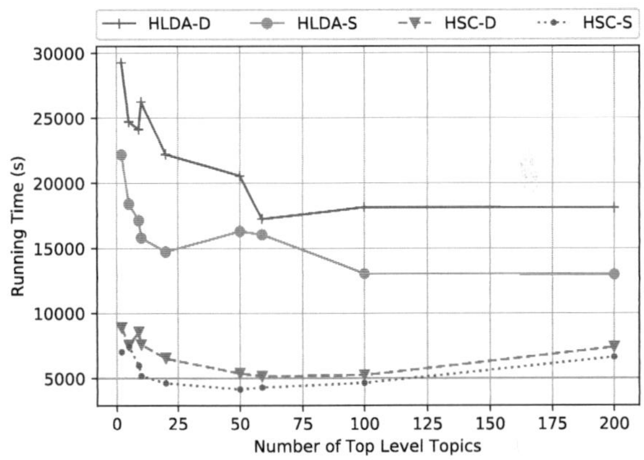

(b) Running time of clustering the Factiva-Marx corpus

Fig. 7: Comparisons of clustering running time

report generation algorithm [19], and hence we would need to carry out topic clustering as fast as we can.

Fig. 7 depicts the running time of clustering the BBC News and Factiva-Marx datasets by different algorithms into two-level clusters on a Dell desktop with a quad-core Intel Xeon 2.67 GHz processor and 12 GB RAM. We choose the top-level clusters numbers $K \in [2, 200]$.

We can see that for both corpora, HSC-S is the fastest, HSC-D is slightly slower, HLDA-D is the slowest, and HLDA-S is in between HLDA-D and HSC-D. This result is expected. We also see that when the number of top-level clusters is small, the two-level clustering running time is high. This is because, for a given corpus, a smaller number of top-level clusters would mean a larger number of second-level clusters, requiring significantly more time to compute. The turning points are around $K = 20$. On the other hand, when the number of top-level clusters is larger, the number of second-level clusters is smaller, which implies a lower time complexity. Using summaries with length ratio equal to 0.3 offers a good trade-off between accuracy and time complexity.

5. Conclusions

We presented a hierarchical topic clustering scheme HTC and four implementations, HLDA-D, HLDA-S, HSC-D, and HSC-S, for generating hierarchical topic clusters in order to discover topic structures over a large document collection with high efficiency and accuracy. Our experiments show that HLDA-S on summaries of length ratio equal to 0.3 offers a good trade-off between accuracy and time complexity.

Acknowledgment

We are grateful to Hao Zhang and Wenjing Yang for their help on implementing Semantic WordRank summarization and LDA clustering.

References

[1] D. M. Blei, A. Y. Ng, and M. I. Jordan, "Latent dirichlet allocation," in *Journal of Machine Learning Research*, 2003.

[2] A. Y. Ng, M. I. Jordan, and Y. Weiss, "On spectral clustering: Analysis and an algorithm," in *Advances in neural information processing systems*, 2002, pp. 849–856.

[3] J. MacQueen *et al.*, "Some methods for classification and analysis of multivariate observations," in *Proceedings of the fifth Berkeley symposium on mathematical statistics and probability*, vol. 1, no. 14. Oakland, CA, USA, 1967, pp. 281–297.

[4] P. J. Rousseeuw and L. Kaufman, "Finding groups in data," *Hoboken: Wiley Online Library*, 1990.

[5] R. T. Ng and J. Han, "Efficient and effective clustering methods for spatial data mining," in *Proceedings of the 20th International Conference on Very Large Data Bases*, ser. VLDB '94. San Francisco, CA, USA: Morgan Kaufmann Publishers Inc., 1994, pp. 144–155. [Online]. Available: http://dl.acm.org/citation.cfm?id=645920.672827

[6] P. Domingos and M. Pazzani, "On the optimality of the simple bayesian classifier under zero-one loss," *Machine learning*, vol. 29, no. 2-3, pp. 103–130, 1997.

[7] T. Hofmann, "Probabilistic latent semantic indexing," in *ACM SIGIR Forum*, vol. 51, no. 2. ACM, 2017, pp. 211–218.

[8] C. Li, Y. Lu, J. Wu, Y. Zhang, Z. Xia, T. Wang, D. Yu, X. Chen, P. Liu, and J. Guo, "Lda meets word2vec: A novel model for academic abstract clustering," in *Companion of the The Web Conference 2018 on The Web Conference 2018*. International World Wide Web Conferences Steering Committee, 2018, pp. 1699–1706.

[9] J. Yin and J. Wang, "A dirichlet multinomial mixture model-based approach for short text clustering," in *Proceedings of the 20th ACM SIGKDD international conference on Knowledge discovery and data mining*. ACM, 2014, pp. 233–242.

[10] J. Xu, P. Wang, G. Tian, B. Xu, J. Zhao, F. Wang, and H. Hao, "Short text clustering via convolutional neural networks," in *Proceedings of NAACL-HLT*, 2015, pp. 62—69.

[11] B. C. Fung, K. Wang, and M. Ester, "Hierarchical document clustering using frequent itemsets," in *Proceedings of the 2003 SIAM international conference on data mining*. SIAM, 2003, pp. 59–70.

[12] C.-J. Lee, C.-C. Hsu, and D.-R. Chen, "A hierarchical document clustering approach with frequent itemsets," *International journal of engineering and technology*, vol. 9, no. 2, p. 174, 2017.

[13] Y. Zhao, G. Karypis, and U. M. Fayyad, "Hierarchical clustering algorithms for document datasets," *Data Mining and Knowledge Discovery*, vol. 10, pp. 141–168, 2005.

[14] S. Vikram and S. Dasgupta, "Interactive bayesian hierarchical clustering," in *International Conference on Machine Learning*, 2016, pp. 2081–2090.

[15] M. Charikar, V. Chatziafratis, and R. Niazadeh, "Hierarchical clustering better than average-linkage," in *SODA*, 2019.

[16] H. Zhang and J. Wang, "Semantic WordRank: Generating Finer Single-Document Summarizations," *ArXiv e-prints*, Sept. 2018.

[17] D. Greene and P. Cunningham, "Practical solutions to the problem of diagonal dominance in kernel document clustering," in *Proc. 23rd International Conference on Machine learning (ICML'06)*. ACM Press, 2006, pp. 377–384.

[18] T. L. Griffiths and M. Steyvers, "Finding scientific topics," *Proceedings of the National academy of Sciences*, vol. 101, no. suppl 1, pp. 5228–5235, 2004.

[19] J. Wang, H. Zhang, C. Zhang, W. Yang, L. Shao, and J. Wang, "An effective scheme for generating an overview report over a very large corpus of documents," *DocEng*, 2019.

Slim LSTMs

Fathi M. Salem
Circuits, Systems, and Neural Networks (CSANN) Lab
Department of Electrical and Computer Engineering
Michigan State University
East Lansing, Micigan 48824–1226
Email:salemf@msu.edu

***Abstract*—Long Short-Term Memory (LSTM) Recurrent Neural networks (RNNs) rely on gating signals, each driven by a function of a weighted sum of at least three components. The LSTM structure and components encompass redundancy and overly increased parameterization. In this paper, we systemically introduce variants of the standard LSTM RNNs, referred to here as Slim LSTMs. These slim variants express aggressively reduced parameterizations to achieve computational saving and/or speedup in (training) performance—while necessarily retaining (validation accuracy) performance comparable to the standard LSTM RNN.**

***Index Terms*—Long Short-Term Memory (LSTM), Recurrent Neural Networks (RNNs), Gated RNNs.**

1. Introduction

In "Deep Learning," Long Short-Term Memory (LSTM) architectures for Recurrent Neural networks (RNNs) is the dominant workhorse in sequence-to-sequence applications. They have shown impressive demonstrated performance in various sequence-to-sequence applications, see e.g., [1], [2], [3] and [4]. A standard LSTM RNN architecture relies on three gating signals. Each gating signal is itself a replica of a simple recurrent neural network with its own parameters (at least *two* matrices and a bias vector). Specifically, each gating signal is an output of a logistic nonlinearity driven by a weighted sum of at least *three* terms: (i) one adaptive weight matrix multiplied by the incoming external vector sequence, (ii) one adaptive weight matrix multiplied by the previous memory/activation state vector, and (iii) one (adaptive) bias vector. This is the basic composition driving the gating mechanism in the gated RNN architectures literature. There are a host of variants starting from simple RNN (sRNN), to basic RNN (bRNN) [5], to more complex gated variants, see, e.g., [3] and [4].

1.1. The rationale in developing the Slim LSTMs:

A key point is to (i) recognize and exploit the role of the internal dynamic "state" that captures the essential information about processing an input signal's time-history profile, and (ii), in time-series signal processing in recurrent systems, there is no need for repeated matrix multiplication of internal states beyond multiplying the (external) input sequence. As a matrix multiplication signifies scaling and rotation (say, mixing) of elements of a signal, one may use only scaling of subsequent processing after the matrix multiplication of the input signal. Scaling can be expressed as a point-wise (Hadamard) multiplication. These two observations are exploited in defining the new family of Slim architectures of the LSTMs.

As the state contains the essential summary information about a network, including the input sequence profile history, one can eliminate (redundant) terms not containing the state, directly or indirectly, in the gating signals. The gating signals' two weights and bias vector update laws depend on the external input signal and/or the previous memory state(s). Thus, there is redundancy in using all three terms to generate the gating signal(s) to achieve effective learning towards a desired (low loss or) high accuracy performance. Exploiting this observation allows for the development of several variant networks with reduced parameters resulting in computational savings.

The view is to consider the gating as control "signals" which essentially only needs a measure of the network's state. In that view, the form of the standard LSTM network is overly redundant in generating such control signals. For example, it is redundant to provide the state (which may be represented by the memory cell or the activation unit, but not both!) and the external input signal to the gating signal.

For one, the derived (gradient-descent) update learning law(s) of the bias vector itself depends on the prior memory state vector and/or the (previous) external input vector. The state vector, again, captures all information pertaining to the signals in the dynamic system history profile— specifically the external input prior (time-) sequence. A present input value may add a new (discounted) information to prior state values; however, it may also bring an instantaneous outlier value corrupted by noisy measurements or external noise. On that basis, we assert forms that eliminate the instantaneous input sample from (all) gating signals. The intent is to strife to retain the accuracy performance of a gated RNN while aggressively reducing the number of (adaptive) parameters to various degrees. Such parameter reduced architectures would speedup execution in training and inference modes and may be more suitable for limited embedded or mobile computing platforms.

From a recurrent dynamic systems view, the qualitative performance is expected to be retained. However, the quantitative performance would of course vary to various degrees as the number of parameters is reduced to various different levels.

This paper collectively presents the network families for Slim LSTM RNNs and shows the interconnections among them. Throughout, we denote the dimension of the input vector (sequence) to be m, and dimension of the hidden unit, and similarly the state (or memory-cell) vector to be n.

More variants will be described in the following sections. We will describe a diverse set of variant networks with the intended goal of providing a host of choices, balancing parameter-reduction and quantitative performance in (validation-testing) accuracy. We have already demonstrated the quantitative performances of these new network variants in recent publications ([6–9])— albeit for initial datasets. Here, we describe the insight and reasoning into the reduced networks' developments in a comprehesive way [5]. We indicate how those network variants link the simple RNN in graded complexity all the way to the full *standard* LSTM network.

2. Background: The Simple and LSTM RNNs

The so-called simple RNN has a recurrent hidden state as in

$$h_t = g(Wx_t + Uh_{t-1} + b) \tag{1}$$

where x_t is the (external) $m-$dimensional input vector at time t, h_t the $n-$dimensional hidden state, g is the (point-wise) activation function, such as the logistic function, the hyperbolic tangent function, or the rectified Linear Unit (ReLU) [2, 3], and W, U *and* b are the appropriately sized parameters (namely, two weights and a bias). Specifically, in this case, W is an $n \times m$ matrix, U is an $n \times n$ matrix, and b is an $n \times 1$ matrix (or vector).

Simple RNN exhibited frequent inability to capture long-term dependencies because the (stochastic) gradients tend to either vanish or explode with long sequences, see [2, 3] and the references therein. The Long Short-Term Memory (LSTM) RNN has been the first network proposed to mitigate the vanishing or exploding gradient problems, see [4] and the references therein.

2.1. The Long Short-Term Memory (LSTM) RNN

The LSTM RNN architecture introduces the "memory cell" to augment the simple RNN architecture of equation (1). Further, it introduces the gating (control) signals to basically incorporate the previous memory value to the new computations. Let the simple RNN computation produce its contribution to an intermediate variable, say $\tilde{c}_t$, and add it in a weighted-sum (element-wise) to the previous value of the internal memory state, say c_{t-1}, to produce the current value of the memory cell (state) c_t. These operations are expressed as the following set of discrete dynamic equations:

$$\tilde{c}_t = g(W_c x_t + U_c h_{t-1} + b_c) \tag{2}$$
$$c_t = f_t \odot c_{t-1} + i_t \odot \tilde{c}_t \tag{3}$$
$$h_t = o_t \odot g(c_t) \tag{4}$$

The weighted sum is implemented in Eqn (3) as element-wise (Hadamard) multiplication denoted by $\odot$ to gating (control) signals i_t and f_t, respectively . The gating signals $i_t,\ f_t\ and\ o_t$ denote, respectively, the *input*, *forget*, and *output* gating signals at (discrete) time or step t [4]. In Eqns (2) and (4), the activation nonlinearity g is typically the hyperbolic tangent function, however other forms are possible, e.g., the logistic function or the rectified Linear Unit (reLU).

These control gating signals are in fact replica of the basic equation (1), with their own replica parameters and simply replacing g by the logistic function. The logistic function limits the gating signals to within 0 and 1. The specific mathematical form of the gating signals are thus expressed as the vector equations:

$$i_t = \sigma(W_i x_t + U_i h_{t-1} + b_i) \tag{5}$$
$$f_t = \sigma(W_f x_t + U_f h_{t-1} + b_f) \tag{6}$$
$$o_t = \sigma(W_o x_t + U_o h_{t-1} + b_o) \tag{7}$$

where σ is the logistic nonlinearity and the parameters for each gate consist of two matrices and a bias vector. Thus, the total number of parameters (represented as matrices and bias vectors) for the 3 gates and the memory cell structure are, respectively, W_i, U_i, b_i, W_f, U_f, b_f, W_o, U_o, b_o, W_c, U_c and b_c. These parameters are all updated at each training step (or mini-batch) and stored. It is immediately noted that the number of parameters in the LSTM model is increased 4-folds from the simple RNN model in Eqn (1). Assume that the cell state c_t is n-dimensional. (Note that the activation and all the gates have the same dimensions). Assume also that the input signal is m-dimensional. Then, the total parameters in the LSTM RNN is equal to $4 \times (n^2 + nm + n)$.

3. Slim LSTMs: reduction within gates

The gating signals in Gated RNNs enlist all of (i) the previous hidden unit or state, (ii) the present input signal, and (iii) a bias, in order to enable the Gated RNN to essentially learn sequence-2-sequence mappings. The dominant adaptive algorithms used in training are varieties of backpropagation through time (BPTT) stochastic gradient descent. The gates, each, simply replicates a simple RNN. All parameters in this LSTM structure are updated using the BPTT stochastic gradient descent to minimize a loss function [4]. The concept of state, which in essence summarizes the information of the Gated RNN up to the present (or previous) time step, contains the information about the profile of the input sequence. Moreover, the parameter update also includes information pertaining to the state (and co-state) of the overall network structure [5, 10].

For tractable and modular realizations, we consider applying the modifications to all gating signals uniformly. Thus we can consider only the modifications to one of the gating signals, say the i-th gating signal, and replicate the modifications in all other gating signals.

A gating signal is driven by 3 components, resulting in 8 possible variations— including the trivial one when all three components are absent. without the external input signal, there 3 non-trivial variants per gate. For efficiency, we consider the 3 variants without the external input sequence as the input sequence over its time/sample horizon is contained in the "state."

3.1. Variant 1: The LSTM_1 RNN

In this variant, each signal gate is computed using the previous hidden state and the bias, thus reducing the total number of parameters from the 3 gate signals, in comparison to the LSTM RNN, by $3 \times nm$.

$$i_t = \sigma(U_i h_{t-1} + b_i) \quad (8)$$
$$f_t = \sigma(U_f h_{t-1} + b_f) \quad (9)$$
$$o_t = \sigma(U_o h_{t-1} + b_o) \quad (10)$$

3.2. Variant 2: The LSTM_2 RNN

In this variant, each signal gate is computed using only the previous hidden state, thus reducing the total number of parameters from the 3 gate signals, in comparison to the LSTM RNN, by $3 \times (nm + n)$.

$$i_t = \sigma(U_i h_{t-1}) \quad (11)$$
$$f_t = \sigma(U_f h_{t-1}) \quad (12)$$
$$o_t = \sigma(U_o h_{t-1}) \quad (13)$$

3.3. Variant 3: The LSTM_3 RNN

In this variant, each gate is computed using only the bias, thus reducing the total number of parameters in the 3 gate signals, in comparison to the LSTM RNN, by $3 \times (nm + n^2)$.

$$i_t = \sigma(b_i) \quad (14)$$
$$f_t = \sigma(b_f) \quad (15)$$
$$o_t = \sigma(b_o) \quad (16)$$

In order to reduce the parameters even further, one replaces the standard multiplications by point-wise multiplications. In the case of the hidden units, the matrices U_* are reduced into (column) vectors of the same dimension as the hidden units (i.e., n). We denote these corresponding vectors by u_* as delineated next.

3.4. Variant 4: The LSTM_4 RNN

In this variant, each gate is computed using only the previous hidden state but with point-wise multiplication. Thus one reduces the total number of parameters, in comparison to the LSTM RNN, by $3 \times (nm + n^2)$.

$$i_t = \sigma(u_i \odot h_{t-1}) \quad (17)$$
$$f_t = \sigma(u_f \odot h_{t-1}) \quad (18)$$
$$o_t = \sigma(u_o \odot h_{t-1}) \quad (19)$$

3.4.1. Variant 4i: The LSTM_4i RNN. In this variant, only the (so-called) input (or update) gate is computed, thus further reducing the total number of parameters.

$$i_t = \sigma(u_i \odot h_{t-1}) \quad (20)$$
$$f_t = \alpha, \qquad 0 \leq |\alpha| \leq 1 \quad (21)$$
$$o_t = 1 \quad (22)$$

α is typically a constant between between 0.5 and 0.99 in order to stabilize the (gated) RNN— in a Bounded Input Bounded Output (BIBO) sense [10]. This model reduces to the more compact form:

$$c_t = \alpha \, c_{t-1} + i_t \odot g(W_c x_t + U_c h_{t-1} + b_c) \quad (23)$$
$$h_t = g(c_t) \quad (24)$$

where c_t is clearly the only state of the network, and the activation, h_t is a (nonlinear) function of the state. This is in contrast to some claims in the literature that consider both c_t and h_t, togther, as states of the network!

3.4.2. Variant 4ib: The LSTM_4ib RNN. Motivated by the bRNN model in [10], we can remove the nonlinearity in eqn [23], and thus use the "equivalent" dynamic architecture with a single activation function $g(.)$, namely,

$$c_t = \alpha \, c_{t-1} + i_t \odot (W_c x_t + U_c h_{t-1} + b_c) \quad (25)$$
$$h_t = g(c_t) \quad (26)$$

3.5. Variant 5: The LSTM_5 RNN

In this variant, each gate is computed using only bias plus the previous hidden state with point-wise multiplication as follows.

$$i_t = \sigma(u_i \odot h_{t-1} + b_i) \quad (27)$$
$$f_t = \sigma(u_f \odot h_{t-1} + b_f) \quad (28)$$
$$o_t = \sigma(u_o \odot h_{t-1} + b_o) \quad (29)$$

Analogous to the previous subsection, we reduce the gating signals further.

3.5.1. Variant 5i: The LSTM_5i RNN. In this variant, only the input gate is used. The other gates are set to constants as follows:

$$i_t = \sigma(u_i \odot h_{t-1} + b_i) \quad (30)$$
$$f_t = \alpha, \qquad 0 \leq |\alpha| \leq 1 \quad (31)$$
$$o_t = 1 \quad (32)$$

α has absolute value less than or equal to 1 for bounded input bounded output (BIBO) stability, but typically is set as a (hyperparameter) constant between 0.5 and 0.99. This model reduces to the more compact form:

$$c_t = \alpha \; c_{t-1} + i_t \odot g(W_c x_t + U_c h_{t-1} + b_c) \quad (33)$$
$$h_t = g(c_t) \quad (34)$$

3.5.2. Variant 5ib: The LSTM_5ib RNN. Again, motivated by the basic RNN (bRNN) model in [10], we can remove the nonlinearity in eqn [33], and thus use the "equivalent" dynamic architecture with a single activation function $g(.)$, namely,

$$c_t = \alpha \; c_{t-1} + i_t \odot (W_c x_t + U_c h_{t-1} + b_c) \quad (35)$$
$$h_t = g(c_t) \quad (36)$$

3.6. Variant 6: The LSTM_6 RNN

In this variant, each gate is computed using only constants.

$$i_t = 1 \quad (37)$$
$$f_t = \alpha, \qquad 0 \leq |\alpha| \leq 1 \quad (38)$$
$$o_t = 1 \quad (39)$$

In Variant_ 6, the overall system equations can compactly be expressed as

$$c_t = \alpha \; c_{t-1} + g(W_c x_t + U_c h_{t-1} + b_c) \quad (40)$$
$$h_t = g(c_t) \quad (41)$$

3.6.1. Variant 6b: The LSTM_6b RNN. Again, motivated by the basic RNN (bRNN) network in [10], we can remove the nonlinearity in eqn [42], and thus use the "equivalent" dynamic architecture with a single activation function $g(.)$, namely,

$$c_t = \alpha \; c_{t-1} + (W_c x_t + U_c h_{t-1} + b_c) \quad (42)$$
$$h_t = g(c_t) \quad (43)$$

This network is in effect the bRNN model reported in [10] with the input vector advanced by one sample.

4. Slim LSTMs: reduction in gates and the memory cell input block

We next apply the reduction to the body of the simple RNN (sRNN) network as the input block within the standard LSTM equations, namely:

$$\tilde{c}_t = g(W_c x_t + U_c h_{t-1} + b_c) \quad (44)$$

It is observed that the external input signal has its entry point to the the LSTM for processing. Its "mixing" matrix, i.e., W_c, is needed for full transformation (scaling and rotation) of the external signal x_t, the bias parameter b_c would likley be needed in case the external signal does not have zero mean. However, the $n \times n$-matrix U_c may be replaced by an $n - d$-vector to retain scaling (point-wise) but not rotation. The main observation is that in propagation over the time horizon, each instant of the vector $\tilde{c}_t$ will be a function of a weighted sum of all components of the external input signal. Thus all "state-vector" components will be "mixed" naturally due the mixing of the external input signal. Thus, one can reduce the parameterization from n^2 to n, and consequently reducing all associated update computation and storage for $n^2 - n$ parameters. For this one matrix, the reduction is $100(1 - 1/n)\%$. For n-d LSTM, this becomes 99% reduction!

The new variants are focusing on the "memory cell input block" of Eqn (44). One leaves the multiplication in the first term that contains the input sequence unchanged, in order to provide mixing multiplication to the incoming input sequence. Here, one only alters the term involving the activation unit h_{t-1} into the g function. The multiplication here can be made point-wise (Hadamard) multiplication which provides scaling but no rotation. The rationale is that the "state" (namely, the memory cell c_t, and consequently the activation h_t), over the sequence horizon, integrates mixtures of the components of the input sequence, and therefore, there is apparent redundancy in further rotations the states. Thus, it is a candidate for point-wise (scaling only) Hadamard multiplication in order to reduce parameterization (while preserving potential performance).

The actions here can generate additional possibilities when counting the possibilities of the presence and absence of each term in comparison to the baseline original LSTM form. The "memory cell input block" equation can generate a total of $2^2 = 4$ variants including the baseline, or 3 new variants. We choose two Cell variants below as follows:

4.1. Variant Cell 1

Here , one replaces the original $n \times n$-matrix U_c by the $n - d$-vector u_c, and applies point-wise (Hadamard) multiplication to the previous hidden activation h_{t-1}. The bias parameter is also present; note that, in the paper, the bias parameter is present in odd-numbered variants.

$$\tilde{c}_t = g(W_c x_t + u_c \odot h_{t-1} + b_c) \tag{45}$$
$$c_t = f_t \odot c_{t-1} + i_t \odot \tilde{c}_t \tag{46}$$
$$h_t = o_t \odot g(c_t) \tag{47}$$

4.2. Variant Cell 2

Here, one replaces the original $n \times n$-matrix U_c by the $n-d$-vector u_c, and applies point-wise (Hadamard) multiplication to the previous hidden activation h_{t-1}. The bias parameter is removed; note that, in his paper, the bias parameter is removed in even-numbered variants.

$$\tilde{c}_t = g(W_c x_t + u_c \odot h_{t-1}) \tag{48}$$
$$c_t = f_t \odot c_{t-1} + i_t \odot \tilde{c}_t \tag{49}$$
$$h_t = o_t \odot g(c_t) \tag{50}$$

It is noted that one may consider these variants in combination (or linked) with the variations introduced on the gating signals to obtain the total possible diverse variations. As an example, we introduce the following reduced variations involving a combination of gating signals and "memory cell" input block reduced parameterization. In the listed variations below, we retain the same variation numbering as before preceded by the letter C to signify that these variants are alterations including the "memory cell" input block.

4.3. Variant C3: The LSTM_C3 RNN

In this variant, each signal gate is computed using the previous hidden state and the bias, thus reducing the total number of parameters from the 3 gate signals, in comparison to the LSTM RNN, by $3 \times nm$.

$$i_t = \sigma(b_i) \tag{51}$$
$$f_t = \sigma(b_f) \tag{52}$$
$$o_t = \sigma(b_o) \tag{53}$$

with the "memory cell" reduced form

$$\tilde{c}_t = g(W_c x_t + u_c \odot h_{t-1} + b_c) \tag{54}$$
$$c_t = f_t \odot c_{t-1} + i_t \odot \tilde{c}_t \tag{55}$$
$$h_t = o_t \odot g(c_t) \tag{56}$$

4.4. Variant C4: The LSTM_C4 RNN

In this variant, each signal gate is computed using the previous hidden state and the bias, thus reducing the total number of parameters from the 3 gate signals, in comparison to the LSTM RNN, by $3 \times nm$.

$$i_t = \sigma(u_i \odot h_{t-1}) \tag{57}$$
$$f_t = \sigma(u_f \odot h_{t-1}) \tag{58}$$
$$o_t = \sigma(u_o \odot h_{t-1}) \tag{59}$$

with the "memory cell" reduced form

$$\tilde{c}_t = g(W_c x_t + u_c \odot h_{t-1} + b_c) \tag{60}$$
$$c_t = f_t \odot c_{t-1} + i_t \odot \tilde{c}_t \tag{61}$$
$$h_t = o_t \odot g(c_t) \tag{62}$$

4.4.1. Variant C4i: The LSTM_C4i RNN. In this variant, only the (so-called) input (or update) gate is computed, thus reducing the total number of parameters.

$$i_t = \sigma(u_i \odot h_{t-1}) \tag{63}$$
$$f_t = \alpha, \qquad 0 \le |\alpha| \le 1 \tag{64}$$
$$o_t = 1 \tag{65}$$

α is typically a constant between between 0.5 and 0.99 to stabilize the (gated) RNN. This model reduces to the more compact form:

$$c_t = \alpha\ c_{t-1} + i_t \odot g(W_c x_t + u_c \odot h_{t-1} + b_c) \tag{66}$$
$$h_t = g(c_t) \tag{67}$$

4.4.2. Variant C4ib: The LSTM_C4ib RNN. Motivated by the bRNN model in [10], we can remove the nonlinearity in eqn [23], and thus use the "equivalent" dynamic architecture with a single activation function $g(.)$), namely,

$$c_t = \alpha\ c_{t-1} + i_t \odot (W_c x_t + u_c \odot h_{t-1} + b_c) \tag{68}$$
$$h_t = g(c_t) \tag{69}$$

4.5. Variant C5: The LSTM_C5 RNN

In this variant, each gate is computed using only bias plus the previous hidden state with point-wise multiplication as follows.

$$i_t = \sigma(u_i \odot h_{t-1} + b_i) \tag{70}$$
$$f_t = \sigma(u_f \odot h_{t-1} + b_f) \tag{71}$$
$$o_t = \sigma(u_o \odot h_{t-1} + b_o) \tag{72}$$

with the "memory cell" reduced form

$$\tilde{c}_t = g(W_c x_t + u_c \odot h_{t-1} + b_c) \tag{73}$$
$$c_t = f_t \odot c_{t-1} + i_t \odot \tilde{c}_t \tag{74}$$
$$h_t = o_t \odot g(c_t) \tag{75}$$

Now, we reduce the gating signals.

4.5.1. Variant C5i: The LSTM_C5i RNN. In this variant, only the input gate is used. The other gates at set to constants. each gate is computed using only the bias.

$$i_t = \sigma(u_i \odot h_{t-1} + b_i) \tag{76}$$
$$f_t = \alpha, \qquad 0 \le |\alpha| \le 1 \tag{77}$$
$$o_t = 1 \tag{78}$$

α, $|\alpha| <= 1$,which is typically a constant between 0.5 and 0.96 to stabilize the (gated) RNN. This model reduces to the more compact form: 56

$$c_t = \alpha\ c_{t-1} + i_t \odot g(W_c x_t + u_c \odot h_{t-1} + b_c) \quad (79)$$
$$h_t = g(c_t) \quad (80)$$

4.5.2. Variant C5ib: The LSTM_C5ib RNN. Again, motivated by the basic RNN (bRNN) model in [10], we can remove the nonlinearity in eqn [33], and thus use the "equivalent" dynamic architecture with a single activation function $g(.)$), namely,

$$c_t = \alpha\ c_{t-1} + i_t \odot (W_c x_t + u_c \odot h_{t-1} + b_c) \quad (81)$$
$$h_t = g(c_t) \quad (82)$$

4.6. Variant C6: The LSTM_C6 RNN

In this variant, each gate is computed using only constants.

$$i_t = 1 \quad (83)$$
$$f_t = \alpha, \qquad 0 \leq |\alpha| \leq 1 \quad (84)$$
$$o_t = 1 \quad (85)$$

In Variant C6, the overall system equations can compactly be expressed as

$$c_t = \alpha\ c_{t-1} + g(W_c x_t + u_c \odot h_{t-1} + b_c) \quad (86)$$
$$h_t = g(c_t) \quad (87)$$

4.6.1. Variant C6b: The LSTM_C5ib RNN. Again, motivated by the basic RNN (bRNN) model in [10], we can remove the nonlinearity in eqn [33], and thus use the "equivalent" dynamic architecture with a single activation function $g(.)$), namely,

$$c_t = \alpha\ c_{t-1} + (W_c x_t + u_c \odot h_{t-1} + b_c) \quad (88)$$
$$h_t = g(c_t) \quad (89)$$

As before, α is a (hyper-parameter) constant typically between between 0.5 and 0.96 for BIBO stability.

Remarks:

1) Particularly in this last variant, as the parameters have been aggressively reduced, the (state) dimension of the network is a critical hyper-parameter that can be increased in order to increase the capacity of performance of the overall variant network.

2) in this variant, as in all other variants, the weight matrix W_c may be replaced with a convolution kernel operations or suitable size.

5. Sample Comparative Experiments

We show sample of numerous experiments with the Slim LSTM networks in the following. The basic architecture has the form in Figure 1 where the LSTM block is defined by the *standard* LSTM RNN or one of the numerous Slim LSTM variants. The dataset used here is the IMDB dataset acquired via the KERAS framework. IMDB Dataset is a binary sentiment classification dataset using 5000 samples for training and 5000 samples for testing.The coding is all using the Keras 2.0 with Tensorflow as a backend (see https://keras.io).

Each sample (review) is truncated or padded to 500 words. The first layer is an embedding layer which is a simple multiplication that transforms words into their corresponding word embedding. The output is then passed to an LSTM layer followed by a dense layer. The adopted network specification from Keras is given in table 1.

TABLE 1. NETWORK SPECIFICATIONS: IMDB DATASETS

Input dimension	500 × 32
Number of hidden units	200
Non-linear function	sigmoid
Output dimension	1
Number of epochs	100
Optimizer	Adam
Batch size	32
Loss function	binary cross-entropy

A schematic representation of the architecture used is given in figure 1.

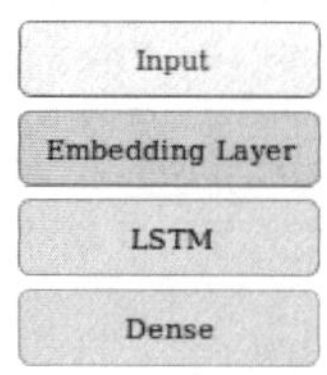

Figure 1. IMDB, Network Architecture Diagram

We now show representative experiments of several variants vis-a-vis the base or *standard* LSTM RNN (denoted in the figures a lstm0). It is noticeable that the performance of the Slim LSTM variants are very competitive and mostly are close to the *standard* LSTM RNN in these experiments.

6. Concluding Remarks

We have introduced a mosaic of new recurrent architectures that *Slim* down the standard LSTM architecture to simpler forms. We have eliminated the redundancy of parameters and in some cases allow for the presence of a single nonlinearity in the memory-cell recurrent network structure. As recurrent neural networks are employed to learn sequence-to-sequence mappings, the question turns to *capacity*, i.e., the existence of a set of parameters in a given architecture (or variant) that enables approximate

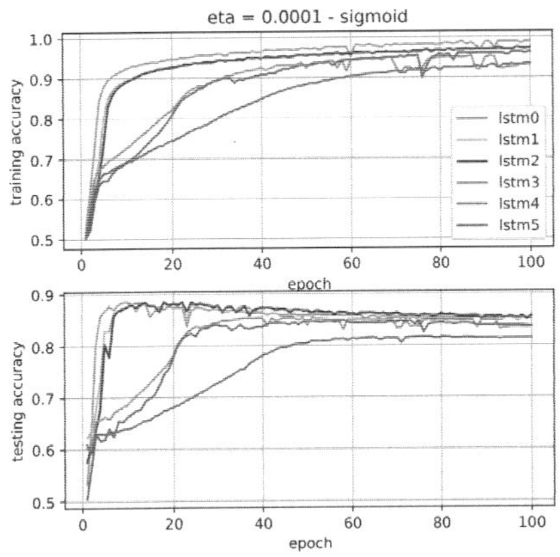

Figure 2. IMDB, Training & Test accuracy, $\sigma = sigmoid, \eta = 1e{-4}$

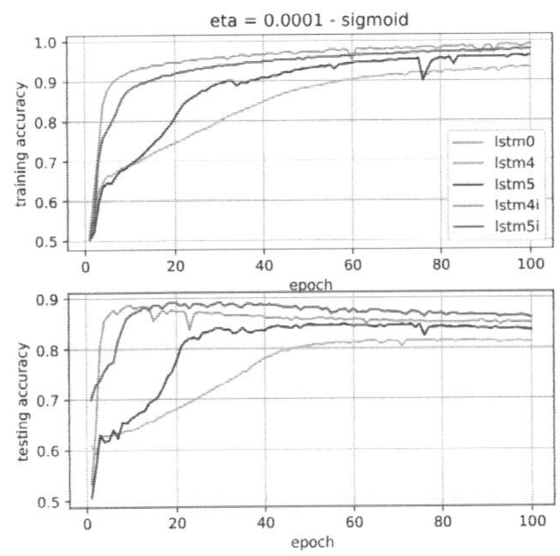

Figure 3. IMDB, Training & Test accuracy, $\sigma = sigmoid, \eta = 1e{-4}$

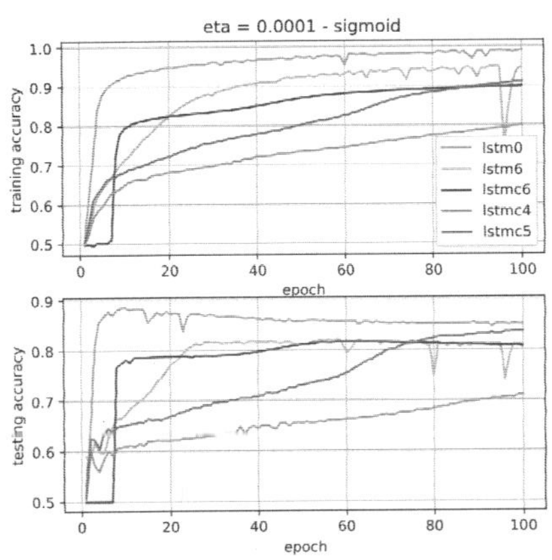

Figure 4. IMDB, Training & Test accuracy, $\sigma = sigmoid, \eta = 1e{-4}$

mappings of finite sequence-to-sequence using the training data— while generalizing on validation/test datasets. In that context, the dimension of the variant would become an important (hyper-) parameter for some Slim LSTMs that could be used to increase the capacity of improved performance.

Many of these variants have already been validated to produce comparable performance to the standard LSTM RNN in recent publications [5–9]. The remaining ones are currently being investigated in case studies.

Acknowledgment

This work was supported in part by the National Science Foundation under grant No. ECCS-1549517.

References

[1] M. Johnson, M. Schuster, Q. V. Le, M. Krikun, Y. Wu, Z. Chen, N. Thorat, F. B. Viégas, M. Wattenberg, G. Corrado, M. Hughes, and J. Dean, "Google's multilingual neural machine translation system: Enabling zero-shot translation," *CoRR*, vol. abs/1611.04558, 2016. [Online]. Available: http://arxiv.org/abs/1611.04558

[2] J. Chung, C. Gulcehre, K. Cho, and Y. Bengio, "Empirical evaluation of gated recurrent neural networks on sequence modeling," *arXiv preprint arXiv:1412.3555*, 2014.

[3] R. Jozefowicz, W. Zaremba, and I. Sutskever, "An empirical exploration of recurrent network architectures," *ICML'15, Processings of the 32nd International Conference on Machine Learning*.

[4] K. Greff, R. K. Srivastava, J. Koutnk, B. R. Steunebrink, and J. Schmidhuber, "Lstm: A search space odyssey," *IEEE transactions on Neural Networks and Learning Systems*, vol. 28, no. 10, pp. 2222–2232, 2017.

[5] F. M. Salem, "Slim lstms," *www.arXiv.com, arXiv:1812.11391*, 2018.

[6] Y. Lu and F. M. Salem, "Simplified gating in long short-term memory (lstm) recurrent neural networks," in *The IEEE 60th International Midwest Symposium on Circuits and Systems*. IEEE, 2017, pp. 1601–1604.

[7] A. Akandeh and F. M. Salem, "Simplified long short-term memory recurrent neural networks: part i," *The World Congress in Computer Science, Computer Engineering & Applied Computing (CSCE'17)*.

[8] ——, "Simplified long short-term memory recurrent neural networks: part ii," *The World Congress in Computer Science, Computer Engineering & Applied Computing (CSCE'17)*.

[9] ——, "Simplified long short-term memory recurrent neural networks: part iii," *The World Congress in Computer Science, Computer Engineering & Applied Computing (CSCE'17)*.

[10] F. M. Salem, "A basic recurrent neural network model," *arXiv preprint arXiv:1612.09022*, 2016.

SESSION

DATA SCIENCE AND APPLICATIONS + MIS AND DATABASES

Chair(s)

TBA

Adaptive Computing and Big Data Analytics for Business Intelligence

E. Sheybani[1] and G. Javidi[2]
[1]Information Systems and Decision Science, University of South Florida, Sarasota, Florida, USA
[2]Information Technology, University of South Florida, Sarasota, Florida, USA

Abstract - *This article describes an innovative and adaptive computational methodology in which big data can be analyzed for business intelligence. Data sources and the data itself are numerous and heterogeneous, and can arise from many business information systems such as management, marketing, finance, distribution, operations, service, and customer support systems. New approaches to use this data can provide a multitude of applications in each domain, from adaptive control to customized billing to predictive maintenance, to name but a few. In the next few years, businesses, large or small, will have to use some form of data analytics to make business decisions. As the Internet becomes more widespread, high-speed data processing, analytics, and reduced response times are becoming more critical than ever.*

Keywords: Business Information Systems, Processing, Adaptive Computing, Business Intelligence, Big Data Analytics

1 Introduction

Data scientist is announced as the sexiest job of the 21st century [1]. Big data is not a fashion. We just started a upheaval that will touch every business and every life on the planet. Here are some facts:

- With data volumes in the past two years being than the entire history of the human beings, the data volumes are exploding.
- Data is produced at a faster pace than ever before, by 2020, 1.7 megabytes will be formed per second per person.
- By 2020, the overall data will grow to around 44 zettabyets.
- In Aug 2016, Facebook was used by over 1 billion people in a single day.
- By 2020, there will be over 6.1 billion smartphone users globally.

Some of the data sources that contribute to this chaotic situation are:

- **Power Grid Data**: Data used by a node in an electric network base-station.
- **Transport Data**: Data such as distance, availability, model, and capacity of a vehicle.
- **Search Engine Data**: Data recovered by search engines from databases.
- **Black Box Data**: This device records data from recordings of microphones and earphones, the performance information of the aircraft, and voices of the flight crew in airplanes, and jets, etc.
- **Social Media Data**: Twitter and Facebook are examples of social media.
- **Stock Exchange Data**: Data about the 'buy' and 'sell' decisions made on the stocks of companies.

2 Characteristics of Big Data: 5 V's

The characteristics of Big Data can be summarized in the following:

1. Volume: The amount of data continues to explode.
2. Velocity: The data generation and movement speed.
3. Veracity: Level of mess and trust in data.
4. Variety: Level of mix in data.
5. Value: Our ability to turn data into value

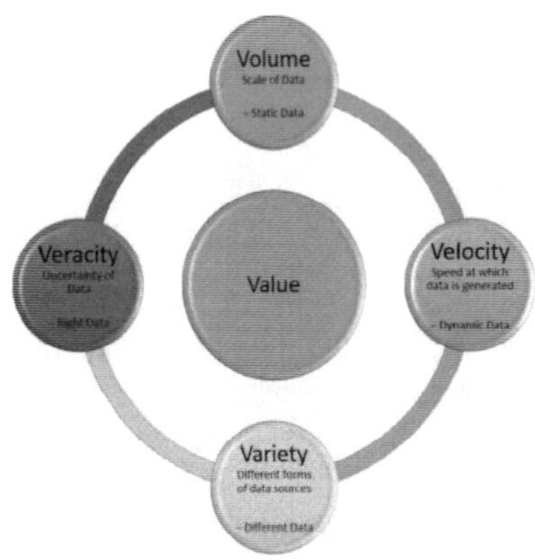

Figure1: Big Data consists of large amounts, fast, messy, and mixed data data [2].

In many ways the uncontrollable growth of big data is similar to pollution. Pollution starts with introducing pollutants into a natural setting, causing unpredictability, ailment, damage, or distress to the system. Likewise, the absolute amount of data being produced today can often "pollute" the corporate "setting" and cause "unpredictability, ailment, damage, or distress for businesses. This phenomenon has been termed information pollution (infolution), pollution caused by the quick burst of data. The influence of infolution can be understood by the total money corporations spend to stockpile additional data:

- Gartner approximates that at least 70 percent of all data in a representative enterprise has not been retrieved within one year.
- Cisco spent $77 million in 2010 to stock data that hasn't been retrieved for a year.

Organizations spend money to adapt the large amounts of data and generate information. The incentive is that 1) Data isn't valuable by itself; it must be labelled, prearranged, examined, united, and cleaned before it can be well-thought-out as information, 2) Information must be managed into a system that aids individuals do something fruitful, such as taking a vital business verdict (Knowledge). In order to help these processes, experts have formed data flowgraphs and replicas that help understand the flow of data within an organization. Figure 2 represents one of these models:

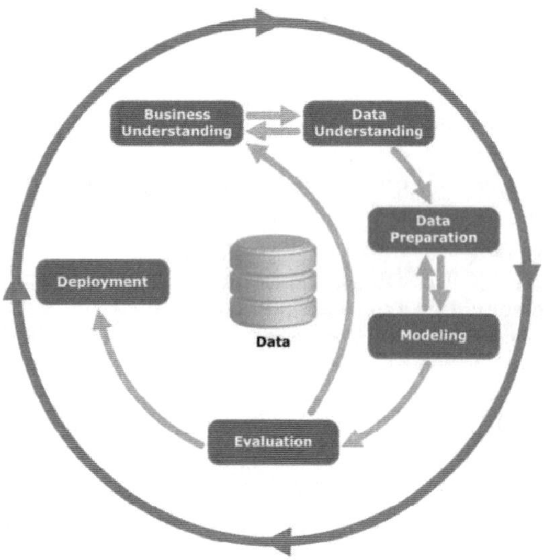

Figure 2: CRoss-Industry Process for Data Mining (CRISP-DM) Model [2]

The CRISP-DM procedure offers a planned method to development of a data mining scheme. It is a powerful and robust method. It is well-known for its prevailing pragmatism, elasticity and practicality when using analytics to resolve prickly business matters. It is the excellent strand that scores high in every customer engagement.

3 Understanding Data is Crucial

Computer experts have developed brilliant computing power and data storage technologies (such as Hadoop) which in turn has made the buildup of big data possible. However, accumulating data and loading information is different from understanding it. Understanding what Big Data means is different from construing little data. So far, outdated statistical approaches and typical statistical tests and computational measures have been used for illustrating scientific interpretations. These were intended to examine small samples taken from large populations. Big Data delivers enormously large samples that occasionally contains all or most of a population. The scale of the chore can cause difficulties for applying computational processes for testing. This does not resonate well with organizations, but it can become worse.

the Big Data models take more time to scrutinize, they also stereotypically comprise many pieces of information about every sample. This is one of the features of Big Data which translates to high dimensionality. High dimensionality might lead to erroneous statistical interpretation and incorrect scientific deductions. For example, a health study may correlate accomplishment with a medicine to a patient's tallness. However, that may only be due to the Big Data information confined on everything from tallness and heaviness to shoe size, eye color, and favorite baseball team. With so many scopes to study, data seems to be significant just by accident.

Another source of error is experimental variations. Big Data often is acquired by combining information from many sources, at different times, using a variety of technologies or methodologies. This creates issues of experimental variations, and statistical biases, and requires us to develop more adaptive and robust procedures to handle the challenges of Big Data. Therefore, we need new computational methods that can adjust themselves to the 5V's of big data.

Additionally, another important factor in dealing with any kind of dataset is visualization. A picture is worth a thousand words and by the same token a graph is worth a thousand data points. Table 1 shows numbers enhanced with graphics. It is obvious that at the first glance, Table 1 conveys more information to the user than just numbers. Therefore, the goals of this research effort have been to 1) Understand how people use visualizations to gain insight, and 2) Design techniques for effective visual analysis.

4 Research and Methodology

The authors have explored different ways to apply advanced signal processing algorithms to analysis and visualization of big data. This is a new approach that paves the road for more effective analysis of big data with promising algorithms. The authors have used wavelet transforms as a possible alternative to data noise reduction, to explore new ways to reduce complexity, and to achieve more efficient dimension reduction methods.

Table 1: Display of dataset with enhanced graphics

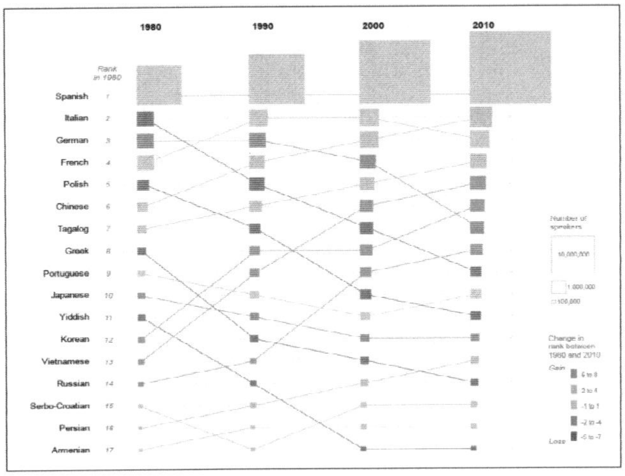

4.1 What is Wavelet Transform?

Wavelets use simple math operations that decompose a datasets into its basic components in frequency, matching each component resolution to its scale. Each small wave (wavelet) is an oscillation like a wave in time with amplitude opening at zero, then growing and declining back to zero. Wavelet excerpt information from dissimilar kinds of data. Wavelet compression analyzes a dataset and converts it to a series of math terms that gets deciphered at the receiver.

4.2 What is Decomposition?

In the case of composite datasets, it is a good practice to decay it to less composite and more controllable datasets. This carries a clear equivalent in data analysis: rather than analyzing a comprehensive dataset, decay it to smaller, more controllable datasets that can be analyzed individually. The core idea is to progressively smooth the data using an iterative procedure and keep the details along the way.

4.3 Fourier Transform (FT) vs. Wavelet Transform (WT)

The commonly used tool for signal analysis is FT, which breaks down a signal into signals of different frequencies. The Fourier Transform shows the frequency components that are present in a signal. The wavelet transform shows the frequency components that are present as well as their location or scale. For a signal that is varying in time, the FT does not show when in time this has happened.

To better understand how these transform filters work, let's use an example. Suppose you are given a smoothie, and you are asked to find its recipe. You could run the smoothie through transform filters to extract each ingredient. Once the components are extracted, recipes are easier to analyze, compare, and modify than the smoothie itself. It is obvious that if you want to get the smoothie back, all you have to do is to blend the ingredients. Using wavelet transforms, if a signal can be separated into ingredients (frequencies, sharpness, drifts, transitions), we can boost the parts we care about, and hide the ones we don't. The random noise can be removed. Additionally, one could gain business intelligence, pro-actively report incidents, target improvements in usability of Big Data, automate Filtering of non-useful data, establishing correlations, extract, transform, and load Big Data, and preprocess data.

5 Results and Discussion

In order to meet the challenges of big data in business information systems the characteristics of our solution include:

- Algorithmic challenges
- Fundamental change in pre/processing
- distributed file-sharing framework for data storage and query
- Parallel processing
- Modular structure
- multiple-layer architecture
- distributed, scalable, and portable solutions
- Hardware Implementation
- Multiscale and multidimensional
- Efficient streaming feature selection method to identify strongly relevant non-redundant features

The adaptivity of the proposed data analysis technique makes it capable of handling information theory and decision making, analysis of large datasets, and scientific computing. The proposed adaptive technique is a new methodology that deals with the translation-invariant and scale-invariant issues of the discrete wavelet transform (DWT): after an input signal is filtered by an input-dependent filter, whose impulse response is calculated by the first two moments of the original input and is built from a scale function of an orthonormal wavelet, an adaptively renormalize signal is obtained. The renormalized signal is then decomposed by using the algorithm of the conventional DWT. The final wavelet transform coefficients are called adaptive wavelet invariant moments, and are both translation-invariant and scale-invariant.

6 Conclusion

In this article, the authors describe a mathematically low-power, low-cost, and low-bandwidth filter that will eliminate signal noise and compress the data for decision-making. Algorithm has been successfully applied to datasets in Cyber Security, e-Health, GIS/RS, Big Data, Nanotechnologies, Advanced Manufacturing, Embedded Systems, Smart Grid, Biomedicine, WSN, System Health, SAR, Bioinformatics, Oceanography, Modeling/Simulation, Data Mining, Visualization, Vibration, RF Communication, Smart Robots, Video Gaming, and Video/Data/Speech/Image Processing.

7 References

[1] Thomas H. Davenport, D.J. Patil, "Data Scientist: The Sexiest Job of the 21st Century", Harvard Business Review, October 2012. https://hbr.org/2012/10/data-scientist-the-sexiest-job-of-the-21st-century

[2] Philip Guo, "Data Science Workflow: Overview and Challenges", Communications of ACM, October 30, 2013. http://cacm.acm.org/blogs/blog-cacm/169199-data-science-workflow-overview-and-challenges/fulltext

[3] Sheybani, Ehsan; Garcia-Otero, Singli; Adnani, Fedra; Javidi, Giti; Deshpande, Manohar (2012). An Algorithm for Real-Time Blind Image Quality Comparison and Assessment. *IJECE*, Vol 2, No 1.

[4] Sheybani, E.O.; Mengshoel, O.J.; Poll, S. (2010). Removing spikes while preserving data and noise using wavelet filter banks. *Proceedings of IEEE Aerospace Conference,* pp. 1 – 10.

[5] Aparna Varde, Elke Rundensteiner, Giti Javidi, Ehsan Sheybani and Jianyu Liang (2007). Learning the Relative Importance of Features in Image Data. *Proceeding of IEEE ICDE's DBRank-07*, Istanbul, Turkey, pp. 237–244.

[6] Sheybani, E., Sankar, R. (2002). A Survey of Telemedicine/ Teleradiology/ Telemammography Network Architectures. *SPIE Journal of Electronic Imaging*.

[7] Sheybani, E. (2011). Dimensionality Reduction and Noise Removal in Wireless Sensor Networks. *New Technologies, Mobility and Security (NTMS), Proceedings of 2011 4th IFIP International Conference on*, pp 1–5, Parice, France.

[8] Sheybani, E.; Javidi, G.; "Dimensionality Reduction and Noise Removal in Wireless Sensor Network Datasets", *Computer and Electrical Engineering, Second International Conference on, ICCEE* '09, Volume: 2, 28-30 Dec. 2009, pp: 674 – 677, Dubai.

[9] Sheybani, E.; Javidi, G.; "Multi-resolution filter banks for enhanced SAR imaging", *Systems and Informatics (ICSAI), 2012 International Conference on*, 19-20 May 2012, pp: 2702 – 2706, Yantai, China.

[10] Huilin Xiong, Tianxu Zhang, Y.S. Moon, "A translation- and scale-invariant adaptive wavelet transform", *IEEE Transactions on Image Processing*, 2000, Volume: 9, Issue: 12, pp. 2100 – 2108.

[11] Ehsan Sheybani, Giti Javidi, "Advanced Image Processing for Analytics in Biomedicine and Bioscience", *Curr Trends in Biomedical Eng & Biosci*. 2017; 6(4).

[12] Sheybani, E. & Javidi, G. "Integrating Software Defined Radio with USRP", *International Journal of Interdisciplinary Telecommunications and Networking*, Vol. 9, Issue 3, pp. 1-9, 2017.

[13] Javidi, G. & Sheybani, E. "Application of Digital Signal Processing in USRP Satellite Signal Detection", *International Journal of Interdisciplinary Telecommunications and Networking*, Vol. 9, Issue 2, pp. 16-25, 2017.

[14] Sheybani, E. & Javidi, G. "Application of Signal Processing in GPS Signal Detection Using USRP", *International Journal of Interdisciplinary Telecommunications and Networking*, Vol. 9, Issue 2, pp. 26-36, 2017.

[15] Luttamaguzi, J, Eslami, A., Brooks, D., Sheybani, E., Javidi, G., Gabriel, P. "Using Simulations and Computational Analyses to Study a Frequency-Modulated Continuous-Wave Radar", International *Journal of Interdisciplinary Telecommunications and Networking*, Vol. 9, Issue 1, pp. 38-51, January-March 2017.

[16] Javidi, G. & Sheybani, E. "Development of a Satellite Communication Emulator for Hyper spectral Microwave Atmosphere Sounder HYMAS ", *International Journal of Interdisciplinary Telecommunication and Networking,* Vol. 7, Issue 2, 2015.

[17] Javidi, G., Sheybani, E. & Mason, D. "Visualization of Real-Time Radar Data by Integration of X-Band Software", *International Journal of Interdisciplinary Telecommunication and Networking*, Vol. 6, Issue. 4, p. 73-82, 2014.

[18] Mukherjee, S., Varde, A. S., Javidi, G., Sheybani, E., "Predictive analysis of engine health for decision support", *SIGKDD Explorations* 15(2): 39-49 (2013).

[19] Sheybani, L. Ralph, G. Javidi, A. Eslami, J. Luttamaguzi, "SNMP-Based RMA Analysis of Wired and Wireless Networks" International Journal of Interdisciplinary Telecommunications and Networking, 5.3, pp. 49-53, 2013.

[20] Sheybani, E., Garcia-Otera, S., Adnani, F., & Javidi, G. "A Fast Algorithm for Automated Quality Control in Surface Engineering", Journal of Surface Engineered Materials and Advanced Technology, 2012, 2, 120-126.

[21] E. Sheybani, "Adaptive Wavelet Filtering for Data Enhancement in Wireless Sensor Networks", Journal of Sensor Technologies, Vol. 2, No. 2, 2012, pp 82-86.

[22] Sheybani, E., Garcia-Otera, S., Adnani, F., & Javidi, G. "A Fast Algorithm for Surface Quality Comparison and Assessment in Advanced and Automated Manufacturing", *International*

Journal of Engineering Research and Innovation, 2012, Vol.4, No. 1, 52-59.

Incremental extraction of a NoSQL database model using an MDA-based process

Amal AIT BRAHIM, Rabah TIGHILT FERHAT and Gilles ZURFLUH
Toulouse Institute of Computer Science Research (IRIT),
Toulouse Capitole University, Toulouse, France

Abstract - *In recent years, the need to use NoSQL systems to store and exploit big data has been steadily increasing. Most of these systems are characterized by the property "schema less" which means absence of the data model when creating a database. This property brings an undeniable flexibility by allowing the evolution of the model during the exploitation of the base. However, the expression of queries requires a precise knowledge of this model. In this paper, we propose an incremental process to extract the model while operating the document-oriented NoSQL database. To do this, we use the Model Driven Architecture (MDA) that provides a formal framework for automatic model transformation. From the insert, delete and update queries executed on the database, we propose formal transformation rules with QVT to generate the physical model of the NoSQL database. An experimentation of the extraction process was performed on a medical application.*

Keywords: Big Data, NoSQL, model extraction, schema less, MDA, QVT.

1 Introduction

The number of digital devices that we use nowadays produces a huge amount of data, known as Big Data that need to be exploited. Usually, who says Big Data, says at least, Volume, Variety and Velocity [5]. Volume is the size of the data set that needs to be processed, Variety describes different data type including factors such as format, structure, and sources and Velocity indicates the speed of data loading and processing. Relational systems that had been for decades the one solution for all databases needs prove to be inadequate for all applications, especially those involving Big Data [1]. Consequently, new type of DBMS, commonly known as "NoSQL" [8], has appeared. These systems are well suited for managing large volume of data with flexible models. They also provide low latency at scale and faster data access [1]. NoSQL covers a wide variety of different systems that were developed to meet specific needs. These systems can be classified into four basic types: key-value, column-oriented, document-oriented and graph-oriented. In this paper, we focus on the third one.

One of the NoSQL key features is that databases can be schema-less. This means, in a table, meanwhile the row is inserted, the attributes names and types are specified. The schema-less property offers undeniable flexibility that facilitates the database model evolution. End-users are able to quickly and easily incorporate new data into their applications without rewriting tables. However, the importance and the necessity of the database model are widely recognized. There is still a need for this model to know how data is structured and related in the database; this is particularly necessary to write declarative queries where tables and columns names are specified.

On the one hand, NoSQL systems have proven their efficiency to handle Big Data. On the other hand, the needs of the NoSQL database model remain up-to-date. Therefore, we are convinced that it's important to provide an automatic approach that extracts the database model within NoSQL systems. To formalize and automate this approach, we have used the Model Driven Architecture (MDA) that is well known as a framework for models automatic transformations. Our approach starts from the user queries and update the database model. For each query provided by the user and applied to the database, the process has mainly two steps: (1) it analyzes the query and (2) update the database model by applying the changes introduced by this user query.

The remainder of the paper is structured as follows. Section 2 motivates our work using a case of study in the healthcare field. Section 3 reviews previous work. Section 4 defines our NoSQL database model extraction process. Section 5 details our experiments as well as the validation of our process. Finally, Section 6 concludes the paper and announces future work.

2 Motivation

To motivate and illustrate our work, we have used a case study in the healthcare filed. This case study concerns international scientific programs for monitoring patients suffering from serious diseases. The main goal of this program is (1) to collect data about diseases development over time, (2) to study interactions between different diseases and (3) to evaluate the short and medium-term effects of their treatments. The medical program can last up to 3 years. Data collected from establishments involved in this kind of program have the features of Big Data (the 3 V):
Volume: the amount of data collected from all the establishments in three years can reach several terabytes.
Variety: data created while monitoring patients come in different types; it could be (1) structured as the patient's vital signs (respiratory rate, blood pressure, etc.), (2) semi-

structured document such as the package leaflets of medicinal products, (3) unstructured such as consultation summaries, paper prescriptions and radiology reports. Velocity: some data are produced in continuous way by sensors; it needs a [near] real time process because it could be integrated into a time-sensitive processes (for example, some measurements, like temperature, require an emergency medical treatment if they cross a given threshold).

This is a typical example in which the use of a NoSQL system is suitable. On the one hand, in the medical application, briefly presented above, the database contains structured data, data of various types and formats (explanatory texts, medical records, x-rays, etc.), and big tables (records of variables produced by sensors). On the other hand, NoSQL data stores are ideally suited for this kind of applications that use large amounts of disparate data. Therefore, we are convinced that a NoSQL DBMS, like MongoDB, is the most adapted system to store the medical database.

As mentioned before, this kind of systems operate on schema-less data model. Nevertheless, there is still a need for the database model in order to know how data is structured and related in the database and then to express queries. Regarding the medical application, doctors enter measures regularly for a cohort of patients. They can also recording new data in cases where the patient's state of health evolve over time. Few months later, they will analyze the entered data in order to follow the evolution of the pathology. For this, they need the database model to express their queries.

In our view, it's important to have a precise and automatic solution that guides and facilitates the database model extraction task within NoSQL systems. For this, we propose the Query2Model process presented in the next section that extracts the physical model of a database stored in MongoDB. This model is expressed using the JSON format.

3 Related work

Several research works have been proposed to extract a NoSQL databases model, mainly for document-oriented databases such as MongoDB. In [11], the authors present a process to extract a model from a collection of JSON documents stored on MongoDB. The model returned by this process is in JSON format; it is obtained by capturing the names of the attributes that appear in the input documents and replacing their values with their types. Attribute values can be atomic, lists, or nested documents.

Authors in [12] propose a model extraction process from a document-oriented NoSQL database that can include several collections. The returned result is not a unified model for the whole database but it is a set of model versions. These versions are stored in JSON format.

More specific to document-oriented databases, we can mention [7] where authors describe a process called BSP (Build Schema Profile) to classify the documents of a collection by applying a set of rules that correspond to the user requirements. These rules are expressed through a decision tree where nodes represent the attributes of the documents and edges specify the conditions on which the classification is based. These conditions reflect either the absence or the presence of an attribute in a document or its value. As in the previous article [12], the result returned by this approach is not a unified model but a set of model versions ; each of them is common to a group of documents.

We can also mention [14] that describes a mapping from a document-oriented NoSQL database to a relational model. The process groups together all documents that have the same fields name. For each class of documents, it generates a table that have as columns the fields names and as rows the fields values.

Another study [15] have proposed a model extraction process from a collection of JSON documents. This process is based on the use of MapReduce. The Map step consists of extracting the schema of each document in the collection by mapping each couple (field, value) into another couple (field, type). The Reduce step consists of unifying all the schemas produced in the Map step in order to provide an overall schema for the input collection. The same authors have proposed in another paper [16] an extension of the process prposed in [15] in order to take into account the parameterization of the extraction at the Reduce step. Thus, the user can choose either to unify all the schemas of the collection, or to unify only the schemas having the same fields (same names and types).

On the other hand, [13] proposes a process for extracting a model from object insertion queries and relations in a graph-oriented databases. The proposed process is based on an MDA architecture and applies two treatments. The first one build a graph (Nodes + Edges) starting from Neo4j queries. The second one consists of extracting an Entity / Association model from the graph returned by the first treatment.

In Table 1, we summarize the previous works using three criteria: the database content (one or several classes), the considered NoSQL system type (document or graph) and the way used to implement links (references, nested data or edges).

	Database content		NoSQL system type		Links					
	One class	Several classes	Document-oriented	Graph-oriented	Intra classe			Inter classes		
					Using references	Using nested data	Using edges	Using references	Using nested data	Using edges
[11]: Klettke et al., 2015	X		X			X				
[12]: Sevilla et al., 2015		X	X			X			X	
[7]: Gallinucci et al., 2018	X		X			X				
[13]: Comyn-Wattiau et al., 2018		X		X			X			X
[14]: Maity et al., 2018	X		X			X				
[15]: Baazizi et al., 2017	X		X			X				
[16]: Baazizi et al., 2019	X		X			X				

Table. 1 Comparative table of previous works

Regarding the state of the art, the solutions proposed in [7], [11], [14], [15] and [16] start from a single collection of documents and take into account only the links implemented using nested data ; the links presented using references are not considered. The process proposed in [12] takes as input a set of collections ; however, only the use of nested data to express links is considered. On the other hand, authors in [13] have worked on graph-oriented systems. This kind of NoSQL systems does not offer many solutions to implement links as like document-oriented systems ; it expresses explicitly links between data using edges. To overcome these limits, we define an automatic process to extract the database model within documents-oriented NoSQL systems. This process process takes into account the links between collections.

4 Query2Model process

This article focuses on extracting the model from a NoSQL database with the "schema less" property. We limit ourselves to the document-oriented type which is the most complete in terms of expression of links (use of references and nesting). For this, we propose the Query2Model process which automatically builds the model of a NoSQL database from update requests submitted by users.

The Query2Model process is based on OMG's Model Driven Architecture [10]. We recall below the outlines of this model transformation approach. MDA is a formal framework for formalizing and automating model transformations. The purpose of this architecture is to describe separately the functional specifications and implementation specifications of an application on a given platform. For this, MDA uses three models representing the abstraction levels of the application. These are (1) the Computational Independent Model (CIM) describing the services that the application must provide to meet the needs of users, (2) the analysis and design model (PIM for Platform Independent Model) which defines the structure and the behavior of the system without indicating the execution platform and (3) the model of code (PSM for Platform Specific Model) which is the projection of a PIM on a particular technical platform. Since the input of our process corresponds to user requests and its output is a physical model, we retain only the PSM level. The extraction of the model from a NoSQL database is done via a sequence of transformations. We will formalize these transformations using the QVT standard (Query View Transformation) defined by the OMG (see Experimentation). Figure 1 shows an overview of our process.

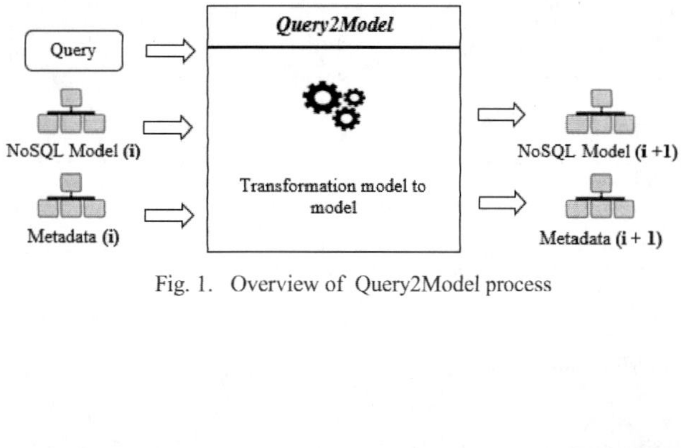

Fig. 1. Overview of Query2Model process

As shown in Figure 1, the input of the Query2Model process consists of three elements: (1) an insert, delete, or modify query, (2) a NoSQL database model, and (3) metadata. Note that at the first execution of the Query2Model process, the NoSQL model and the metadata are empty; these will be created and updated as requests are processed. Thus, for each new update request, the process proceeds as follows: (1) It analyzes the query against the model and available metadata, (2) It updates the model and enriches the metadata to allow the processing of future requests.

In the following sections, we detail the components of Query2Model by specifying the inputs / outputs as well as the transformation rules.

4.1 Inputs/ Outputs

4.1.1 Insertion query

An insertion query Q^I is defined as a pair (Cll, FL) where:

- $Q^I.Cll$ is the name of the collection on which Q^I is executed,
- $Q^I.FL = AFL \cup CFL$ is the set of fields that appear on Q^I, where:
  - $AFL = \{afl_1, \dots, afl_k\}$ is the set of atomic fields, where: $\forall$ i $\in$ [1..k], an atomic field $afl_i \in AFL$ is defined as a pair (N, V) where:
    - $afl_i.N$ is the name of afl_i,
    - $afl_i.V$ is the value of afl_i,
  - $CFL = \{cfl_1, \dots, cfl_l\}$ is the set of complex fields, where: $\forall$ j $\in$ [1..l], a complex field $cfl_j \in CFL$ is defined as a pair (N, FL') where:
    - $cfl_j.N$ is the name of cfl_j,
    - $cfl_j.FL' \in FL$ is the set of fields that cfl_j contains. These fields can be atomic or complex.

4.1.2 Delete query

A delete query Q^D is defined as a pair (Cll, Id) where:

- $Q^D.Cll$ is the name of the collection on which Q^D is executed,
- $Q^D.Id$ is the identifier of the document to delete.

4.1.3 Update query

An update query Q^U is defined as a triple (Cll, Id, FL) where:

- $Q^U.Cll$ is the collection name mentioned in Q^U,
- $Q^U.Id$ is the identifier of the document to update,
- $Q^U.FL = AFL \cup CFL$ is a set of fields to update in the document where the identifier is Id, where:
  - $AFL = \{afl_1, \dots, afl_k\}$ is a set of atomic fields, where : $\forall$ i $\in$ [1..k], an atomic field $afl_i \in AFL$ is defined by a couple (N, V) where:
    - $afl_i.N$ is the field name,
    - $afl_i.V$ is the field value.

- $CFL = \{cfl_1, \dots, cfl_l\}$ is a set of complex fields, where: $\forall$ j $\in$ [1..l], a complex field $cfl_j \in CFL$ is defined by a couple (N, FL') where:
  - $cfl_j.N$ is the field name,
  - $cfl_j.FL' \in FL$ is a set of fields that compose cfl_j. These fields can be either atomic or complex.

Query metamodel is shown in Figure2; this metamodel describes the main concepts used in insertion, update and delete queries.

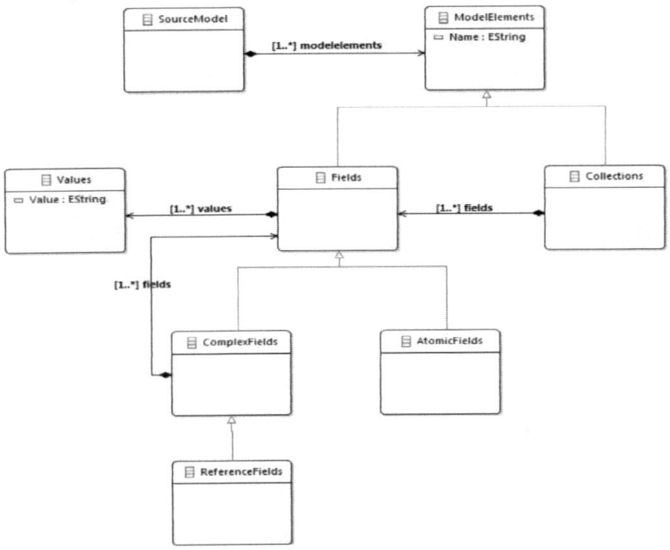

Fig. 2. Query metamodel

4.1.4 NoSQL model

The NoSQL model is stored in a JSON objet noted O^M. This is defined as a pair (Id, CAT), where:

- $O^M.Id$ is the identifier of the object O^M,
- $O^M.CAT = \{cat_1, \dots, cat_n\}$ is the set of complex attributes, where: $\forall$ i $\in$ [1..n], a complex attribute cat_i is defined as a pair (N, AT) where:
  - $cat_i.N$ is the name of cat_i. It corresponds to the name of a collection in the database,
  - $cat_i.AT = AAT \cup CAT'$ is a set of attributes of the collection, where:
    - $AAT = \{aat_1, \dots, aat_k\}$ is the set of atomic attributes of the collection, where: $\forall$ j $\in$ [1..k], an atomic attribute aat_j is defined as a pair (N, T) where:
      - $aat_j.N$ is the name of aat_j,
      - $aat_j.T$ is the type of aat_j.
    - $CAT' = \{cat_1', \dots, cat_l'\}$ is the set of complex attributes of the collection, where: $\forall$ j $\in$ [1..l], a complex attribute cat_j' is defined as a pair (N, AT') where:
      - $cat_j'.N$ is the name of cat_j',
      - $cat_j'.AT'$ is the set of attributes that cat_j' contains. These attributes can be atomic or complex.

4.1.5 Metadata

Metadata is stored in a JSON objet noted O^{MD}. This is defined as a pair (Id, CAT), where:

- $O^{MD}.Id$ is the identifier of the object O^{MD},
- $O^{MD}.CAT = \{cat_1, \dots, cat_n\}$ is the set of complex attributes, where: $\forall$ i $\in$ [1..n], a complex attribute cat_i is defined as a pair (N, AT) where:
  - $cat_i.N$ is the name of cat_i. It corresponds to the name of a collection in the database,
  - $cat_i.AT = AAT \cup CAT'$ is a set of attributes of the collection, where:
    - $AAT = \{aat_1, \dots, aat_k\}$ is the set of atomic attributes of the collection, where: $\forall$ j $\in$ [1..k], an atomic attribute aat_j is defined as a pair (N, Cpt) where:
      - $aat_j.N$ is the name of aat_j,
      - $aat_j.Cpt$ is the number of occurrences of aat_j in the collection where it appears,
    - $CAT' = \{cat_1', \dots, cat_l'\}$ is the set of complex attributes of the collection, where: $\forall$ j $\in$ [1..l], a complex attribute cat_j' is defined as a pair (N, AT') where:
      - $cat_j'.N$ is the name of cat_j',
      - $cat_j'.AT'$ is the set of attributes that cat_j' contains. These attributes can be atomic or complex.

We present the concepts used to describe the NoSQL model and the metadata through the meta-model of Figure 3.

4.2 Transformation rules

In this section, we present our Query2Model process as a sequence of transformation rules described below for each type of query.

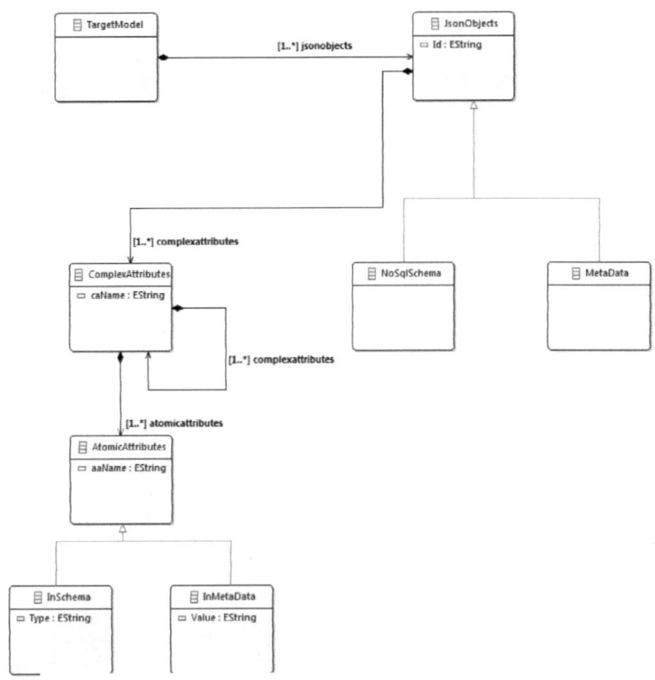

Fig. 3. Metadata and NoSQL metamodel

4.2.1 Case of an insertion query

Triggered by an insert query containing the name of the collection and a set of fields of the form (Name, Value), Query2Model process proceeds as follows:

Step 1: It compares the elements of the query with the current model of the collection and updates it, if necessary.
Step 2: It enriches metadata that will be used later for the treatment of delete query.

Formally, for each insertion query Q^I, Query2Model process applies rules R1 and R2:

R1: Each pair (Name, Value) in the insertion query is transformed into a pair (Name, Type) in the model as follows:

- If there is an attribute $cat_i \in O^M.CAT$, where i ∈ [1..n], and $cat_i.N = Q^I.Cll$, then:

- For each field $afl_j \in Q^I.AFL$, with j ∈ [1..k] :

- Transform the pair $(afl_j.N,\ afl_j.V)$ into a pair $(afl_j.N, afl_j.T)$.

- If there is not an attribute $aat_j \in cat_i.AAT$, with i ∈ [1..n] and j ∈ [1..k], where: $aat_j.N = afl_j.N$ and $aat_j.T = afl_j.T$, then:

- Create a pair $(aat_j.N,\ aat_j.T)$ and add it to $cat_i.AAT$, as:

- $aat_j.N = afl_j.N$,

- $aat_j.T$ is generated based on afl_j.

- Else:

- Create an attribute $cat_i \in O^M.CAT$, with i ∈ [1..n], as $cat_i.N = Q^I.Cll$

- For each field $afl_j \in Q^I.AFL$, with j ∈ [1..k] :

- Create a pair $(aat_j.N,\ aat_j.T)$ and add it to $cat_i.AAT$, as:

- $aat_j.N = afl_j.N$

- $aat_j.T$ is generated based on afl_j.

R2: Each pair (Name, Value) in the insertion query is transformed into a pair (Name, Cpt) in the metadata as follows:

- If there is an attribute $cat_i \in O^{MD}.CAT$, with i ∈ [1..n], as $cat_i.N = Q^I.Cll$, then:

- For each field $afl_j \in Q^I.AFL$, with j ∈ [1..k]:

- Transform the pair $(afl_j.N,\ afl_j.V)$ into a pair $(afl_j.N, afl_j.Cpt)$.

- If there is not an attribute $aat_j \in cat_i.AAT$, with i ∈ [1..n] and j [1..k], as: $aat_j.N = afl_j.N$ and $aat_j.T = afl_j.T$, then:

- Create a pair $(aat_j.N, aat_j.Cpt)$ and add it to $cat_i.AAT$, as:

- $aat_j.N = afl_j.N$

- $aat_j.Cpt = 1$

- Else,

- Update the pair $(aat_j.N, aat_j.Cpt)$, as:

- $aat_j.N = afl_j.N$

- $aat_j.Cpt = aat_j.Cpt + 1$

- Else,

- Create an attribute $cat_i \in O^{MD}.CAT$, with i ∈ [1..n], as: $cat_i.N = Q^I.Cll$

- For each field $afl_j \in Q^I.AFL$, with j ∈ [1..k] :

- Create a pair $(aat_j.N, aat_j.Cpt)$ and add it to $cat_i.AAT$, as:

- $aat_j.N = afl_j.N$

- $aat_j.Cpt = 1$.

4.2.2 Case of a delete query

A delete query contains the name of the collection and the identifier of the document to be deleted. Query2Model process treats this type of queries as follows:
Step 1: It recalculate the model based on the current metadata of the collection.
Step 2: It updates the metadata.
Formally, for each delete query Q^D, Query2Model process applies rules R3 and R4:

R3: Each field of the document whose identifier is Id is transformed as follows:

- Look for the attribute $cat_i \in O^{MD}.CAT$, with i ∈ [1..n], where $cat_i.N = Q^D.Cll$:

- Find the corresponding pair $(aat_j.N,\ aat_j.Cpt)$, as $aat_j \in cat_i.AAT$, with i ∈ [1..n] and j ∈ [1..k]

- If $aat_j.Cpt = 1$, then:

- Delete the corresponding pair $(aat_j.N,\ aat_j.T)$ from the model O^M.

R4: Each pair $(aat_j.N,\ aat_j.T)$ deleted from the model O^M, is transformed into a pair $(aat_j.N,\ aat_j.Cpt)$ in metadata O^{MD}

- Look for the attribute $cat_i \in O^{MD}.CAT$, with i ∈ [1..n], as $cat_i.N = Q^D.Cll$:

- $aat_j.Cpt = aat_j.Cpt - 1$

4.2.3 Case of an update query

An update query contains the name of the collection, the identifier of the document to be modified and a set of fields of the form (Name, Value) to be updated in the document in question. The Query2Model process treats this type of queries as follows:

Step 1: It updates the model based on the current metadata of the collection

Step 2: It updates the metadata for future queries.

Formally, for each change request Q^U, the Query2Model process applies the following rules:

R5: If it is an insertion of a field in the document in question, then apply R1 and R2.

R6: If it is a deletion of a field in the document, then apply R3 and R4.

R7: If it is about renaming a field in the document, then:

- Look for $cat_i \in O^{MD}.CAT$, with i $\in$ [1..n], and $cat_i.N = Q^U.Cll$:

 - Find the corresponding pair $(aat_j.N,\ aat_j.Cpt)$, where $aat_j \in cat_i.AAT$, i $\in$ [1..n] and j $\in$ [1..k]

  - If $aat_j.Cpt = 1$, then:

   - Delete the corresponding pair $(aat_j.N,\ aat_j.T)$ from the model O^M and create another pair with the new attribute name.

   - Delete the corresponding pair $(aat_j.N,\ aat_j.Cpt)$ from the metadata O^{MD} and create another pair with the new attribute name.

  - Else:

   - Keep the corresponding pair $(aat_j.N, aat_j.T)$ in the model O^M and create another with the new attribute name.

   - Keep the corresponding pair $(aat_j.N, aat_j.Cpt)$ in the metadata O^{MD} and create another with the new attribute name.

R8: If it is about updating the value of a field in the document, then:

- Look for $cat_i \in O^M.CAT$, with i $\in$ [1..n], and $cat_i.N = \ Q^U.Cll$:

 - Find the corresponding pair $(aat_j.N,\ aat_j.T)$, where $aat_j \in cat_i.AAT$, i $\in$ [1..n] and j $\in$ [1..k]

  - If the two values of the field are not of the same type, then:

   - If $aat_j.Cpt = 1$, then:

    - Delete the corresponding pair $(aat_j.N,\ aat_j.T)$ in the model $O^M$and create another pair with the new attribute type.

   - Else:

    - Keep the corresponding pair $(aat_j.N,\ aat_j.T)$ in the model O^M and create another pair with the new attribute type.

    - Keep the corresponding pair $(aat_j.N,\ aat_j.Cpt)$ in the metadata O^{MD} by decreasing Cpt and create another pair with the new attribute type.

5 Experiments and validation

5.1 Experiments

To demonstrate the practical applicability of our work, we have implemented the process defined above in Eclipse Modeling Framework (EMF) that provides a convenient environment for formalizing transformations. It combines a set of several powerful modeling standards. Among these standards we used: (1) XML Metadata Interchange (XMI) for exchanging metadata information via XML and (2) Query / View / Transformation (QVT) language for specifying transformations. Transformations presented in section 4.2 are expressed as a sequence of elementary steps that builds the resulting NoSQL model step by step from the input query. First, we implement the transformation rules by means of the QVT plugin provided within EMF. Then, we test the transformation by running the QVT script. This script takes as input (1) the current database model version and (2) a query provided by the user and returns as output the NoSQL database model new version.

To illustrate this, we build an insert query using the standard-based XML Metadata Interchange (XMI) format. The QVT script is then executed on this query to update the complex field that contain the model of the collection provided in the insert query. The result after running the script is provided in the form of XMI file.

5.2 Validation

5.2.1 Experimental environment

Our problem is to extract the model of a database managed by a NoSQL system. Such a feature is intended for users who do not know the data structure (developer who has not created the database, decision makers, etc.); its major interest is to allow the expression of queries as can be done in relational systems. The experiments of our proposal were carried out on a cluster composed of 3 machines. Each machine has the following specifications: Intel Core i5, 8 GB of RAM and 2 TB of disk. One of these machines is configured to act as a master; the other two machines have slave status. To implement our solution, we used [17] AND [18] to generate data. We produced a 3TB dataset in the form of JSON files. These files were loaded into MongoDB using shell commands.

5.2.2 Query set

For our experiment, we have considered four kinds of queries: **(1)** those using one collection (example : select the patients whose age is between 10 and 70), **(2)** queries that use two related collections with the link is expressed using a monovalued reference field (example: we want the name of doctor who has performed the consultation number 41), **(3)** queries that use two related collections with the link is expressed using a multivalued reference field (example: select the antecedents of patient "DUPONT David"), **(4)** queries that use two related collections with the link is expressed using nested data. Table 2 shows the comparison results between our solution and those proposed in [11], [12], [7], [14], [15] and [16] regarding the expression of queries. Note, however, that we only consider works that deal with document-oriented NoSQL databases. Thus, we have excluded the work of [13] which uses a graph-oriented database. For each query we have considered to perform this comparison, we indicate if it can be formulated using the model obtained by each solution proposed in the mentioned works.

Query category	[11]	[12]	[7]	[14]	[15]	[16]	QueryToModel
(1)	X	X	X	X	X	X	X
(2)							X
(3)							X
(4)		X					X

Table. 2 Comparison results between our solution and state of the art

Table 2 shows that the absence of taking into account the links between collections in the referenced works [11], [12], [7], [14], [15] and [16], does not make it possible to write complex queries. Considering for example the following query that applies a join between the Patients collection and the Doctors collection:

db.Patients.aggregate (
[
{$ lookup: {from: "Doctors", localField: "Treating-Doctors._id", foreignField: "_id", as: "Doctors"}}
])

We can see that we can not write this query if we do not visualize the link between Patients and Doctors.

6 Conclusion and perspectives

Our work is part of the evolution of databases towards Big Data. They are currently focused on the extraction mechanisms of the model of a NoSQL database "schema less" to allow the expression of queries by end-users. In this article, we have proposed an automatic process that builds the physical model of a NoSQL database as it is used. This process is based on the Model Driven Architecture (MDA) architecture that provides a formal framework for automating model transformations. Our process generates a NoSQL physical model from insert, delete and update queries by applying a sequence of transformations formalized with the QVT standard. The returned model describes the structure of the collections that make up the database as well as the links between them. We have experimented our process on the case of a medical application that deals with scientific programs for the follow-up of pathologies; the database is stored on the MongoDB system.

Regarding future work, we aim to enrich our process so that it can take into consideration the diversity of particular cases related to the data entered. In fact, when feeding the database, users can enter incorrect data: misspelled field names, values associated with the same field of different types, etc. The current version of our process is based on consistent strategies, but the result may not be entirely satisfactory to users.

7 References

[1] Angadi, A. B., Angadi, A. B., & Gull, K. C. (2013). Growth of New Databases & Analysis of NOSQL Datastores. International Journal of Advanced Research in Computer Science and Software Engineering, 3, 1307-1319.

[2] Abdelhedi, F., Brahim, A. A., Atigui, F., & Zurfluh, G. (2017, August). MDA-Based Approach for NoSQL Databases Modelling. In International Conference on Big Data Analytics and Knowledge Discovery (pp. 88-102). Springer, Cham.

[3] Bondiombouy, C. (2015). Query processing in cloud multistore systems. In BDA : Bases de Données Avancées.

[4] Budinsky, F., Steinberg, D., Ellersick, R., Grose, T. J., & Merks, E. (2004). Eclipse modeling framework: a developer's guide. Addison-Wesley Professional.

[5] Chen, CL Philip et Zhang, Chun-Yang. Data-intensive applications, challenges, techniques and technologies: A survey on Big Data. Information Sciences, 2014, vol. 275, p. 314-347.

[6] Douglas, L., 2001. 3d data management: Controlling data volume, velocity and variety. Gartner. Retrieved, 6, 2001.

[7] Gallinucci, E., Golfarelli, M., & Rizzi, S. (2018). Schema profiling of document-oriented databases. Information Systems, 75, 13-25.

[8] Han, Jing, Haihong, E., LE, Guan, et al. Survey on NoSQL database. Pervasive computing and applications (ICPCA), 2011 6th international conference on. IEEE, 2011. p. 363-366.

[9] Harrison, G. (2015). Next Generation Databases : NoSQLand Big Data. Apress.

[10] Hutchinson, J., Rouncefield, M., & Whittle, J. (2011, May). Model-driven engineering practices in industry. In Proceedings of the 33rd International Conference on Software Engineering (pp. 633-642). ACM.

[11] Klettke, M., U. Störl, et S. Scherzinger (2015). Schema extraction and structural outlier detection for json-based nosql data stores. Datenbanksysteme für Business, Technologie und Web (BTW 2015).

[12] Sevilla, Diego Ruiz, Severino Feliciano Morales, and Jesús García Molina. "Inferring versioned schemas from NoSQL databases and its applications." International Conference on Conceptual Modeling. Springer, Cham, 2015.

[13] Comyn-Wattiau, I., & Akoka, J. (2017, December). Model driven reverse engineering of NoSQL property graph databases: The case of Neo4j. In 2017 IEEE International Conference on Big Data (Big Data) (pp. 453-458). IEEE.

[14] Maity, B., Acharya, A., Goto, T., & Sen, S. (2018, June). A Framework to Convert NoSQL to Relational Model. In Proceedings of the 6th ACM/ACIS International Conference on Applied Computing and Information Technology (pp. 1-6). ACM.

[15] Baazizi, M. A., Lahmar, H. B., Colazzo, D., Ghelli, G., & Sartiani, C. (2017, March). Schema inference for massive JSON datasets. In Extending Database Technology (EDBT).

[16] Baazizi, M. A., Colazzo, D., Ghelli, G., & Sartiani, C. (2019). Parametric schema inference for massive JSON datasets. The VLDB Journal, 1-25.

[17] Generate Test Data (2018) http://www.convertcsv.com/generate-test-data.htm Online; 5 July 2018.

[18] JSON Generator (2018) http://www.json-generator.com/. Online; 5 July 2018.

Developing a Methodology for the Identification of Alternative NoSQL Data Models via Observation of Relational Database Usage

Paul M. Beach[1], Brent T. Langhals[1], Michael R. Grimaila[1], Douglas D. Hodson[2], Ryan D. L. Engle[1]
[1]Dept. of Systems Engineering, Air Force Institute of Technology, Wright-Patterson AFB, OH
[2]Dept. of Electrical & Computer Engineering, Air Force Institute of Technology, Wright-Patterson AFB, OH

Abstract – *NoSQL databases are largely synonymous with Big Data applications, however there is existing research to support their usage for smaller scale applications (even on a single desktop). This work seeks to reinforce this notion by proposing a methodology to identify when a NoSQL database may be better suited than an existing Relational Database Management System (RDBMS). First, approaches to characterizing database workloads are discussed, along with a summary of relevant benchmarking metrics. Then, we present a methodology for evaluating the suitability of an existing RDBMS against possible alternative NoSQL databases.*

Keywords: Benchmarking, data models, database, database systems, NoSQL.

1 Introduction

The present era of Big Data has given rise to a number of novel approaches and supporting technologies for coping with the ever-increasing amounts of data that many organizations attempt to collect and use. The volumes, velocities and varieties of data collected, inherent characteristics of "Big Data", have increasingly proven traditional relational data databases as inadequate. This challenge has led to the emergence of a new class of database systems (often referred to as NoSQL systems), which are not based upon the traditional relational model [1].

Although these systems were initially borne out of a need to deal with massive datasets hosted across large clusters of computers utilizing commodity hardware, previous research has highlighted the value in considering the use of these NoSQL systems in a single desktop configuration (citing reasons such as efficient write performance and fast, low-latency access, among others) [2]. Our research extends this effort and considers the possibility that there are relational database systems operating today which may benefit from better performance using a key-value, document, column, or graph data model, i.e. one supported by a NoSQL data model.

There are several reasons why an existing system may be using a relational data model when a different data model would be more appropriate. One possibility is that the application developer was unfamiliar with the recent development of the NoSQL data models when they designed the system. Alternatively, the usage of a database system may have evolved over time from a point when a relational data model made the most sense, to something different which more closely aligns with a NoSQL data model.

Regardless of the underlying reason for the mismatch, our research serves as an exploratory effort towards proposing a methodology for identifying a more suitable NoSQL database type based solely on observations of interactions with an existing relational database. In particular, we are characterizing a user's workload against the existing database and matching the workload to relevant benchmark metrics designed to identify a more suitable solution. The remainder of the paper is organized as follows. In Section 2, a comparison of relational and NoSQL data models is presented. Section 3 discusses existing approaches towards defining database workloads and benchmark metrics are discussed. Section 4 presents the proposed methodology. Section 5 walks the reader through a hypothetical use case for the proposed methodology and the paper is concluded in Section 6.

2 Data Models

Due to its ubiquitous usage, the uses of the relational data model are likely well understood by many audiences. However, a brief review of the NoSQL data models and their relative advantages and disadvantages over the relational model provides a foundation for the topics that follow.

2.1 Key-value

Key-value (KV) stores rely on a simple data model predicated on a simple structure involving a key and its associated value. In this data model, the key is a unique identifier for the data and is comparable to maps, dictionaries, and associative arrays which all organize data using non-integer indexing. Additionally, the set of employable keys are not pre-defined. In fact, this model grants extensive freedom to the user for key definition. Likewise, the associated value may vary greatly from strings, to numbers, or even binary large objects (BLOBs) among others. This data is considered "opaque" to the model because limited information is known about the stored data itself [3]–[5].

Storage and retrieval of data is also relatively simple as operations are typically focused on keys. In fact, operations on key-value stores are typically limited to three options: storing (putting) a value by a key, retrieving (getting) a value for a key or deleting a value by its key. In effect, this model does not provide the ability to query by examining the contents of a stored value.

In contrast to a relational model, queries that are relatively easy to perform against values, e.g., SELECT * FROM Table WHERE value=X, are no longer feasible. Additionally, atomic operations can only be performed on a single key-value pair at a time. Another limitation of the key-value model is that it becomes much more difficult to efficiently store and retrieve related pieces of data, since the data model does not provide a native mechanism to track relationships between key-value pairs. If relationship management is necessary, the user must do so externally from the KV model. Furthermore, KV stores require no pre-defined schema unlike relational implementations [3].

Finally, although the key-value model theoretically can store any type of value, a practical consideration to consider is that databases employing the KV model will have an upper limit on the size of the stored value [3]. Despite these limitations, one of the primary motivations for using a database implementation based on the key-value model is that they tend to be extremely performant [5].

2.2 Document

In this data model, documents are characterized as "self-describing, hierarchical tree data structures," with a flexible schema that allows one document to differ from another [5]. This is contrasted with the relational model, in which all tuples of a given entity are required to have the same attributes [6]. Although the document data model lacks a means of joining documents the way the relational model does, the ability to flexibly store documents nested within another document is one approach to satisfying this objective. Like the other non-relational implementations, attributes may be added to documents without defining a schema [3].

Similar to the key-value model, atomic operations across documents are not possible in the document model. On the other hand, document databases are able to execute queries based on the stored values, so they differ from key-value stores but are similar to relational databases in this regard [3].

2.3 Column Family

Superficially, relational and column family databases may appear similar since they both employ rows, columns and, effectively, tables. However there are notable differences between their underlying data models. In a column family model, data are uniquely identified by both a row and column name. Additionally, columns may be grouped together to form column families. This organization improves performance when reading and writing related data because it is stored together [4], [7]. Similar to KV stores, atomic operations in column families are limited to operating only a single row. Again, this contrasts with the relational capability to execute multi-row transactions in a single operation [3].

One of the strengths of the column family over relational model is its ability to store only the data that is of interest. Thus, rows may or may not contain values for every column, i.e., be sparse. This design enables column family databases to potentially span millions of columns in an efficient manner whereas relational databases must store null values if there are non-relevant or empty fields. This approach becomes substantially less tenable for relational databases when large numbers of sparsely populated fields are commonplace. Additionally, columns may be added at any time to an existing data store which contrasts with the relational requirement to update the existing database structure definition (i.e., schema) prior to adding an attribute [4].

2.4 Graph

Graph databases represent data using nodes and relationships between nodes, which is useful for storing information about highly interrelated objects. The graph data model (and the databases that employ it) make querying across related data easier and more efficient than would be possible using a relational data model (which would require many joins, and/or recursive queries, if supported by the particular RDMBS) [3].

3 Benchmarking NoSQL Databases

The earliest usage of the term "NoSQL" in the context of non-relational databases dates back to 2009 [5], and some of the earliest examples of what we would consider today to be a NoSQL database were being designed only a few years earlier [8]. Still, in the relatively brief period since then there has been ample interest from practitioners and researchers alike to look at ways of benchmarking the performance of these systems. This section examines previous approaches of benchmarking NoSQL databases found in the literature which focus on how the usage (i.e., workload) and performance (i.e., metrics) of these systems can be characterized

3.1 Workloads

One way of defining workloads in a database system is "requests made by the users of a system" [9]. Depending on the kinds and frequency of requests that users are making to a database system, the burden upon that system will vary. Thus, a first step towards understanding how an existing database system is being employed will require a means of assessing the existing workload on that system. Three approaches were identified in the literature, including "Big Data distributed tasks", "standardized queries" and "core workloads".

A Big Data application-based approach to defining database workloads considers Big Data workloads as being comprised of one or more core computational tasks common in Big Data processing, such as sorting, word counting, grep, cryptographic hashing, matrix multiplication, random sampling, graph traversal, and so on [10], [11]. While this bottom-up, "building blocks" approach to creating a database workload is an interesting method for comparing Big Data processing frameworks (e.g., Apache Hadoop), the scope of this research (non-"Big Data", single box workloads) does not extend to such frameworks so the usefulness of this approach would be limited.

Another observed approach for testing database workloads is to employ a set of predefined "standardized queries", which are queries representative of tasks that would be performed in real-world systems (e.g., "List the top 10 states in descending order with at least 10 customers who during a given month bought products with the price tag at least 20% higher than the average price of products in the same category") [12], [13]. Similar to the Big Data application-based approach to assembling workloads, this is an excellent top-down approach for comparing the overall performance of two or more big data processing frameworks. However, the methodology presented in section 4 relies upon the ability to generalize observable queries (i.e. not predefined), which would be a non-trivial endeavor with this approach. Therefore, a third approach is considered.

One of the most common benchmarking frameworks used to assess NoSQL databases is the Yahoo! Cloud Serving Benchmark (YCSB) [14]. This framework was designed by engineers from Yahoo! to benchmark various databases used in cloud-based settings. One of the reasons for its popularity is the fact that it was designed to be extensible so that researchers could easily incorporate additional databases or customize the workloads to suit their needs [15].

YCSB comes with a set of six predefined "core workloads" (Workloads A through F) that generically represent typical usage patterns of various types of applications. Core workloads are defined by a fractional breakdown of the read, update, insert, and scan operations that will be executed by the benchmark and a random distribution that determines which record to read or write to. For example, Workload A is considered an "update heavy" workload, and is configured to perform a 50%/50% mix of reads and writes using a Zipfian distribution in order to represent an application such as a session store (Zipfian distributions represent situations where a few records are very popular and commonly accessed, while the majority are not frequently accessed). Workload B is considered a "read mostly" workload, and is configured to perform read queries 95% of the time and write queries the remaining 5%, also using the Zipfian distribution. The example application of Workload B is photo tagging, where most operations are reading tags with an occasional write [15].

This method has the best potential for being adapted to this research, since it is conceivable to develop software that can analyze the behavior of an existing database workload by evaluating the queries based on keyword extraction (i.e., looking for "SELECT", "UPDATE", "DELETE", etc.). This approach will be discussed further in the Methodology section.

3.2 Metrics

A number of studies have been conducted to measure the performance of databases using a variety of benchmarking metrics, to include metrics related to CRUD (create, read, update, and delete) operations and system performance.

The most prevalent types of benchmarking metrics that were observed involve assessing CRUD operations on NoSQL databases. Given the simplicity of the key-value data model, many types of NoSQL databases can support this model, even those typically associated with other data models (e.g., MongoDB, Cassandra, etc.) and as such it appears to be the most widely studied [16]. The Yahoo! Cloud Serving Benchmark (YCSB), is designed to test NoSQL databases supporting this key-value model [15]. Additionally, there have been many other studies that conducted research on the performance of CRUD operations for various types of NoSQL databases [16]–[27].

Beyond simple CRUD performance measurements, other studies have looked at aspects of the host system's performance in order to gain insights about the performance of NoSQL databases and/or Big Data workloads. For instance, the utilization of system metrics such as CPU and memory utilization, I/O wait times, memory, disk and network bandwidth utilization, cache misses, branch misprediction rates and energy-efficiency are a few of the metrics that have been used to date in previous studies [10], [13], [28]–[32]. However, it has also been pointed out that such "micro benchmarks" do not necessarily indicate how a given benchmark will perform on different hardware, potentially limiting their usefulness [33].

A consolidated summarization of these benchmarking metrics is provided in Table 1.

Table 1: Benchmarking Metrics Discussed in the Literature.

Metric	Description
CRUD Operations	
Create	Time required to insert a new value
Read	Time required to read a value
Update	Time required to update a value
Delete	Time required to delete a value
System Performance	
CPU utilization rates	Percentage of CPU utilization
I/O wait times	Percentage of time CPU is waiting
Memory I/O bandwidth	Rate of memory data transfer (in MBps)
Memory utilization	Percentage of memory utilization
Disk I/O bandwidth	Rate of disk data transfer (in MBps)
Network I/O bandwidth	Rate of network data transfer (in MBps)
Cache misses per kilo instructions	Number of times a cache lookup failed
Branch mispredict rate	Percentage of branch mispredictions
Energy-efficiency	Power consumption of a system (in Watts)

4 A Proposed Methodology

In this section, we offer a proposed methodology for identifying suitable NoSQL database alternatives to an existing RDBMS.

4.1 Step 1: Monitor Current Usage

The process begins by observing the current usage of an existing RDBMS system (see Fig. 1). This step is intended to collect information about the queries being performed against the RDMBS by all users, as well as the collection of metrics identified in Table 1. Since we are attempting to characterize the usage of the system as a whole, queries for the entire system are gathered (rather than per user). Information about the queries should include the Structured Query Language (SQL) code being sent to the RDBMS as well as the response from the database. A sufficient number of queries should be collected to ensure that a representative sample has been captured. Also, information about the overall size of the database is captured.

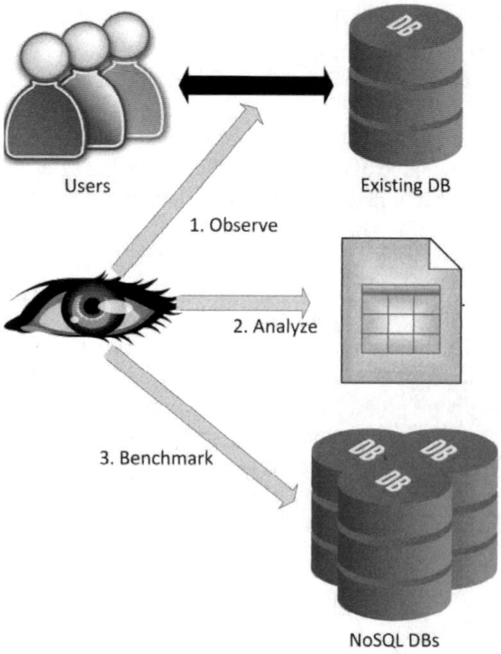

Fig. 1. Proposed methodology.

4.2 Step 2: Analyze Observed Usage

After collecting the necessary information in the first step, the next step involves analyzing the collected data in order to characterize the current system's workload. The SQL queries and associated responses are parsed in order to extract three attributes pertaining to the types of queries being presented: core workload classification(s), query frequency, and data volume.

As described in section 3.1, core workload classifications(s) refers to a fractional breakdown of the queries based on the read, update, insert, and read/modify/write mixture. To establish this ratio, the SQL commands are parsed to extract and tabulate the relevant SELECT, UPDATE, INSERT INTO, and/or DELETE commands. For the slightly more complex read/modify/write workload, a sequence of a SELECT command followed by an UPDATE/INSERT/DELETE with matching WHERE clauses would apply.

Query frequency is an average measurement of how many queries are being performed per unit of time against the database. This attribute gives a measure of the intensity of the database's usage.

Query complexity can be categorized as either simple or complex. Simple queries are those that can access data via a unique identifier or range of identifiers or values, while a complex query would be anything else (e.g., queries using aggregate function such as AVG, COUNT, MAX, MIN and SUM, or relational queries using JOIN, IN and EXISTS, etc.) [6], [34].

Finally, data volume is a measurement of the average volume of data being stored or retrieved from the database for any given query. These could be given discrete categorizations such as small for queries containing values less than 1 kilobyte in size, medium for queries with values between 1 kilobyte and 1 terabyte in size, and large for anything exceeding 1 terabyte per query [34]. Alternatively, for a simpler approach a scalar value for the observed average can be used.

4.3 Step 3: Run Benchmark Tests

Finally, the outputs from step 2 are used as inputs for a battery of benchmark tests (using YCSB or another similar benchmark tool) to assess the performance of similarly resourced NoSQL databases (i.e., in terms of CPU, memory, and storage). More concretely, the benchmark tool should be configured to use a core workload mixture analogous to the mixture observed on the existing system, queries should be ran as frequently as those observed on the existing system, and the volume of data being sent and received should similarly be based on that seen on the existing system.

Once the benchmark tests have been executed, the resulting metrics are be compared to those gathered during the observation of the existing system in step 1. NoSQL databases showing improvements in CRUD operation metrics may indicate a more suitable choice of database (assuming the improved CRUD operation(s) are of interest/value to the user). Additionally, improvements in system performance metrics may indicate that better performance could be obtained with a NoSQL system, or that similar performance can be achieved with less hardware. Finally, the relative sizes of the databases can be compared to determine if there is any advantage of one over the other in terms of storage costs.

5 Hypothetical Use Case

To provide a more concrete example of our proposed approach, we present the following hypothetical use case. In this example, we begin by observing a common RDMBS (MySQL) supporting an online forum system.

Online forums typically consist of a number of distinct entities such as subforums, discussion threads, comments, and users. Subforums organize discussion topics into related areas, which consist of discussion threads. The discussion threads are ordered by recency (the most recently commented upon threads are generally presented first, replacing threads that have not recently been commented on), and these threads are composed of individual comments. Finally, it should be noted that the comments are made by the users who visit the forum. In reality, there may be many more relevant entities in a realistic forum system (e.g., messages between users).

For the sake of this example, consider a user visiting an individual subforum, where they would be presented with a list of discussion threads that are ordered by recency of comments within each discussion thread. Usage patterns of such a system would typically involve a high-read workload (e.g., 95%) and a low-write workload (e.g., 5%), since forums are often used for community discussions where one user makes a comment that is subsequently read by many other users. Also, the most recent discussions are typically the ones being browsed at any given time, so access patterns would follow a distribution where the most recent information is accessed more often.

A typical RDBMS system such as MySQL would organize this database with a normalized schema keeping each of these entities (i.e. subforums, discussion threads, comments, and users) separate. Thus, when the user visits a subforum a series of many SQL queries would need be issued to collect and then present the proper information to the user. For example, first the system would need to query a list of all threads in the subforum that the user was visiting, which would be a relatively simple SELECT query. However, in order to know the correct order to display them in, each of the comments for each of the discussion threads would need to be queried and sorted by most recent, requiring individual SELECT statements with an ORDER BY clause for each topic. Finally, when discussion threads are listed in subforums, they also typically include information about the most recent post, such as when it was made and by which user. Therefore, another batch of SELECT statements using JOIN operators would be required to obtain the proper usernames associated with each of the most recent comments for each discussion thread.

In the proposed methodology, we would begin by monitoring the usage of the MySQL database, collecting the SQL queries described above. As mentioned, due to the usage patterns of this system, 95% of the entries would be a SELECT statement of some type to collect the necessary discussion threads, comments and user information, and about 5% would be UPDATE or INSERT operations.

After the queries are collected, the second step of our methodology can be accomplished with a simple script to parse the collected queries for the SQL keywords of interest, tabulating each to determine the precise workload breakdown ratio. Also, the total number of queries over the observed period of time are gathered to arrive at an average frequency, and the average size of the queries and their responses are averaged to determine a representative value for the data volume to be used in the benchmark tests.

Finally, the third step of the methodology would consist of running benchmark tests using similarly sized NoSQL databases. In this scenario, the benchmark tests employ the YCSB benchmarking tool against each of the four NoSQL databases. The tool is configured with the core workload classification, target number of operations per second, and average value size. After the tests are run, the results can be compared to the performance observed in step 1. The output in Table 2 shows a representative example of the difference in performance between the two databases. The experimental setup that generated these results employed YCSB's Workload B (95% reads, 5% update) to execute 100,000 operations, modified to use a "latest" distribution (which selects records on a basis that the most recently inserted ones will be selected more often [15]), mirroring the usage pattern described above for online forums. These results were generated on virtual machines operating Ubuntu 18.04 LTS equipped with 4 GB RAM and 4 CPU cores (Intel i7-8650U @ 1.90GHz).

In contrast to the organization of the MySQL database, the nested structure of a document database (such as MongoDB), lends itself well to the structure of an online forum. Each

Table 2: Benchmarking Results (smaller is better).

	MySQL	MongoDB
Total execution time (in seconds)	22.947	15.637
Average read time (in microseconds)	184.89	147.514
Average update time (in microseconds)	933.226	250.929

subforum is a document, which will refence other nested documents for the individual discussion threads. These threads can contain all of the comments, along with the associated user information embedded within them since NoSQL data models are typically denormalized. As a result of this structure, reads (which comprise the majority of operations in this system) would be optimized, and can be expected to perform more quickly. Thus, it is anticipated that the results will remain consistent with real-world testing of similar scenarios, and that the benchmark test for the document database (i.e., MongoDB) would indicate that this data model may be a more suitable selection for this use case [35].

6 Conclusions and Future Work

This work demonstrates a possible approach for characterizing observed workloads against an RDBMS, and further it proposes a method to suggest suitable NoSQL databases based on the observed workloads for the existing RDBMS.

Because of the abstractions involved in the underlying data models, this approach can be used to suggest when switching to a NoSQL database may be a preferred solution (in terms of increased performance and/or reduced hardware requirements), however it cannot guarantee that this is the case. Knowing for certain that switching to a NoSQL data model would be a more suitable choice would likely require empirical testing using the actual system's users and original data (properly transformed into the appropriate NoSQL data model).

Future work includes empirical testing of this methodology to further support the validity of this approach. Also, additional attributes about the observed queries such as query complexity (e.g., are the queries simple SELECT statements, or do they involve more complex operations such as JOIN), and the development of a corresponding supervised learning decision tree model to facilitate the inclusion of multiple criteria in a decision model.

Acknowledgment

Funding for this research was provided as part of the Air Force Office of Scientific Research grant 18RT0095 in support of Dynamic Data Driven Application Systems, PI: Dr. Eric Blasch.

Disclaimer

The views expressed in this paper are those of the authors and do not reflect the official policy or position of the U.S. Air Force, the Department of Defense, or the U.S. Government.

7 References

[1] A. B. M. Moniruzzaman and S. A. Hossain, "NoSQL Database: New Era of Databases for Big data Analytics - Classification, Characteristics and Comparison," *Int. J. Database Theory Appl.*, vol. 6, no. 4, p. 14, 2013.

[2] R. D. L. Engle, B. T. Langhals, M. R. Grimaila, and D. D. Hodson, "The Case for NoSQL on a Single Desktop," presented at the International Conference on Information and Knowledge Engineering, Las Vegas, NV, 2018, p. 4.

[3] D. Sullivan, *NoSQL for mere mortals*. Hoboken, NJ: Addison-Wesley, 2015.

[4] R. Hecht and S. Jablonski, "NoSQL evaluation: A use case oriented survey," in *2011 International Conference on Cloud and Service Computing*, Hong Kong, China, 2011, pp. 336–341.

[5] P. J. Sadalage and M. Fowler, *NoSQL distilled: a brief guide to the emerging world of polyglot persistence*. Upper Saddle River, NJ: Addison-Wesley, 2013.

[6] P. Pratt, *A Guide to SQL*, Seventh. Boston, MA: Thomson Course Technology.

[7] G. Copeland and S. Khoshafian, "A Decomposition Storage Model," *ACM SIGMOD Rec.*, vol. 14, no. 4, pp. 268–279, 1985.

[8] F. Chang *et al.*, "Bigtable: A Distributed Storage System for Structured Data," *ACM Trans. Comput. Syst.*, vol. 26, no. 2, pp. 1–26, Jun. 2008.

[9] R. Jain, *The art of computer systems performance analysis: techniques for experimental design, measurement, simulation, and modeling*. New York: Wiley, 1991.

[10] W. Gao *et al.*, "Data Motifs: A Lens Towards Fully Understanding Big Data and AI Workloads," *ArXiv180808512 Cs*, Aug. 2018.

[11] F. Ahmad, S. Lee, M. Thottethodi, and T. N. Vijaykumar, "PUMA: Purdue MapReduce Benchmarks Suite," Purdue University, ECE Technical Reports TR-ECE-12-11, 2012.

[12] Transaction Processing Performance Council, "Transaction Processing Performance Council - TPC Express Big Bench (TPCx-BB) Standard Specification Version 1." 2016.

[13] D. Richins, T. Ahmed, R. Clapp, and V. Janapa Reddi, "Amdahl's Law in Big Data Analytics: Alive and Kicking in TPCx-BB (BigBench)," in *2018 IEEE International Symposium on High Performance Computer Architecture (HPCA)*, Vienna, 2018, pp. 630–642.

[14] V. Abramova and J. Bernardino, "NoSQL databases: MongoDB vs cassandra," in *Proceedings of the International C* Conference on Computer Science and Software Engineering - C3S2E '13*, Porto, Portugal, 2013, pp. 14–22.

[15] B. F. Cooper, A. Silberstein, E. Tam, R. Ramakrishnan, and R. Sears, "Benchmarking cloud serving systems with YCSB," in *Proceedings of the 1st ACM symposium on Cloud computing - SoCC '10*, Indianapolis, Indiana, USA, 2010, p. 143.

[16] Y. Li and S. Manoharan, "A performance comparison of SQL and NoSQL databases," in *2013 IEEE Pacific Rim Conference on Communications, Computers and Signal Processing (PACRIM)*, Victoria, BC, Canada, 2013, pp. 15–19.

[17] V. D. Jogi and A. Sinha, "Performance evaluation of MySQL, Cassandra and HBase for heavy write operation," in *2016 3rd International Conference on Recent Advances in Information Technology (RAIT)*, Dhanbad, India, 2016, pp. 586–590.

[18] A. Boicea, F. Radulescu, and L. I. Agapin, "MongoDB vs Oracle -- Database Comparison," in *2012 Third International Conference on Emerging Intelligent Data and Web Technologies*, Bucharest, Romania, 2012, pp. 330–335.

[19] S. Islam, K. Lee, A. Fekete, and A. Liu, "How a consumer can measure elasticity for cloud platforms," in *Proceedings of the third joint WOSP/SIPEW international conference on Performance Engineering - ICPE '12*, Boston, Massachusetts, USA, 2012, p. 85.

[20] J. Klein, I. Gorton, N. Ernst, P. Donohoe, K. Pham, and C. Matser, "Performance Evaluation of NoSQL Databases: A Case Study," in *Proceedings of the 1st Workshop on Performance Analysis of Big Data Systems - PABS '15*, Austin, Texas, USA, 2015, pp. 5–10.

[21] D. Carstoiu, E. Lepadatu, and M. Gaspar, "Hbase - non SQL Database, Performances Evaluation," *Int. J. Adv. Comput. Technol.*, vol. 2, no. 5, p. 11, 2010.

[22] G. Ladwig and A. Harth, "CumulusRDF: Linked Data Management on Nested Key-Value Stores," presented at the The 7th International Workshop on Scalable Semantic Web Knowledge Base Systems, 2011, p. 13.

[23] B. Atikoglu, Y. Xu, and E. Frachtenberg, "Workload Analysis of a Large-Scale Key-Value Store," in *ACM SIGMETRICS Performance Evaluation Review*, 2012, vol. 40 (1), pp. 53–64.

[24] E. Dede, M. Govindaraju, D. Gunter, R. S. Canon, and L. Ramakrishnan, "Performance evaluation of a MongoDB and hadoop platform for scientific data analysis," in *Proceedings of the 4th ACM workshop on Scientific cloud computing - Science Cloud '13*, New York, New York, USA, 2013, p. 13.

[25] A. Flores, S. Ramirez, R. Toasa, J. Vargas, R. U.- Barrionuevo, and J. M. Lavin, "Performance Evaluation of NoSQL and SQL Queries in Response Time for the E-government," in *2018 International Conference on eDemocracy & eGovernment (ICEDEG)*, Ambato, 2018, pp. 257–262.

[26] C.-O. Truică, F. Rădulescu, A. Boicea, and I. Bucur, "Performance evaluation for CRUD operations in asynchronously replicated document oriented database," *2015 20th Int. Conf. Control Syst. Comput. Sci.*, pp. 191–196, May 2015.

[27] R. Aniceto *et al.*, "Evaluating the Cassandra NoSQL Database Approach for Genomic Data Persistency," *Int. J. Genomics*, vol. 2015, pp. 1–7, 2015.

[28] H. Boral and D. DeWitt, "A methodology for database system performance evaluation," in *Proceedings of the 1984 ACM SIGMOD international conference on Management of data*, 1984.

[29] A. T. Kabakus and R. Kara, "A performance evaluation of in-memory databases," *J. King Saud Univ. - Comput. Inf. Sci.*, vol. 29, no. 4, pp. 520–525, Oct. 2017.

[30] Z. Jia, L. Wang, J. Zhan, L. Zhang, and C. Luo, "Characterizing data analysis workloads in data centers," in *2013 IEEE International Symposium on Workload Characterization (IISWC)*, Portland, OR, USA, 2013, pp. 66–76.

[31] L. Wang *et al.*, "BigDataBench: a Big Data Benchmark Suite from Internet Services," *2014 IEEE 20th Int. Symp. High Perform. Comput. Archit. HPCA*, pp. 488–499, Feb. 2014.

[32] R. Panda and L. K. John, "Proxy Benchmarks for Emerging Big-data Workloads," in *26th International Conference on Parallel Architectures and Compilation Techniques (PACT)*, 2017, pp. 105–116.

[33] Y. Chen, S. Alspaugh, and R. Katz, "Interactive Analytical Processing in Big Data Systems: A Cross-Industry Study of MapReduce Workloads," *ArXiv12084174 Cs*, Aug. 2012.

[34] R. D. L. Engle, "A Methodology for Evaluating Relational and NoSQL Databases for Small-scale Storage and Retrieval," Air Force Institute of Technology, 2018.

[35] C. Gyorodi, R. Gyorodi, G. Pecherle, and A. Olah, "A comparative study: MongoDB vs. MySQL," in *2015 13th International Conference on Engineering of Modern Electric Systems (EMES)*, Oradea, Romania, 2015, pp. 1–6.

Improving the Quality of Homeless Dataset

Ting Liu
Computer Science Department
Data Science Program
Siena College
Loudonville, USA
tliu@siena.edu

Keith Grable
Computer Science Department
Siena College
Loudonville, USA
kw28grab@siena.edu

Ruth Kassel
Academic Community Engagement
Siena College
Loudonville, USA
rkassel@siena.edu

Hamza Memon
Computer Science Department
Siena College
Loudonville, USA
h01memo@alum.siena.edu

Mark Eliseo
Computer Science Department
Siena College
Loudonville, USA
mc12elis@siena.edu

Luke Mckenna
Computer Science Department
Siena College
Loudonville, USA
lr10mcke@siena.edu

Michael Lostritto
Computer Science Department
Siena College
Loudonville, USA
ma25lost@siena.edu

***Abstract* — The quality of homeless data is always a serious issue because of information silos and lack of experienced staff. In this paper, we demonstrate a toolkit that achieved two main approaches. The first one is to identify the records from different shelters that belong to same person and merge them. We started from deduplication algorithm from U.S. Department of Housing and Urban Development (HUD) and made a significant improvement by adding new features, such as household id, into deduplication process. The second approach is to automatically detect and report the errors hidden in the dataset, which is a very tedious task for human being. This toolkit significantly improves the quality of homeless data and relieved the heavy burden of data quality control from people tremendously so that they can spend more time on data analysis and critical thinking that can improve the quality of their service to homeless people.**

***Index Terms*—Data Quality, HMIS, Data Accuracy, Deduplication, Homeless**

Type: Regular research paper

I. Introduction

A Homeless Management Information System (HMIS) [1] established by the U.S. Department of Housing and Urban Development (HUD) is a database system used to collect client-level data and data on the provision of housing and services to homeless individuals and families and persons at risk of homelessness. Each Continuum of Care (CoC) is responsible for data collection and report the statistics and analysis from the data to HUD annually, which will help policymakers, researchers, service agencies, and other community stakeholders understand homeless issues accurately and then create effective and efficient strategy to serve homeless people. Therefore, how much the data can reflect the actual information in the real world is vitally important.

According to HUD determined standard[2], the issues of the data quality in HMIS system can be classified into four categories,

- Timeliness of Data
  Information collected from clients served by homeless programs (part of HMIS system) should be entered in the database in time to guarantee the reports/analysis sent to HUD tell the current status of homeless.
- Data Completeness
  To have a better comprehension of the clients, the collected data should contain all required information of all clients get served by some programs. Both missing whole client information and incomplete client records can cause serious issues. For example, when multiple records belonging to same person fails to be merged, the number of people can be severely skewed to larger number.
- Data Accuracy
  Collected data should be as accurate as possible to represent the information of the clients. The inaccurate information can be caused by either client (intentionally or unintentionally) or data entry staff (without enough training). Same as data completeness issue, inaccurate/wrong information generates wrong report that can mislead policymakers significantly.
- Data Consistency
  Consistency of data collection refers to interpretation of the data fields by data entry staff has to be consistent. Therefore, data entry training is important and necessary.

CoCs currently have two ways for data quality control, 1) train data entry staff, 2) validate the data regularly to reduce data quality issues. HMIS system also provides deduplication tool to automatically merge records of same person collected from different shelters. However, CoCs have to check other data issues manually, which is a very time-consuming job. In this paper, we report a data validation system that,

- Improves the accuracy of the deduplication tool in HMIS system
- Reports the conflicts in the duplicates found through deduplication process. For example, when coming back

[1] https://www.hudexchange.info/programs/hmis/
[2] https://www.hudexchange.info/resources/documents/EnhancingHMISDataQuality.pdf

to the same shelter, some member of the family got original household id but different personal ids.

- Automatically detect and report other quality issues in the data.

Our goal is to liberate people from such heavy burden and tedious job so that they can have more time on data analysis and critical thinking and thus can provide better service to homeless people and produce high quality reports to HUD.

This paper has five sections, section one explains the homeless dataset collected by our community partner, CARES Inc[3]. Section two discusses related research regarding deduplication process. Section three describes the deduplication algorithm used in HMIS system. Section four discusses the issues found in the algorithm with improvements. Section five demonstrate other validation process in our system. Finally, section six describes the conclusion and future work.

II. Homeless Data

CARES, Inc, who act as HMIS System Administrators for 13 CoCs in New York state, is our local community partner. We are collaborating tightly focusing on quality improvement of homeless data and novel ideas of data analysis/interpretation. The provided homeless data by CARES was acquired from shelters or any homeless programs in 27 counties around capital area of New York State (Figure 1) in August 2017. The dataset records the information of clients who used the homeless service between 2005 and 2016. The dataset contains twelve files, Client, Disabilities, Enrollment, EnrollmentCoC, Exit, Export, Funder., IncomeBenefits, Project, ProjectCoC,

Figure 1 CARES is administrating the homeless shelters and programs in the 27 highlight *counties* in New York State

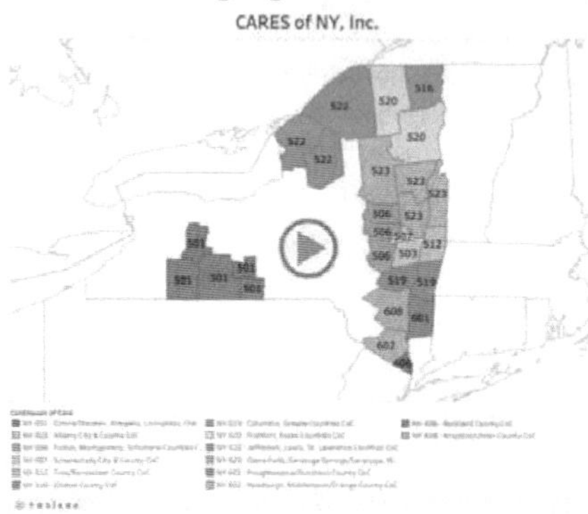

Site, and UniqueIDkey. Table 1 shows the dimensions of four example files. Client table collects 89,677 (rows) individual information on 36 categories (columns), such as Name (including first name, last name, middle name, and name suffix), Social Security Number (SSN), Date of Birth (DOB), Gender, etc. To protect client privacy, all confidential information, such as client's name, SSN, and personal ID are double-hashed before the data released to Siena college (Table 2). This data has finished deduplication process at shelters' level. So if one person used a shelter multiple times, he/she should have only one record. It makes the enrollment number (Table 1) is bigger than client number. On the other hand, exit number (Table 1) is less than enrollment, which indicates that people are still in HMIS system and using the service. Since HMIS is a big and complex system, HUD built a dictionary[4] with detailed description of the tables.

File	Rows	Columns
Client	89,677	36
Enrollment	130,466	101
Exit	122,428	27
Site	197	14

Table 1 Overview of Four Data Files

III. Related Research on Deduplication Process

Deduplication is not a trivial task since there is no standard/global indicator for identification. It often requires a combination of different factors according to what information can be utilized from data. There are two main types of deduplication methodologies, deterministic and probabilistic approaches. In deterministic approach, the deduplication process is based on a set of heuristic rules [5][6]. Domain experts will first find a list of features from the dataset that are good indicators for data linkage. In the linked Surveillance, Epidemiology and End-Results (SEER)-Medicare data [8], SSN, name, gender, and date of Birth are found as most effective features for linkage process. Then rules are generated using one or a combination of the features and evaluated. Those can achieve above the certain threshold will be kept for the deduplication process. For example, one rule used for SEER data to merge two records if they match on name, month of Birth, gender, and seven digits of SSN.

The second main type is probabilistic approach [2][3][7]. By combining a feature's probabilities of both correct matches and false matches, the weight of the feature is calculated as an indicator how much this feature can contribute deduplication process [2]. Different from deterministic approach, it is no longer "all-or-nothing" and for each match, system can tell how confident this match would be according to the weights of features of the rule for deduplication process. Some recent approaches also employ supervised/semi-supervised machine learning algorithms to let system automatically decide what features would be involved and the way of combination by learning from the training dataset [1][4]. However, the

PersonalID	FirstName	LastName	NameDataQuality	SSN	SSNDataQuality	DOB	DOBDataQuality	
38b4ceda7	aafa3c96770c175071aef4a e7b007440e8c1cee3	38a7f7e89000772466e3a6 ee361226d97575b11d	1	20258d6a69e5216362c364cf 4ad5db378f6aa3fbb979	1	1/4/74	1	...
edf940d9e	4ae911039f50e7f7988f334 ebf4b567e558942bf	91179bd6f18d08d960a6c4 2bb9058ceb1aafaad4	1	0646461a0f5bb24f1b0932c8 0a3c20b4277a046c9253	1	9/7/81	1	
26cb0d358	838595b69b27bbe7f7c55e 110a97eba0db266c8e	86ed62e7eb1ae069b1e75 20aec3778fa48dcb4b2	1	10866be49633daa60a7a0dfb 90ad68f2ab5dc97cfd85	1	4/9/69	1	

Table 2 A few examples of client information

probabilistic approach heavily depends on the size and quality of training data to have features' weight statistically significant. Therefore, many deduplication processes, including the one in HMIS system, are still using deterministic approach.

IV. HMIS Deduplication Algorithm

Deduplication is an extremely important part of homeless data cleaning and quality improving process since the data from different shelters does not communicate with each other. One person can have multiple client records while moving from one shelter to another. Therefore, to study the data merged from different shelters and create high qualified reports to support policy making, it is necessary to deduplicate the data before analysis.

With the collaboration between McCormack Graduate School of Policy Studies, University of Massachusetts Boston and Change and Strategy Solutions for HUD, a deduplication tool[5] is developed within the HMIS system to aggregate data collected from local shelters and merge the duplicate records of same person.

This rule-based algorithm, called AWARDS, employed the various combinations of social security number (SSN), first name, last name, date of Birth (DOB), and gender to decide whether two records from homeless database belong to the same person. It was tested using a test set with 400 records and achieved 96% accuracy[6], which is very high.

AWARDS contains two tests to find potential match record. In test one, for any two clients' records, if their SSNs[7] match and two of the first name, last name, and DOB[8] match then the two records are marked as duplicates.

In test two, the threshold of the criteria is lower with two filters introduced to avoid introducing too many false alarms. Here is the three steps for this test,

First Name	Last Name	Social Security Number	Date of Birth	Gender
3702adf3bc6e22453e6f82b29c bad8dc89f1db89	262f2d9cb68d9cd7f9877d04 7056f78d902119be	0976c33070792f3e43fa9135d3 62c1d9bdb697b58995	2/28/1984	1
3702adf3bc6e22453e6f82b29c bad8dc89f1db89	262f2d9cb68d9cd7f9877d04 7056f78d902119be	0976c33070792f3e43fa9135d3 62c1d9bdb697b58995	2/28/1994	1
29624ce5d077bf0bab9c979331 26242a957eb017	ad508f3c41bcf16b28ded2c e6b7df75248a2c41d	1237462b22f189cc3b46170669 4e56f0f1ec5a7b826b	7/16/1989	0
29624ce5d077bf0bab9c979331 26242a957eb017	ad508f3c41bcf16b28ded2c e6b7df75248a2c41d	1237462b22f189cc3b46170669 4e56f0f1ec5a7b826b	7/16/1984	0
cf396d355b9f2a47c68e2f8f077 fb97dd0549006	4ae911039f50e7f7988f334e bf4b567e558942bf	1345b98b4715a2f5770cbb302f 5a8580a14c2ef78e98	5/3/1964	1
cf396d355b9f2a47c68e2f8f077 fb97dd0549006	4ae911039f50e7f7988f334e bf4b567e558942bf	1345b98b4715a2f5770cbb302f 5a8580a14c2ef78e98	12/3/1964	1

Table 3 Two record pairs passed test one criteria but DOB mismatched

1. Pair of client records will pass if either full SSNs (the nine social security number) are matching or two of first name, last name, DOB, and partially reported SSNs are matching.
2. The passed pairs will be sent to a filter to compare six criteria, Gender, Name Suffix, Day of Birth, Month of Birth, Year of Birth, and partially reported SSNs (the last four digits of SSN). If a pair fails two or more matches, it will be filtered out.
3. The left pairs then will be sent to the second filter, twin check filter. In this filter, two clients will marked as twin if 1) they have same Last Names and DOBs but not First Names (must not blank), 2) SSNs also do not match (either different or at least one is null), and 3)the matching clients are under 18 at admission.

The duplicates found by both tests then will be merged as one record. So far, the merging strategy is to use the latest record of the duplicates as the final record with the assumption that the latest one has the most updated information.

V. Deduplication Issues and Improvement

The original deduplication algorithm is implemented inside HMIS system using SQL scripts and we re-implemented HUD deduplication algorithm in java that can be applied on both csv files and database. After applying our deduplication process to homeless dataset, 16460 duplicates were found from test one and 10212 matches were generated from test 2. The unique client number drops to 63005, which is 29.7% less than the original data size. Even though the accuracy is high (96%), the test data set contains only 400 records, which is too small. Therefore, we analyzed the duplicates and do find some issues, which will be discussed in this section with proposed solutions.

While looking into failure cases from test one, we noticed that 389 pairs of clients that have same fully reported SSNs but fail the other criteria. One reason is that parents will assign their own SSNs to their children some time if they were born in homeless shelters and we found 86 such cases. Another reason is that people's First Name and Last Name were mistakenly swapped by inexperienced staff or volunteers of homeless shelter, which is a common input error. To accommodate this issue, we cross compared the First Name and Last Name of any two records if they have different First Name and Last Name. This method found 4706 pairs of records have First Name and Last Name switched. By combining with same SSN criterion, this new method finds 171 extra duplicates.

Another failure analysis is on Date of Birth (DOB) errors, which can be either typos or wrong information provided by clients. We compared day, month, and year of DOB separately from all duplicates found in test one that have different DOBs and found that 94% of the mismatches are caused by one different day, month, or year.

Table 3 show three example pairs that passed test one exam with different DOBs. The first pair has different years, 1984 vs 1994. It could be caused by typo since button "8" and "9" are next to each other on keyboard. The second pair also has different number, 9" vs "4", which could be caused by the ambiguity of hand writings. The last pair has different months, 5 vs 12, which have very different pronunciation and also hand writings. Therefore, it is possible that the client provided conflict information. According to the observation of homeless

[5]https://www.hudexchange.info/resources/documents/TechnicalGuidelinesForUnduplicatingAndDeIdentifyingClientRecords.pdf

[6] Page 28 in Technical Guidelines for Unduplicating and De-identifying HMIS Client Records

[7] SSN must to be fully reported and be neither "000000000" nor "999999999".

[8] The content of the three fields cannot be empty

shelters' staff, it happened quite frequently that clients provided conflict information from time to time.

According to this new finding, we propose to change DOB matching rule in test one to that if any two of day, month, and year match, then the two DOBs will be considered as identical. This new rule will definitely find more matches missed by DOB mistakes. However, according to HMIS deduplication technique report, this rule could introduce too many false positives, especially when using same Day and Month since "in a group of 45 people, there is a 90% chance that two people have the same birthday (year of birth is not included)"[9]. However, this claim missed one key point that DOB is just one of four criteria in test one. With the criteria of same SSN and one same either First Name or Last Name, the maximum number of records that have same two of Day/Month/Year is 3. From the simulation program, the possibility of 3 people having same Day and Month of Birth is less than 1%. Therefore, this new rule won't introduce a lot of noises and by adding this modification in test one, we found extra 114 pairs of duplicates.

In test two, a twin check filter is employed to avoid merging information from twins (children less than 18 years old) since they can share a lot of same information such as Last Name, DOB, and Gender and therefore will be treated as duplicates. However, this filter is quite problematic since it allows empty SSN during matching because some infants born in homeless shelters do not have SSN. Even though this is a reasonable argument, this filter could introduce a lot of noises when the same kid enrolled in another shelter with different First Name, e.g. Full First Name used in one place and Nick Name used in another place.

PersonalID	First Name	Last Name	SSN	DOB	Gender
fea3d5d6c	8fe39603c5d8ad444279f1 10d4ecb29477292f68	718d1ad6a9001d18ecd59 daec6886e63f86d2b64		8/12/2011	0
f6eb5b4d5	4542955467970e208c69b d744442423a1c11cd8a	718d1ad6a9001d18ecd59 daec6886e63f86d2b64		8/12/2011	0

Table 4 One pair is found as Twin by Twin Check

To confirm our hypothesis, we looked into 100 randomly picked pairs of records filtered by twin check criteria and found that the accurate rate is only 9%, which confirms our concern. Most issues come from the situation that no SSN is involved in the check. Table 4 displays an example pair found by Twin Check. According the filter, the two records should belong to twin sisters, but they actually came from two households (Table 5) that used two different shelters at different time. Incidentally, both households have one head and three children[10]. From client information in Table 6, we can see that except the first name of these two records from table 4, all other information of these two households are perfectly matching. This is just one family using homeless service twice and there are no twins in this family. However, the current deduplication algorithm will merge the records of all other household members but the two caught by the twin check, which is a mistake. This twin check filter totally prevented

Personal ID	EntryDate	HouseholdID	RelationshipToHoH
91c652a32	11/22/2016	131568	1
d7b75a8be	11/22/2016	131568	2
f6eb5b4d5	11/22/2016	131568	2
a285611e4	11/22/2016	131568	2

Personal ID	EntryDate	HouseholdID	RelationshipToHoH
460c86f42	7/31/2015	213110	1
03ea8a55c	7/31/2015	213110	2
fea3d5d6c	7/31/2015	213110	2
a4a0fb786	7/31/2015	213110	2

Table 5 The enrollment information of two households that have the two children from Table 4

1121 pairs of records being merged. Most of them are actually good matching and this error could cause very negative impact for those researchers whose study focuses on youth and children.

PersonalID	First Name	Last Name	SSN	DOB
91c652a32	0aaa497903d65169946c2e a40323b808b6c40930	718d1ad6a9001d18ecd59 daec6886e63f86d2b64	0637e93afd625288b9c9df4 9a5efcf5f535d966cc94f	9/14/1981
d7b75a8be	5b3d60e653d9790dddb6f 1333301ea81caae014f	7f74392a04c2a112186c94 c36fe41738572de608		3/18/2010
f6eb5b4d5	4542955467970e208c69b d744442423a1c11cd8a	718d1ad6a9001d18ecd59 daec6886e63f86d2b64		8/12/2011
a285611e4	c2bdb186e0c870412b5d6 07e430d1f03239bf964	718d1ad6a9001d18ecd59 daec6886e63f86d2b64		12/20/2012

PersonalID	First Name	Last Name	SSN	DOB
460c86f42	0aaa497903d65169946c2e a40323b808b6c40930	718d1ad6a9001d18ecd59 daec6886e63f86d2b64	0637e93afd625288b9c9df4 9a5efcf5f535d966cc94f	9/14/1981
03ea8a55c	5b3d60e653d9790dddb6f 1333301ea81caae014f	8ed3f7f5428de76323f0ae c11382bfc7b9a0fc26		3/18/2010
fea3d5d6c	8fe39603c5d8ad444279f1 10d4ecb29477292f68	718d1ad6a9001d18ecd59 daec6886e63f86d2b64		8/12/2011
a4a0fb786	c2bdb186e0c870412b5d6 07e430d1f03239bf964	718d1ad6a9001d18ecd59 daec6886e63f86d2b64		12/20/2012

Table 6 The members' profile of the two families in Table 5

To solve this problem, we first collaborated with our community partner, CARES Inc, and homeless shelters in Albany county to understand more about the families in HMIS system. According to their observations, records of infants and their parents can be merged by mistake under some circumstance. For example, when the infants were born in shelters, their parents sometime used parents' information to

PersonalID	First Name	Last Name	SSN	DOB	Gender
770f14cba	4d276a5828471f33324b521 2cd4ac6b09d89320d	3aa61303c74d188b34b7 ed61bdcb2a848359e1cb	05865135bd528d26f678f25 e00373ab209831cb49ac7	2/16/1981	1
c220ef404	4d276a5828471f33324b521 2cd4ac6b09d89320d	3aa61303c74d188b34b7 ed61bdcb2a848359e1cb	05865135bd528d26f678f25 e00373ab209831cb49ac7	10/16/2007	1

Table 7 Two client records have identical information except DOB

Personal ID	EntryDate	HouseholdID	RelationshipToHoH
770f14cba	5/1/2014	200964	1
bacac0d94	5/1/2014	200964	3
c220ef404	5/1/2014	200964	2
cc12c5cbc	5/1/2014	200964	2

Table 8 One family enrollment information

register their children except the DOB. Table 7 displays a sample case that the two records will be merged during test one exam. However, the enrollment information of in table 8 shows that the two records in table 7 actually belong to two individuals, a father and a son of one family who enrolled into

[9] For a clear explanation of this, see http://www.mste.uiuc.edu/reese/birthday/intro.html

[10] In the last column of relationship to household Head, 1 means self, 2 means Head of household's child

homeless service in May 1st, 2014. Therefore, in addition to avoid the mismatches between twins, we should also add a function to prevent other mismatches like those between parents and their children. To accomplish this, we redesigned twin check algorithm by adding more effective features.

The first new feature we plan to use is the time that people spent in shelters. If two records were from different shelters and have stay time periods overlapped, this would be an indicator that these two records should not be merged since no one can stay in multiple shelters at the same time. However, during the case study, we noticed that the enrollment date is usually accurate but the exit date is vague because people sometime left shelters without checking out. In addition, people are actually allowed to stay in multiple programs at the same time. One good example is that when people were enrolled in permanent housing program and waiting for its readiness, they were allowed stay in transitional housing program and wait. In that case, the records will have people enrolled in both programs at the same time. Therefore, this feature wouldn't be able to buy us accurate result.

The second new feature we focused on is household id. Records with same household id belong to members from same family and therefore shouldn't be compared and merged even though they contain identical information (e.g. two records from table 7). To verify our hypothesis, we looked into those matched records who share the same household id. We found that deduplication actually made the correct merge in some cases. Table 9 showed a family with five members who used a shelter two times. Since it is the same shelter, when this family returned in 2016, same household id was assigned but only two family members got their original personal id and new personal ids were given to the other three members. However, when comparing their personal information from client table (Table 10), we can see that the information of these three members from two enrollment is perfectly matched (only one member missed SSN for 2015 enrollment). This is not a single case issue since we found 162 pairs of records who had same

Personal ID	EntryDate	HouseholdID	RelationshipToHoH
b4c96942a	7/28/2015	131392	1
c399e2d12	7/28/2015	131392	2
cf0334bd1	7/28/2015	131392	2
5ad1ca636	7/28/2015	131392	2
cd1de946e	7/28/2015	131392	5
b4c96942a	10/4/2016	131392	1
5ad1ca636	10/4/2016	131392	2
29b22263b	10/4/2016	131392	3
ee7e79cb7	10/4/2016	131392	2
051f91a12	10/4/2016	131392	2

Table 9 Example of one family enrolled the same shelter twice

household id and met deduplication criteria but were given different personal ids. This must be a mistake made either during the deduplication process from HMIS system or by inexperienced staff.

Because of such quality issue, household id itself would not be able to work well in deduplication process. Therefore, we

PersonalID	First Name	Last Name	SSN	DOB	Gender
c399e2d12	a276ad14a112baebd87cf 72390c8c810e612af95	c8974246f022572bdb30d f6b06ef40b7e49e3f1b	0740ecc40d3ccc9cf7880c08 27806c8649f528e4856b	9/23/2010	1
cf0334bd1	6b711670513c9a66bbb2 fd2796bc8a3b009fc566	c8974246f022572bdb30d f6b06ef40b7e49e3f1b		3/21/2008	1
cd1de946e	a90e498652985c99de3e 2eb8960b2d0f60731df7	c8974246f022572bdb30d f6b06ef40b7e49e3f1b	1215c738d6d7c42c08320a2 67274032c418c37ac422a	4/2/1977	1
29b22263b	a90e498652985c99de3e 2eb8960b2d0f60731df7	c8974246f022572bdb30d f6b06ef40b7e49e3f1b	1215c738d6d7c42c08320a2 67274032c418c37ac422a	4/2/1977	1
ee7e79cb7	a276ad14a112baebd87cf 72390c8c810e612af95	c8974246f022572bdb30d f6b06ef40b7e49e3f1b	0740ecc40d3ccc9cf7880c08 27806c8649f528e4856b	9/23/2010	1
051f91a12	6b711670513c9a66bbb2 fd2796bc8a3b009fc566	c8974246f022572bdb30d f6b06ef40b7e49e3f1b	05298581b587d44b747c054 d02ec356dd6cdee42370d	3/21/2008	1

Table 10. Those family members from table 9 who do not have same personal id with each other

introduced another feature, enrollment time, to work with household id together as a new filter, which means that do not merge those records with same household id and same enrollment time. It worked very well to prevent false deduplicates among family members. However, this filter won't be applied for those families that used the service multiple times because records the family members will have different enrollment times and/or different household ids if they went to different shelters. (Examples from Table 4 and 5)

The current HMIS deduplication system will merge all records as long as their similarities pass test one or test two exam. However, if one record has multiple matches with those records with same household id who enrolled at the same time, only one of the matches should be picked according to the new filter. To do so, we designed a scoring system (Table 11) that will assign similarity scores to all matched pairs. SSN is the key matching criterion, therefore it gets the highest score, 2, if full SSN matched but -2 if different (both records have full SSN). For other supporting features, such as First Name, Last Name, Partial SSN, and DOB, matching score is 1. Since we allow DOB partial match (two matching out of Day/Month/Year), its score is 0.5. Name Suffix and Gender are only used as filter, their matching score is only 0.5[11]. With this

Matching Result	First Name, Last Name, Partial SSN	NameSuffix, Gender	SSN	DOB
Identical	1	0.5	2	1
Patrial Match	0	0	0	0.5
At least one null	0	0	0	0
Not Matched	-1	-0.5	-2	-1

Table 11 Scoring system to evaluate how similar two records matched to each other

new scoring system, we are able to correctly merge records of family members when they use HMIS system multiple times.

We replaced the old twin check filter with the filter plus the scoring system in test two exam and also test one exam. It reduced the 1121 twins found by previous system to 50. The rest were actually two records of same child using homeless service at different time and should be merged. In addition, the new filter and scoring method found extra 204 pairs of false duplicates.

[11] This scoring method may still make mistakes when identifying records of twins without SSN who used their full names during their first registration but nick names when they came back to the service

The new deduplication system found 1510 either new duplicates or wrong previous duplicates. Comparing with total 27873 duplicates, the performance of new system improved 6%. Also, we have delivered all our findings and novel filter methods to CARES Inc. They are communicating with the vendors who design and host the HMIS database system to request the improvement of deduplication process in HMIS system.

VI. Merge Duplicated Record

In original deduplication system, when merging duplicated records, the information from latest enrollment is always used. However, the latest enrollment information doesn't mean it is most updated and complete information. We saw many cases that clients report more completed information from previous enrollments. Therefore, we designed a new merging algorithm to find the most reliable information as the final profile of a client. In addition, the new merging algorithm works at attribute level instead of record level, which means for each attribute, the value with best quality will be can be chosen. Therefore, the information of the final client record can come from different duplicates. Table 12 displayed three groups of duplicated records. We will use these records as examples to explain our new merging algorithm, which has four steps while picking the values from the duplicated records,

PersonalID	First Name	Last Name	SSN	DOB	Gender
246413844	5db49cbd13e1087e128e bdd0f3d1c11c12e07bf3	3db1ac7ac11677aa59409 8f0fae754a78c88b13f		11/11/1999	0
e9240420a	5db49cbd13e1087e128e bdd0f3d1c11c12e07bf3	3db1ac7ac11677aa59409 8f0fae754a78c88b13f	10287e2f1726cf935257e6f4 e14ab77e03b6bc6fdcae	11/11/1999	9
478702839	aafa3c96770c175071aef 4ae7b007440e8c1cee3	5e8003c2286f2c2d03149 e77bdb98b53a91fe360	12659747ce44abf220407a6 0902e285f0eaa589e8030	11/2/1964	0
5494bd69a	aafa3c96770c175071aef 4ae7b007440e8c1cee3	5e8003c2286f2c2d03149 e77bdb98b53a91fe360	12659747ce44abf220407a6 0902e285f0eaa589e8030	1/2/1964	
f47e83a3b	aafa3c96770c175071aef 4ae7b007440e8c1cee3	5e8003c2286f2c2d03149 e77bdb98b53a91fe360	12659747ce44abf220407a6 0902e285f0eaa589e8030	11/2/1964	0
635476054	34e52e97ab396d929291 1c3a0b4790b4ebd265e9	999db2929bc664bbb270 bbbb3d366e62c3790d1b	07801c3c4526c935fa9bd7b 8694a491599fc51e6855b	10/2/2010	0
1c3ac0236	34e52e97ab396d929291 1c3a0b4790b4ebd265e9	178f004991c9922d0e124 e807f9928f1055e11a2	07801c3c4526c935fa9bd7b 8694a491599fc51e6855b	10/3/2010	0
3a3966a19	34e52e97ab396d929291 1c3a0b4790b4ebd265e9	999db2929bc664bbb270 bbbb3d366e62c3790d1b	07801c3c4526c935fa9bd7b 8694a491599fc51e6855b	10/9/2010	0

Table 12 Merging examples

- If all values of one attribute are identical, the value will be used, e.g. First Name and Last Name in group one from Table 11.
- If one value has more complete information, it will be picked. The gender attribute from group one, one is 9, which means client refused to report the information. Therefore, the other value, 0, will be used. The other examples fit this rule is SSN in group one and Gender in group 2.
- When one field has conflict values with same completeness, the one having majority vote will be used. When processing DOB from group 2 and Last Name from group 3, system will apply this rule to choose the value
- If there is not majority vote, the value from latest enrollment will be used. Group 3 has three different DOBs, according to the enrollment dates, 6/21/2012, 3/19/2012, 8/29/2016, the DOB value, 10/9/2010, from the third record will be the final DOB value of this person.

By applying this new merging process, 27873 records (31%) were merged and because the most accurate and complete information were applied for these merged records, the quality of the database are improved too. We are still evaluating how significant the improvement is.

VII. Automatically Generate Error Report

To report homeless status to HUD every year, CARES Inc has to put tremendous time and effort on quality control by manually going through the collected data of current year. In many cases, they have to go back to previous years' records for reference. This tedious task consumes so much of the resource that they are always short of time/energy for data analysis and critical thinking. Therefore, we build a tool that is able to automatically check the quality of homeless data and reports the found errors. Our tool currently focuses on two type of quality checks.

One is to report errors found from deduplication process. From the duplicates, the system also collects those pairs that have conflict information on client name, SSN, DOB, and Gender. Table 13 shows number of conflicts from both test one and test two exams. We can see that the duplicates from test two have a lot more conflict information. This is reasonable since all identical pairs have been picked by test one exam. We separate the last two rows in the table from other conflict information because we are confident that the pairs here are problematic and CARES Inc should set higher priority to work on them.

Source	Number
Test One	2726
Test Two	10419
First Name and Last Name in Wrong Sequence	3386
Same HouseHold ID but Have Different Personal ID	162

Table 13 Deduplicated pairs with conflict information

Another quality control effort we made focuses on quality fields in client table. There are three attributes, Name, SSN, and DOB that have quality fields. Table 14 shows the categories defined for SSN quality field and their meanings. With the description from quality field, we should know the quality of data in the corresponding attribute and then we can plan to how to use it. However, in many cases, the category from a quality field doesn't tell the actual status of the data in the attribute. We have seen SSN quality field is 1 but SSN is empty.

To find all such mistakes, we wrote a method to check whether the category value in the quality field correctly describes the information saved in corresponding attributes.

Category	Description
1	Full SSN Reported
2	Partial/Approximate SSN Reported
8	Client doesn't know
9	Client refused
99	Data not collected

Table 14 SSN Quality Category

Category	Number
Name	628
SSN	2749
DOB	1270

Table 15 Number of records having conflict information comparing quality field value with its attribute value

For any found errors, we save and report them based on the category. Table 15 lists the number of records with inaccurate descriptions.

From both data quality checking processes, we totally reported 8195 errors or 9597 possible errors that haven't been able to be dig out by CARES Inc. (the numbers from last two rows in Table 13 are included in first two rows of the table) This quality checking tool will definitely improve data quality control both efficiently and effectively.

Conclusions and Future Work

In this paper, we present our collaboration with CARES Inc. to help them improve the quality of homeless dataset. We redesigned the deduplication algorithm from HMIS system that improved 6% of system performance. During the merging process, we employed the most accurate and complete information to form new records from duplicates instead of using the latest one, which makes the merged records more complete and reliable. In addition, we built a quality control tool to detect and report data quality problems that haven't been found before. In the future, we plan to continue this study and keep working on the following issues,

Continue improving deduplication process. We will work with CARES Inc. to build hashed table to save names and their nicknames. With the table, we are able to find more matches on First Name. It can also help solve the issue in twin checks in our new filter.

Automated Data analysis. We started building tools for our partners, including CARES Inc. and local homeless shelters for data analysis. One of ongoing research projects is to look into the qualitative data (interviews between shelter's staff and homeless people) and see if we can find pattern(s) from successful cases that can be used to train shelter's staff to improve the quality of their service.

Share the data. We are building an online platform and plan to put our data over there for researchers and organizations who would like help homeless people to share and study homeless data. We finished the database and are still building the web interface. It will be ready in near future and the work will be reported in another publication.

4. Build dynamic vulnerable index. When people apply for HMIS service, they will be evaluated based on a vulnerable index and only those pass a certain threshold will be enrolled into the system. However, this evaluation is done manually and hard to track. Therefore, we plan to integrate this index as part of database and will be automatically updated regularly based on people's current situation. It will make the system more efficient and productive to find the population who can support themselves and check them out and pinpoint the most vulnerable group and put more resource to them.

IX. Acknowledgement

We thanks to Center for Academic Community Engagement (ACE) helped link us with our community partners CARES Inc. and homeless shelters and coordinate this work. We also appreciate Center for Undergraduate Research and Creative (CURCA) who provided financial support to both students and faculties during summer.

References

[1] Bilenko MY, Mooney RJ, Learnable similarity functions and their application to record linkage and clustering, University of Texas at Austin, Austin, TX, 2006

[2] Cohen W, Ravikumar P, and Fienberg S. A comparison of string distance metrics for name-matching tasks. IIWEB, pages 73-78, 2003.

[3] Fellegi IP, Sunter AB. A theory for record linkage. J Am Stat Assoc. 1969; 64(328):1183-210.

[4] Freitas J, Pappa GL, Silva AS, Goncalves MA, Moura E S, Veloso A, Laender AHF, de Carvalho M G, Active learning genetic programming for record deduplication, IEEE Congress on Evolutionary Computation, pp. 1-8, 2010.

[5] Potosky AL, Riley GF, Lubitz JD, et al. Potential for cancer related health services research using a linked Medicare-tumor registry database. Med Care. 1993; 31(8):732-48. PMID: 8336512.

[6] Rathbone J, Carter M, Hoffmann T, Glasziou P. Better duplicate detection for systematic reviewers: evaluation of systematic review assistant-deduplication module. Systematic Rev. 2015; 4(1):6.

[7] Tejada S, Knoblock C A, and Minton S. 2001. Learning object identification rules for information integration. Information Systems 26(8):607–633.

[8] Virnig BA, Warren JL, Cooper GS, Klabunde CN, Schussler N, Freeman J. Studying radiation therapy using SEER-Medicare-linked data. Med Care 2002;40: Suppl IV:49-54

SESSION

INFORMATION AND KNOWLEDGE EXTRACTION AND ENGINEERING + APPLICATIONS

Chair(s)

TBA

A new Bid Process Information System based on data warehouse specification for decision-making

1st Manel Zekri
Department of Computer Science
Faculty of Sciences of Tunis
Tunisia
manel.zekri@fst.utm.tn

2nd Sahbi Zahaf
Department of Computer Science.
Higher Institute of Computer Science
Tunisia
sahbi@zahaf.net

3rd Sadok Ben Yahia
Department of Computer Science
Faculty of Sciences of Tunis
Tunisia
sadok.benyahia@fst.utm.tn

Abstract—**The Bid Process Information System (BPIS) which supports the business process should be made more performant by ensuring greater levels of flexibility and interoperability between devices. Moreover, the specification of this system has to deal with the three fit problems. To this end, four dimensions have been identified in order to cope with potential failures: operational, organizational, decision-making, and cooperative dimensions. In this paper, we focus on the decision-making dimension of the BPIS and propose an operational approach for representing data warehouse scheme based on an ontology that captures the multidimensional bid-knowledge.**

Index Terms—**Bid Process, Information System, Data Warehouse, Conceptual Data Model, Multidimensional Design, Ontology;**

I. INTRODUCTION

The bid process which corresponds to the conceptual phase of the lifecycle of a product is a particular environment for the exploitation of business process [8]. It interacts upstream and involves other processes being design process. It aims to examine the feasibility of the bid before negotiating any contract with any owner following a pre-study carried out before a project launch.

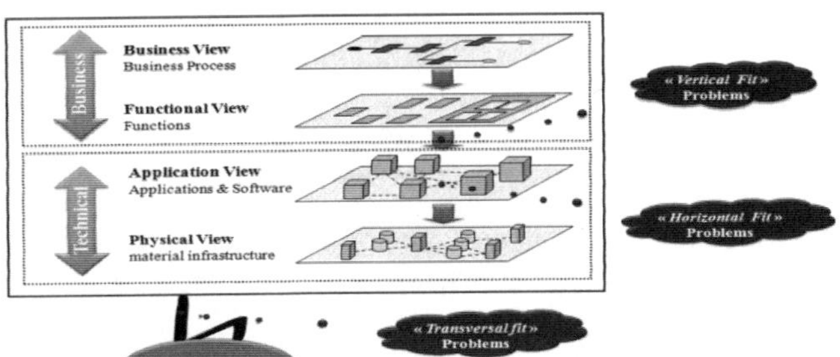

Fig. 1: Enterprise Architecture I.S reference model [7]: three fit problems [18] [19].

The IS (Information System) [7] that allows to run the bid process (Bid Process Information System or BPIS) must be [19] [18]: integrated, flexible and interoperable. Nevertheless, the enterprise architecture approach [7], on which we rely to implement this system, has to deal with "three fit" problems: vertical, horizontal and transversal fit (Fig. 1). Such problems handicap the exploitation of these three criteria [19]. The "vertical fit" represents the problems of integration from a business infrastructure, which is abstract, to a technical infrastructure, which represents implementations. The "horizontal fit" translates not only the softwares problems of identification (induced by the "vertical fit" problems) that can cover the entire infrastructure of the company's business, but also the intra-applicative communications problems (internal interoperability); the purpose being to ensure the interactions between softwares of the same technical infrastructure in the company. The "transversal fit" translates the inter-applicative communications problems (external interoperability carried out dynamically through a network). Therefore, we define an IS that supports four dimensions which are operational, organizational, decision-making, and cooperative dimensions [19]. As for the decision-making dimension of the BPIS, data warehouse is mainly used for making better decisions that can improve the business of organizations and optimize bid process [9], [2]. Hence, building a data warehouse is a complex task that aims at satisfying the needs of decision makers. One of the key points to the success of a bid data warehousing project is the design of the multidimensional schema [1] [6]. In this paper, we propose a method that uses ontologies for multidimensional design of bid data warehouses from an operational data source [5]. In addition, we present an ontology-based method for data modeling schema that eventually covers different phases of the data warehouse lifecycle, and takes into account the users by considering their personalized needs as well as their bid knowledge.

This work is organized as follows.The second section is a description of the solution to the"three fit" problems. The third section shows the related work: extending Multidimensional Ontology [11]. The fourth section describes the design approach. then we end this work by a conclusion and some prospects of future works.

Identify applicable funding agency here. If none, delete this.

II. Resolution of the "three fit" problems: BPIS integrated, flexible and interoperable

We have identified four dimensions to deal with "three fit" problems [19], [18]:

- the operational dimension that serves to specify the bid exploitation process by undertaking a specific project;
- the organizational dimension which allow the management and saving of the set of skills and knowledge that the company acquired in previous bid auctions;
- the decision-making dimension which aims at optimizing the right decision-making by the company in bid auctions; and
- the cooperative dimension which aims at ensuring intra-entreprise communication (internal interoperability) and at planning the inter-entreprise communication on demand, in order to achieve a common goal (dynamic interoperability).

We suggest fulfilling these dimensions while relying on the following hypothesis [19], [18] such as shown in Figure 2. The ERP (Enterprise Resources Planning) aims at build the techno-economic proposal of an offer in order to cover the operational dimension. In addition, the organizational memory covers the organizational dimension [10]. Moreover, a data warehouse will evaluate a set of solutions that make this proposal operational [16] to cover the decision-making dimension [19].

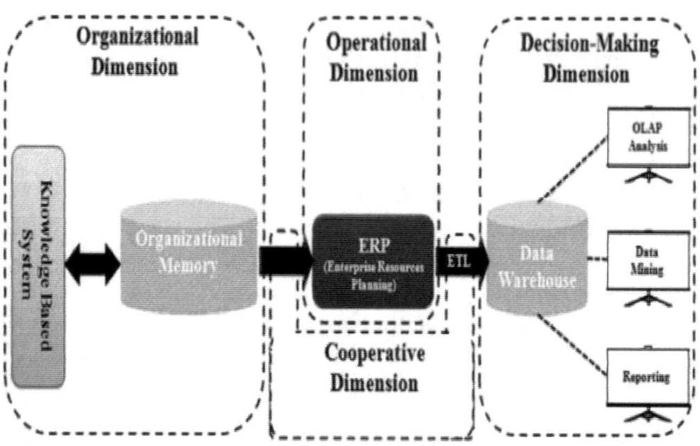

Fig. 2: The Bid Process Information System (BPIS) [19]

III. Related Work: Extending Multidimensional Ontology

In data warehouse design, different modeling techniques are used to represent the multidimensional concepts extracted from data sources, as well as the sources themselves. It can be ER diagram, UML diagram or graphs [8], etc. Unlike ontologies, which are ready for computing, these techniques are conceptual formalizations intended to graphically represent the domain and not used for querying and reasoning. This work is a continuation to a previous research [8], [21] and it aims at integrating ontologies in the data warehouse design process [13]. Therefore, the starting point was the meta-model of data warehouse scheme [21]. The multidimensional ontology [20] is a representation of knowledge dedicated to decision-making dimension [19], [18]. It specifies the multidimensional concepts and their semantic and multidimensional relations [14]. Its use covers different steps of the data warehouse life-cycle. During these steps, it assists the designer to solve problems of data sources heterogeneity. In the OLAP requirement specification step, the decisional ontology helps to validate the multidimensional concepts (fact, measure, dimension, etc.) and relations between these concepts. It, also prevents associations between concepts not semantically associable (e.g. associating fact-to-fact, dimension-to-dimension, hierarchy-to-fact, etc.). Various approaches were proposed to guide creating ontologies [1] [6], we mainly based the multidimensional ontology construction process on the approach proposed in [3]. While other techniques (mentioned above) for representing multidimensional knowledge are an appropriate choice for their respective approaches, their use ends when the task of designing the data warehouse is accomplished. On the other hand, the multidimensional ontology can still be useful. It can cover the various phases of the life cycle of a decision-making dimension [19], [18] , that is to say, from the requirements specification, the design of data warehouse and data marts [4], until the exploitation and evolution phases. This is convenient because the recent DBMSs allow storing ontologies alongside data in the same database structure [2]. Such database is called OBDB (ontology-based database). Ontologies are scalable and extendable, and they showed their effectiveness for IS and requirements specification [3]. More concretely and in the same way, as ontologies are used for clarifying the semantics of data sources, they are used to identify and manage semantic conflicts between concepts. This allows us to add as many extensions as needed to the multidimensional ontology to cover the various phases of the life cycle of a decision-making dimension [19], [18] . To demonstrate this aspect, we have proposed an extension that represents the operational data source conceptual schema, in this case, an ER diagram [21].

IV. The data warehouse lifecycle: ontology-based method for data modeling schema

In this section, we will present an overview of the first phase of the approach which we adopted. It is progressive and iterative. The assistance of the designer throughout this construction is optional. The approach can be executed autonomously, but the intervening of a designer during validation steps is recommended and will result in better output.

A domain ontology contains knowledge that is a semantic representation of the multidimensional concepts. This representation is often complete because of its generality. Hence, multidimensional concepts which could be useful for the decision-makers will be contained in the domain ontology. We design the steps of the data warehouse lifecycle which is an ontology-based method for data modeling schema in Figure 3.

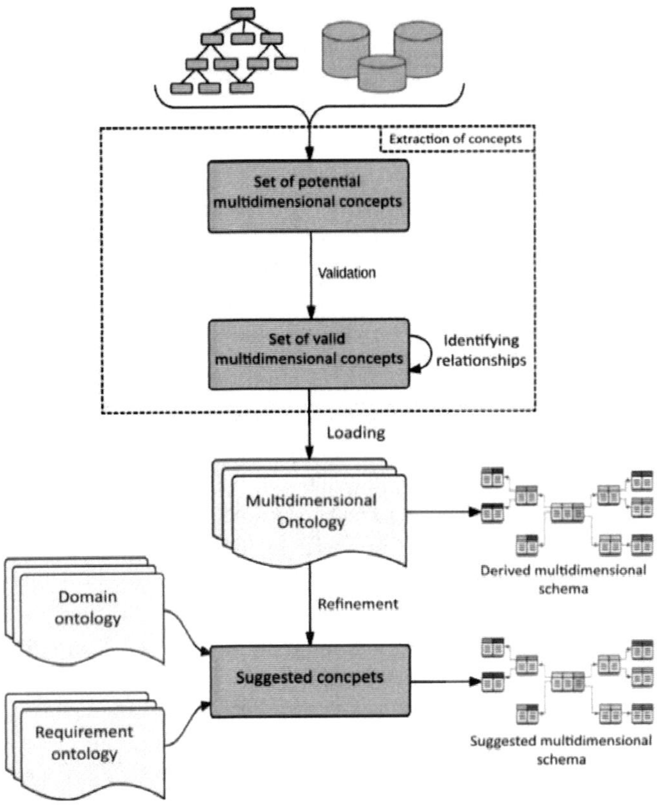

Fig. 3: The data warehouse lifecycle: ontology-based method for data modeling schema [20].

1) Exploiting ontologies: As mentioned, domain ontology contains knowledge about a specific domain. This knowledge is a formal and semantic representation of the multidimensional concepts of the domain. Although this representation is general, it is often complete. So if there are other multidimensional concepts, which might be useful for decision makers, they will be contained in the domain ontology.
In the following, we propose a second multidimensional schema that contains other multidimensional concepts that do not exist in the data source. This schema, which we will call "suggested multidimensional schema", proposes to introduce new concepts that we recommend to add to the derived scheme in order to improve the data warehouse. The contribution will be, for example, the addition of a new dimension to an existing fact, or even the addition of a new fact and therefore a new star. The derived multidimensional schema will be contained in the suggested multidimensional schema. To generate the suggested multidimensional scheme, we follow the following steps:

1) Choosing a domain ontology: By using ontology libraries, this first step aims at choosing a domain ontology that corresponds to our warehousing project.
2) Analyze the domain ontology: The goal of this step is to extract the multidimensional concepts from the domain ontology. We analyze the domain ontology. This will give us interesting concepts to build the conceptual model. We use the ontology and its reasoning ability to perform the task of analysis. Since ontology can capture the concepts of a domain in a formal and semantic way, each source of the data warehouse can be represented using an ontology.
3) Analyze requirements: Develop a requirement tree to obtain information on the needs of decision-makers.
4) Correspondence: In this step, we will match the concepts in the analysis step of the domain ontology and the needs analysis step, and between the derived multidimensional schema.
5) Propose the suggested multidimensional scheme: This is the final step of the approach.

Here, we introduce an algorithm to automatically identify the interesting concepts available in the global ontology representing the source. The output of this algorithm is a list of multidimensional concepts existing in the source.

Algorithm 1: ANALYSE ONTOLOGY OF FACT IDENTIFICATION

Data: Domain Ontology
Result: List of fact
Identify(O);
Begin
for *for each class in O* **do**
  for *each attribut in class* **do**
    if *is_num(attribut)* **then**
      list_num = list_num + attribut
      attr_num ++;
    end
    else
      list_nom_num= liste_non_num + attribut;
    end
    total_attr++;
  end
  r= attr_num / total_attr;
  if *r> seuil* **then**
    fact=class;
    fact.list_measure=list$_n um; fact.list_level = list_non_num;$
  end
end
End

For each attribute (e.g. dataproperty) of the concept class under consideration, we compute the ratio "r" of the numerical attributes with respect to the total number of attributes (r=attr_num / total_attr). Concepts with a ratio above the threshold are marked as facts. The threshold is a numerical value that must be chosen arbitrarily by the designer. The numeric attributes of the fact are identified as measurements (list_num) and the non-numeric attributes (list_non_num) are identified as levels.

Algorithm 2 is used to identify the dimensions of the facts obtained as a result of algorithm 1:

Algorithm 2: ANALYSE ONTOLOGY OF DIMENSION IDENTIFICATION

```
Data: Fact
Result: List of dimensions
Begin
Identify_dimensions(fact);
linked_conceptslinked = list_concepts_linked_to (fact);
for each concept in Linked_concept do
    if maxCardinalité == n & minCardinalité == 1 then
        list_dim = list_dim + concept;
    end
end
End
```

The aim is to identify the dimensions of a given fact. This algorithm is applied to all the facts of the list resulting from algorithm 1. We begin by identifying the list of concepts related to "fact". We rely on the cardinalities of relations with "fact" to identify the dimensions. The concepts related to "fact" by a relation 1..n, are added to the list of dimensions of this fact.

A. Multidimensional Relationships

After defining the concepts of the multidimensional ontology, we need to specify the relationships that exist between them. Each relationship is of the form Relation (X, Y), where Relation is a binary predicate, and X and Y are concepts. We define the relationships described below through the schema given in Figure 4.

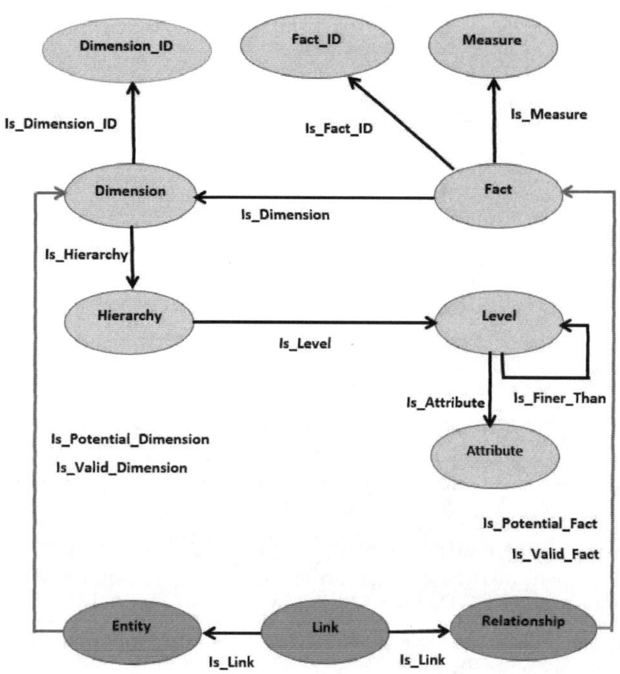

Fig. 4: Graphical representation of multidimensional relationships of ontology.

Both multidimensional concepts and relationships are presented in the bellow:

- Is_Fact_ID (***FID, F***) where Fact_ID (***FID***), Fact (***F***) and ***FID*** is the Id of ***F***.
- Is_Measure (***M,F***) where Measure (***M***), Fact (***F***) and ***M*** is a Measure of ***F***.
- Is_Dimension (***D, F***) where Dimension (***D***), Fact (***F***) and ***D*** is a Dimension of ***F***.
- Is_Dimension_ID (***DID, D***) where Dimension_ID (***DID***), Dimension (***D***) and ***DID*** is the Id of ***D***.
- Is_Hierarchy (***H, D***) where Hierarchy (***H***), Dimension (***D***) and ***H*** is a Hierarchy of ***D***.
- Is_Level (***L,H***) where Level (***L***), Hierarchy (***H***) and ***L*** is a level of ***H***.
- Is_Attribute (***A, L***) where Attribute (***A***), Level (***L***) and ***A*** is an Attribute of ***L***.
- Is_Finer_Than (***Li, Lj***) where Level (***Li***), Level (***Lj***), ***Li*** and ***Lj***are from the same Hierarchy and ***Li*** has a finer granularity that ***Lj***.

With the aim of ensuring the availability of data, we consider the data sources that are represented in a conceptual data model for the production base. In the next step, we extract the multidimensional concepts. It is divided into three stages that are repeated for each multidimensional concept. Thus, we determine a set of potential multidimensional, using extraction rules.

B. Fact extraction

Facts describe the daily activities of the bid companies. These activities result in transactions and produce trans-action objects. A transaction object is an entity registering the details of an event such as the payment of the bid proposition, etc. These entities are the most interesting for the data warehouse and are the basis for the construction of the fact tables. However, they are not all important. Thus, we must choose those that have an interest in the decision making. Usually a transaction object is a complex object containing multiple pieces of information. Therefore its modeling requires its decomposition into associated sub-objects. In the ER model, a transaction object may be represented in one of two forms:

- An entity connected to an association;
- Two entities linked by an association

In order to determine "***Fp***" (set of potential facts), we define the following heuristic:

HF: All transaction objects are potential facts. For each identified transaction object identified, we associate a more descriptive name, which will be the name of the fact. These facts are necessarily all pertinent, thus a validation phase where the designer may intervene is essential to retain a subset of valid facts (***Fv***).

C. Measure extraction

As we previously stated, a transaction object is the result of the bid companies activities. Accordingly, the attributes may be measurements of a fact that are encapsulated in the transaction object. The following heuristics determine the potential measures:

Hm1: Mp (***fv***) contains the non-key numeric attributes belonging to the transaction object representing "***fv***".

Hm2: If the attribute is a Boolean, we add to Mp (fv) the number of instances corresponding to the values"True" and "False" of this attribute.

- Fv: a valid fact from the previous step;
- Mp (***fv***): the set of potential measures of "***fv***";
- Mv (***fv***): the set of measures of "***fv***" approved by the designer, which is a subset of "Mp (***fv***)".

The extraction of measures is also followed by a validation step by the designer in order to determine Mv (***fv***) which elements satisfy the following assertion:

$$\forall \boldsymbol{fv} \in \boldsymbol{Fv}, \forall \boldsymbol{m} \in \boldsymbol{Mv}(\boldsymbol{fv}) \rightarrow \boldsymbol{Is\_measure}(\boldsymbol{m}, \boldsymbol{fv}) \quad (1)$$

D. Decision extraction

Extraction of dimensions is based on a second type of object called base object. A base object determines the details of an event by answering the questions "who", "what", "when", "where" and "how" related to a transaction object. For example, the Bid Project event is defined by several components such as (Owner: who bought) and (Bid Proposition: we sold what). A base object completes the meaning of the event represented by a transaction object thus providing additional details. Each object corresponding to one of these questions, and directly or indirectly linked to a transaction object is a potential dimension for the fact representing the transaction object. The extraction of dimensions consists of determining the name, **ID** and hierarchy(s) through these heuristics:

Hd1: Any base object directly or indirectly connected to the transaction object of "***fv***)" is a potential dimension of "***fv***".

Hd2: All **IDs** of a base object obtained by **Hd1** is an "***id***" of "***d***".

- Dp (***fv***): the set of potential dimensions of "***fv***";
- Dv (***fv***): the set of valid dimensions of "***fv***"; which is a subset of "Dp (***fv***)";
- d: ***a*** dimension;
- idd: the "***id***" of a dimension "***d***",

The validation step produces two subsets **Dv** (***fv***) and **IDDv** (***fv***), satisfying the following assertion:

$$\forall \boldsymbol{fv} \in \boldsymbol{Fv}, \forall \boldsymbol{d} \in \boldsymbol{Dv}(\boldsymbol{fv}), \exists \boldsymbol{dimension\_id}(\boldsymbol{did}) \rightarrow \boldsymbol{Is\_dimension}(\boldsymbol{d}, \boldsymbol{fv}) \wedge \boldsymbol{Is\_dimension}(\boldsymbol{idd}, \boldsymbol{d}) \quad (2)$$

E. Attributes extraction

We define the following heuristics to determine the potential attributes:

Ha1: Any attribute belonging to the base object containing "***idd***" is a potential attribute of "***d***".

Ha2: Any attributes belonging to a base object that generated a valid dimension "***dv***" is a potential attribute of "***dv***".

The validation step produces a set of valid attributes "***Av***", satisfying the following assertion:

$$\forall \boldsymbol{av} \in \boldsymbol{Av}(\boldsymbol{dv}) \rightarrow \boldsymbol{Is\_attribute}(\boldsymbol{av}, \boldsymbol{dv}) \quad (3)$$

Each extracted element becomes an individual (i.e. instance) of the concept that represents its role.

V. The Utility of Applying This Approach in the Knowledge of the Bid Process

Working on a specific bid implies the intervention of several collaborators. Certainly, these contributors exchange knowledge and information flows. However, its environmental differences lead to various representations and interpretations of knowledge ("horizontal fit" problems). Such failures are described in terms of five conflicts: the syntactic conflicts are the results of different terminologies used by stakeholders on the same domain. The structural conflicts are related to different levels of abstraction which aim at classifying knowledge within a virtual company (bid staff). The semantic conflicts concern the ambiguity that emerges due to the stakeholders' reasoning in the development of the techno-economic proposal. Heterogeneities conflicts are due to the diversity of data sources. The contextual conflicts are mainly from environmental scalability problems. Thus, stakeholders can evolve in different environments. In this context, we can deduce that the multidimensional schemas permit to overcome the "horizontal fit" problems with these various conflicts and manage the knowledge of bid process.

VI. Conclusion and Perspectives

In this work, we tried to define the characteristics of the decision-making dimension of the BPIS. Thus, we have presented an approach for representing data warehouse schema based on an ontology that captures the multidimensional knowledge. We discussed one possible for extending the multidimensional ontology to eventually cover different phases of the data warehouse life cycle. We focused on the design phase, and showed how the use of the multidimensional ontology combined with an extension can be beneficial. In the future we intend to continue to explore the possibility of extending ontologies by considering bid ontologies as extensions that could be used to improve the resulting data warehouse schema; in addition to real cases of the implementation of the approach.

References

[1] A. Abrán, J.J. Cuadrado, E. García-Barriocanal, O. Mendes, S. Sánchez-Alonso, and M.A. Sicilia, "Engineering the ontology for the SWEBOK: Issues and techniques. In Ontologies for software engineering and software technology." Springer, Berlin, Heidelberg: 103-121, 2006.

[2] L. Bellatreche, P. Valduriez, and T. Morzy. Advances in Databases and Information Systems. Information Systems Frontiers, 20(1): 1-6, 2018.

[3] F. Bentayeb, N. Maïz, H. Mahboubi, C. Favre, S. Loudcher, N. Harbi and J. Darmont. "Innovative Approaches for efficiently Warehousing Complex Data from the Web. In Business intelligence applications and the web: Models, systems and technologies." IGI Global: 26-52, 2012.

[4] A. Bonifati, F. Cattaneo, S. Ceri, A. Fuggetta and S. Paraboschi. "Designing data marts for data warehouses. ACM transactions on software engineering and methodology." 10(4): 452-483, 2001.

[5] S. Borgo, P. Hitzler and O. Kutz (Eds.). "Formal Ontology in Information Systems": Proceedings of the 10th International Conference: IOS Press.(Vol. 306), 2018.

[6] C. Calero, F. Ruiz, and M. Piattini (Eds.). "Ontologies for software engineering and software technology." Springer Science Business Media, 2006.

[7] X. Fourrier-Morel, P. Grojean, G. Plouin, and C. Rognon. "SOA The guide of SI architecture". Dunod, Paris, 2008.

[8] E. Gallinucci, M. Golfarelli, and S. Rizzi. "Schema profiling of document-oriented databases." Information Systems, 75: 13-25, 2018.

[9] M. Golfarelli, and S. Rizzi. " A survey on temporal data warehousing". International Journal of Data Warehousing and Mining, 5(1): 1-17, 2009.

[10] K.D. Gronwald, (2017). "Integrated Business Information Systems: A Holistic View of the Linked Business Process Chain ERP-SCM-CRM-BI-Big Data." Springer, 2017.

[11] T.R. Gruber. " A translation approach to portable ontology specifications." Knowledge acquisition, 5(2): 199-220, 1993.

[12] N. Guarino. "Some ontological principles for designing upper level lexical resources." arXiv preprint cmp-lg/9809002, 1998.

[13] S. Khouri, I. Boukhari, L. Bellatreche, E. Sardet, J. Stéphane, and B. Michael. "Ontology-based structured web data warehouses for sustainable interoperability: requirement modeling, design methodology and tool." Computers in industry 63(8): 799-812,2012.

[14] J.N. Mazon, J. Lechtenbörger, and J. Trujillo." A survey on summarizability issues in multidimensional modeling." Data Knowledge Engineering 68(12): 1452-1469, 2009.

[15] E. Ovchinnikova and K.U. Kühnberger. "Aspects of automatic ontology extension: Adapting and regeneralizing dynamic updates'.' 72: 51-60, 2006

[16] C. Phipps, and K.C. Davis. "Automating data warehouse conceptual schema design and evaluation." In DMDW (2): 23-32, 2002.

[17] R. Kimball. "The Data Warehouse Toolkit: Practical Techniques for Building Dimensional Data Warehouses.", 1996.

[18] S. Zahaf and F. Gargouri. "ERP Inter-enterprises for the Operational Dimension of the Urbanized Bid Process Information System." Journal of Procedia Technology 16: 813-823, 2014.

[19] S. Zahaf and F. Gargouri. "Business and technical characteristics of the Bid-Process Information System". WorldComp: 52-60, 2017.

[20] M. Zekri. "Automatisation de la conception et la mise en œuvre d'un entrepôt de données générique." Ph.D. Thesis. University of Tunis El Manar, Tunisia, 2015.

[21] M. Zekri, I. Marsit and A. Abdellatif. "A New Data Warehouse Approach Using Graph." IEEE ICEBE:65-70, 2011.

Content based Segmentation of News Articles using Feature Similarity based K Nearest Neighbor

Taeho Jo
School of Game
Hongik University
Sejong, South Korea
tjo018@hongik.ac.kr

***Abstract*—This research proposes the modified KNN version which considers the feature similarity as well as the feature value similarity as a text segmentation tool. We need techniques of text segmentation for retrieving only relevant part from a long text and the task is mapped into a classification task to which the modified KNN version is applied. In the proposed system, adjacent paragraph pairs are generated from a text by sliding a window and they are classified into boundary or continuance. The proposed approach is validated as the better one in segmenting long text articles in various domain. In the next research, the task will be advanced into the temporal topic analysis which generates an ordered list of topics from an article.**

I. Introduction

The text segmentation is referred to the process of segmenting a long text into subtexts based on its contents. A full text is partitioned into paragraphs by the carriage return or sentences by one of punctuation marks; it is a trivial task which is out of this research scope. The scope is restricted to the process of segmenting a long text which deals with multiple topics into subtexts each of which deals with a topic. In this research, the text segmentation is mapped into a binary classification where an adjacent paragraph pair is classified into boundary or continuance, and the modified KNN version will applied to the task. In this section, we describe briefly the motivation, the idea, and the validation of this research.

Let us consider the motivations for doing this research. The text segmentation is necessary for permitting partial retrieval which retrieves only relevant text parts rather than entire full texts in information retrieval systems. The text segmentation may be mapped into a binary classification where each adjacent paragraph pair is classified into boundary or continuance, and the KNN algorithm is a simple approach to the data classification for starting to modify machine learning algorithms. Words which are features for encoding texts into numerical vectors have their own semantic relations with other. In this research, by introducing the feature similarity as well as the feature value similarity, we expect the discriminations among numerical vectors to be improved.

In this research, we apply the proposed KNN version to the text segmentation task. The task is interpreted into the binary classification where each adjacent paragraph pair is classified into boundary or continuance. In the proposed system, adjacent paragraph pairs are generated from the text which is given as the input, by sliding the two sized window to the temporal sequence of paragraphs, and boundaries is put between the adjacent paragraph pairs which are classified into boundary. The KNN is modified into the version where the similarity between the test example and each training example is based on both the feature similarity and the feature value similarity. This research is intended to improve the discriminations among numerical vectors, by considering the similarities among features, as well as ones among feature values.

In this research, we will validate empirically the proposed approach to the text segmentation as the better version than the traditional KNN version. We generate adjacent paragraph pairs from the collections of news articles: NewsPage.com and 20NewsGroups. The traditional KNN version and the proposed version are compared with each other. We observe the better results of the proposed KNN version in classifying each paragraph pair into boundary or continuance. It potentially possible to reduce the dimension by considering the feature similarity.

Let us mention the organization of this research. In Section II, we explore the previous works which are relevant to this research. In Section III, we describe in detail what we propose in this research. In Section IV, we validate empirically the proposed approach by comparing it with the traditional one. In Section V, we mention the significances of this research and the remaining tasks as the conclusion.

II. Previous Works

Let us survey the previous cases of encoding texts into structured forms for using the machine learning algorithms to text mining tasks. The three main problems, huge dimensionality, sparse distribution, and poor transparency, have existed inherently in encoding them into numerical vectors. In previous works, various schemes of preprocessing texts have been proposed, in order to solve the problems. In this survey, we focus on the process of encoding texts into alternative structured forms to numerical vectors. In other words, this section is intended to explore previous works on solutions to the problems.

Let us mention the popularity of encoding texts into numerical vectors, and the proposal and the application of string kernels as the solution to the above problems. In 2002, Sebastiani presented the numerical vectors are the standard representations of texts in applying the machine learning algorithms to the text classifications [4]. In 2002, Lodhi et al. proposed the string kernel as a kernel function of raw texts in using the SVM (Support Vector Machine) to the text classification [5]. In 2004, Lesile et al. used the version of SVM which proposed by Lodhi et al. to the protein classification [6]. In 2004, Kate and Mooney used also the SVM version for classifying sentences by their meanings [7].

It was proposed that texts are encoded into tables instead of numerical vectors, as the solutions to the above problems. In 2008, Jo and Cho proposed the table matching algorithm as the approach to text classification [8]. In 2008, Jo applied also his proposed approach to the text clustering, as well as the text categorization [12]. In 2011, Jo described as the technique of automatic text classification in his patent document [10]. In 2015, Jo improved the table matching algorithm into its more stable version [11].

Previously, it was proposed that texts should be encoded into string vectors as other structured forms. In 2008, Jo modified the k means algorithm into the version which processes string vectors as the approach to the text clustering[12]. In 2010, Jo modified the two supervised learning algorithms, the KNN and the SVM, into the version as the improved approaches to the text classification [13]. In 2010, Jo proposed the unsupervised neural networks, called Neural Text Self Organizer, which receives the string vector as its input data [14]. In 2010, Jo applied the supervised neural networks, called Neural Text Categorizer, which gets a string vector as its input, as the approach to the text classification [15].

The above previous works proposed the string kernel as the kernel function of raw texts in the SVM, and tables and string vectors as representations of texts, in order to solve the problems. Because the string kernel takes very much computation time for computing their values, it was used for processing short strings or sentences rather than texts. In the previous works on encoding texts into tables, only table matching algorithm was proposed; there is no attempt to modify the machine algorithms into their table based version. In the previous works on encoding texts into string vectors, only frequency was considered for defining features of string vectors. Words which are used as features of numerical vectors which represent texts have their semantic similarities among them, so the similarities will be used for processing sparse numerical vectors, in this research.

III. Proposed Approach

This section is concerned with what we propose in this research. The text segmentation is mapped into a binary classification task where each adjacent paragraph pair is classified into boundary or continuance. We propose the similarity metric which considers the feature similarity, as well as the feature value one, and modify the KNN algorithm into version which computes a similarity between a training example and a test example by the similarity metric. The modified version is applied to the text segmentation which is viewed as the text classification task, but it should be distinguished from the topic based text categorization. In this section, we describe what is proposed in this research.

Figure 1 illustrates the process of mapping the text segmentation into a binary classification. The text is given as the input, it is converted into adjacent paragraphs pairs by sliding it with the two sized window, and the pairs are encoded into numerical vectors. Each paragraph pair is classified into boundary or continuance, and boundaries are located between paragraph pairs which are classified into boundary. Sample paragraph pairs are collected domain by domain as shown in Figure 2. The task may be mapped into the regression task, where difference degrees between two paragraphs are estimated as continuous values.

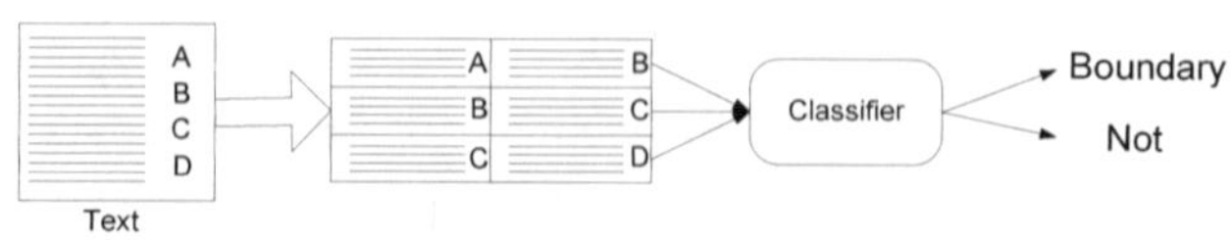

Figure 1. Mapping Text Segmentation into Binary Classification

Figure 2 presents the proposed KNN algorithm. In advance, the training texts are encoded into numerical vectors. A novice text is encoded into a numerical vector, its similarities with the numerical vectors which represent the training ones by equation which is proposed in [17], and the most k similar training texts are selected its nearest neighbors. The label of the novice text is decided by voting ones of the nearest neighbors. We may consider the KNN variants which are derived from this version by discriminating the similarities and the attributes.

Let us explain how to apply the proposed KNN algorithm to the text segmentation task. The sample paragraph pairs which are labeled with boundary or continuance are gathered domain by domain as shown in Figure 2, and they are encoded into numerical vectors. By sliding paragraphs, a list of adjacent paragraph pairs is generated from the text which is assumed to be tagged with its own domain, and their similarities with sample ones in the corresponding domain are computed. For each paragraph pair, its k nearest sample ones are selected and its label is decided by voting their labels. Boundaries are located between paragraph pairs which are classified with boundary.

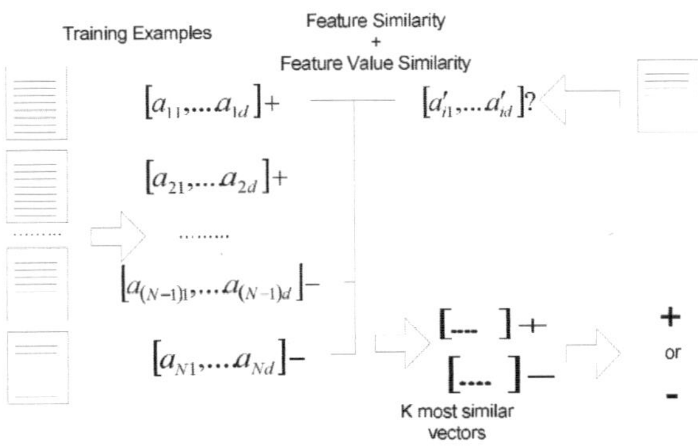

Figure 2. The Proposed Version of KNN

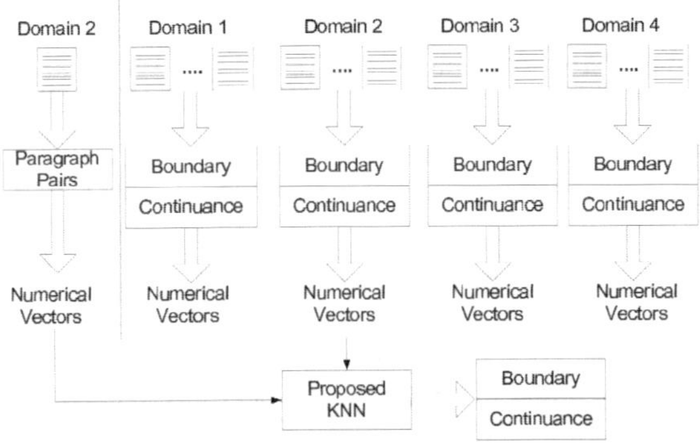

Figure 3. Text Segmentation: Domain Dependent Classification

The task in this research should be distinguished from the topic based text categorization, even if both tasks belong to the classification task. In the topic based text categorization, sample texts are collected independently of domain, whereas in the text segmentation, sample paragraph pairs should be done domain by domain. In the former, a topic or a category is absolutely assigned to each text, whereas in the latter, one of the two categories, is assigned to each paragraph pair, depending on content based difference between two adjacent paragraphs. In the text categorization, a text is classified, depending on its content which is related with a category or a topic, whereas in the text segmentation, it is classified, depending on its semantic difference degree between paragraphs. The process of applying the proposed KNN to the text segmentation is described in [16].

IV. Experiments

This section is concerned with the experiments for validating the better performance of the proposed version on the collection: NewsPage.com. We interpret the text segmentation into the binary classification where each adjacent paragraph pair is classified into boundary and continuance, and, by sliding window on paragraphs of each text, gather the paragraph pairs which are labeled with one of the two categories, from the collection, topic by topic. Each paragraph pair is classified exclusively into one of the two labels. We fix the input size as 50 dimensions of numerical vectors, and use the accuracy as the evaluation measure. Therefore, this section is intended to observe the performance of the both versions of KNN in the four different domains.

In Table I, we specify the text collection, NewsPage.com, which is used in this set of experiments. The collection was used for evaluating approaches to text categorization tasks in previous works [?]. In each category, we extract 250 adjacent paragraph pairs and label them with boundary or continuance, keeping the complete balance over the two labels. In each category, the set of 250 paragraph pairs is partitioned into the training set of 200 ones and the test set of 50 ones. Each text is segmented into paragraphs by a carriage return, and adjacent paragraph pairs are generated by sliding two sized window on the list of paragraphs.

Table I
The Number of Texts and Paragraph Pairs in NewsPage.com

Category	#Texts	#Training Pairs	#Test Pairs
Business	500	200 (100+100)	50 (25+25)
Health	500	200 (100+100)	50 (25+25)
Internet	500	200 (100+100)	50 (25+25)
Sports	500	200 (100+100)	50 (25+25)

Let us mention the experimental process for validating empirically the proposed approach to the task of text segmentation. We collect the sample paragraphs which are labeled with boundary or continuance in each of the four topics: Business, Sports, Internet, and Health, and encode them into numerical vectors. For each of 50 examples, the KNN computes its similarities with the 200 training examples, and selects the three similarity training examples as its nearest neighbors. This set of experiments consists of the four independent binary classifications each of in which each paragraph is classified into one of the two labels by the two versions of KNN algorithm. We compute the classification accuracy by dividing the number of correctly classified test examples by the number of test examples, for evaluating the both versions.

In Figure 4, we illustrate the experimental results from classifying each adjacent paragraph pair into boundary or continuance, using the both versions of KNN algorithm. The y-axis indicates the accuracy which is the rate of the correctly classified examples in the test set. Each group in the x-axis means the domain within which the text summarization which is viewed as a binary classification is performed, independently. In each group, the gray bar and the black bar indicate the accuracies of the traditional version and the proposed version of the KNN algorithm. The most right group in Figure 4 consists of the averages over the accuracies of the left four groups, and the input size which is the dimension of numerical vectors is set to 50.

Let us make the discussions on the results from doing the text segmentation, using the both versions of KNN

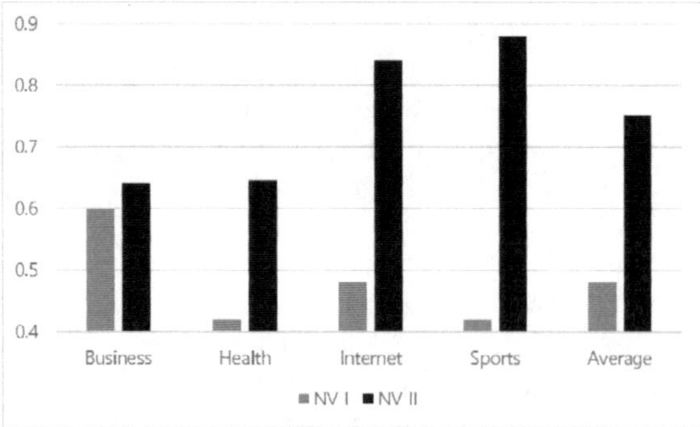

Figure 4. Results from Segmenting Texts in Text Collection: NewsPage.com

algorithm, as shown in Figure 4. The accuracy which is the performance measure of this classification task is in the range between 0.4 and 0.9. The proposed version of KNN algorithm works strongly better in the three domains, Health, Internet, and Sports. However, it loses in the domain, Business. In spite of that, from this set of experiments, we conclude the proposed version works better than traditional one, in averaging over the four cases.

V. Conclusion

The proposed approach should be applied and validated in the specialized domains: engineering, medicine, science, and law, and it should be customized to the suitable version. We may consider similarities among only some essential features rather than among all features, to cut down the computation time. We develop and combine various schemes of computing the similarities among features. By adopting the proposed approach, we will develop the text segmentation system as a real version.

VI. Acknowledgement

This work was supported by 2018 Hongik University Research Fund.

References

[1] T. Mitchell, Machine Learning, McGraw-Hill, 1997.

[2] C. D. Manning and H. Schutze, Foundations of Statistical Natural Language Processing, MIT Press, 1999.

[3] T. Jo, "The Implementation of Dynamic Document Organization using Text Categorization and Text Clustering" PhD Dissertation of University of Ottawa, 2006.

[4] F. Sebastiani, "Machine Learning in Automated Text Categorization", pp1-47, ACM Computing Survey, Vol 34, No 1, 2002.

[5] H. Lodhi, C. Saunders, J. Shawe-Taylor, N. Cristianini, and C. Watkins, "Text Classification with String Kernels", pp419-444, Journal of Machine Learning Research, Vol 2, No 2, 2002.

[6] C. S. Leslie, E. Eskin, A. Cohen, J. Weston, and W. S. Noble, "Mismatch String Kernels for Discriminative Protein Classification", pp467-476, Bioinformatics, Vol 20, No 4, 2004.

[7] R. J. Kate and R. J. Mooney, "Using String Kernels for Learning Semantic Parsers", pp913-920, Proceedings of the 21st International Conference on Computational Linguistics and the 44th annual meeting of the Association for Computational Linguistics, 2006.

[8] T. Jo and D. Cho, "Index based Approach for Text Categorization",International Journal of Mathematics and Computers in Simulation, Vol 2, No 1, 2008.

[9] T. Jo, "Single Pass Algorithm for Text Clustering by Encoding Documents into Tables", pp1749-1757, Journal of Korea Multimedia Society, Vol 11, No 12, 2008.

[10] T. Jo, "Device and Method for Categorizing Electronic Document Automatically", Patent Document, 10-2009-0041272, 10-1071495, 2011.

[11] T. Jo, "Normalized Table Matching Algorithm as Approach to Text Categorization", pp839-849, Soft Computing, Vol 19, No 4, 2015.

[12] T. Jo, "Inverted Index based Modified Version of K-Means Algorithm for Text Clustering", pp67-76, Journal of Information Processing Systems, Vol 4, No 2, 2008.

[13] T. Jo, "Representationof Texts into String Vectors for Text Categorization", pp110-127, Journal of Computing Science and Engineering, Vol 4, No 2, 2010.

[14] T. Jo, "NTSO (Neural Text Self Organizer): A New Neural Network for Text Clustering", pp31-43, Journal of Network Technology, Vol 1, No 1, 2010.

[15] T. Jo, "NTC (Neural Text Categorizer): Neural Network for Text Categorization", pp83-96, International Journal of Information Studies, Vol 2, No 2, 2010.

[16] T. Jo, "K Nearest Neighbors for Text Segmentation with Feature Similarity", DOI: 10.1109/ICCCCEE.2017.7866706, Proceedings of International Conference on Communication, Control, Computing and Electronics Engineering, 2017.

[17] T. Jo, "Text Categorization using K Nearest Neighbor with Feature Similarity", submitted, The Proceedings of International Conference on Green and Human Information Technology, 2018.

Using IPhone for Identifying Objects

C. McTague and Z. Wang
Department of Computer Science, Virginia Wesleyan University, Virginia Beach, Virginia, USA

Abstract - *Knowing things around us such as poison ivy, etc. is important. Using the "Smart Camera" in IPhone can be easily for the identification of everyday items. The application introduced here can be used to identify anything in categories such as trees, animals, food, vehicles, consumer goods, and generic objects. This application utilizes Apples available machine learning models, the IPhone camera, and the IPhone photo storage to assist in the identification and storage of the objects captured by the camera. The research applies machine learning and deep learning by using the Swift computer language to develop a practical and functional application.*

Keywords: Deep Learning, IPhone App, Machine Learning, Swift language, VGG16 Model, Xcode IDE

1 Introduction

In past decades, smart phones and AI have played an important role in our daily life [1]. With the popular use of the smart phone, this research is a demonstration of Machine Learning and Deep Learning technologies that assists in everyday tasks. The Smart Camera's purpose is to render assistance to the user when it comes to identifying some objects they are looking at. Theses object can include but are not limited to, trees, animals, food, vehicles, consumer goods, and generic objects. The idea behind this app is to render assistance to children or adults when they are trying to learn about what they are looking at. This app could be useful in early childhood development when learning about shapes and general house hold objects [2][3][4].

The paper is organized in the following sections. The system design is introduced in the next section. In Section 3, the details of the main modules for case study are presented as well as the code samples. Conclusion is given in Section 4.

2 System Design

This App is constructed using simple, single page design to minimize the learning curve the user would need to overcome to utilize the app. As this app is intended for all ages, simplicity was a key consideration when constructing this app [5].

The page shown in Figure 1 is the loading screen when first starting up the app. This page includes the short title of the app, as well as the related information such as authors. This page only appears while the rest of the app is loading up. It generally only is visible for about one to three seconds at a time.

The main page of the App (shown in Figure 2) is a view finders for the camera and the identification label located at the bottom in the gray bar. When this page is loaded, the screen will show what the IPhone's back camera is seeing.

In order for the Smart Camera Application to be useful to the user, the following subjects have to be implemented.

- A meaningful title
- A view finder for the user to focus the camera on
- An identification label to display what the object might be.
- A confidence percentage that shows the likelihood it is what the identification label says it is.
- Use the VGG16 model provided by Apple to identify the objects in real time.
- A notification to inform the users of the screenshotted item.
- An informative start up screen that displays the projects name, author, professor, and University logo.

Figure 1. The start up page

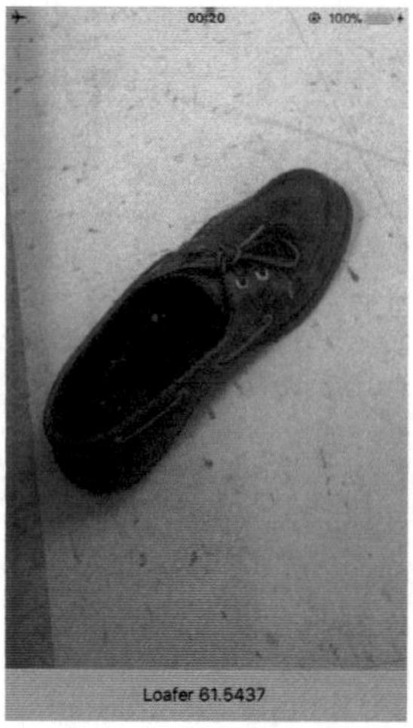

Figure 2. The controller page

3 Case Study

In the section, the main modules with code samples in the system are described as follows.

3.1 The viewController Class

The view controller is the main class where the app is setup. Within this class there are a couple functions such as viewDidLoad() and captureOutput() that are implemented to configure this application. Other various functions are located within the viewController to implement the behaviors needed for this app such as Notification Center permissions and changing the way Notifications are displayed when the app is in the foreground.

3.2 The viewDidLoad() function

This method is where the User Interface is loaded and constructed. This includes establishing the Notification Center for the Screenshot notification, the AVCaptureSession to connect to the camera, the AVCaptureVideoPreviewLayer which is used for the on-screen view finder, and finally sets up the confidence label at the bottom of the screen.

```
override func viewDidLoad()
{       super.viewDidLoad()
// allows notification center to
display alerts while app is in
foreground
        UNUserNotificationCenter.curren
t().delegate = self
        //check if app can use
notification center
        initNotificationSetupCheck()

        //starting up the camera
        let captureSession =
AVCaptureSession()
        // make preview in full res
        captureSession.sessionPreset =
AVCaptureSession.Preset.high

        guard let captureDevice =
AVCaptureDevice.default(for: .video)
else { return }

        guard let input = try?
AVCaptureDeviceInput(device:
captureDevice)
                                   else { return
                        }

        captureSession.addInput(input)
        captureSession.startRunning()

        let previewLayer =
AVCaptureVideoPreviewLayer(session:
captureSession)
        view.layer.addSublayer(previewL
ayer)
        previewLayer.frame = view.frame
//add preview to the frame

        let dataOutput =
AVCaptureVideoDataOutput()
        dataOutput.setSampleBufferDeleg
ate(self, queue: DispatchQueue(label:
"videoQueue"))
        captureSession.addOutput(dataOu
tput)

        // continually running to
detect screenshots
```

```
        detectScreenShot { () -> () in
        let content =
UNMutableNotificationContent()
        content.title = "Screenshot!"
        content.body = "Your screenshot
has been stored in your camera roll"
        content.badge = 1

        let trigger =
UNTimeIntervalNotificationTrigger(timeI
nterval: 1, repeats: false)// trigger
and deley note by 1 second
        let request =
UNNotificationRequest(identifier:
"Screenshot", content: content,
trigger: trigger) // build the request
to notify
        UNUserNotificationCenter.curren
t().add(request, withCompletionHandler:
nil)
            print("Screenshot
detected") //debug code only seen in
xcode
        }
        setupICLabel()
    }
```

3.3 The detectScreenShot() function

This command is located inside the viewDidLoad() method and is used to call the detectScreenShot() method later in the program. This command itself sets up the content of the notification. Once the method is called, it will still not display the notification properly. Due to the native API for Swift, notifications are not displayed when the current application is in the foreground. Therefore the function userNotificationCenter() was used to override this API and allow the notification to be shown one second after the screen shot was taken.

3.4 The catpureOutput() function

This function is where the AVCapturedOutput() from the camera is ran through the VGG16 pre-taught model. Once the request is finished by the VGG16 pre-taught model, the answer is returned and displayed in the form of the confidence label at the bottom of the screen. This is running continually so objects are being identified every second.

3.5 The setupICLabel() function

This method sets up the confidence label and assigns its given properties like size, color, and location. It also adds the label as a sub view of the view controller so when the viewController loads app, the label is output on the screen.

```
fileprivate func setupICLabel()
{       view.addSubview(identifierLabel
)
        identifierLabel.bottomAnchor.co
nstraint(equalTo: view.bottomAnchor,
constant: 0).isActive = true
        identifierLabel.leftAnchor.cons
traint(equalTo:
view.leftAnchor).isActive = true
        identifierLabel.rightAnchor.con
straint(equalTo:
view.rightAnchor).isActive = true
        identifierLabel.heightAnchor.co
nstraint(equalToConstant: 50).isActive
= true
        identifierLabel.shadowColor =
UIColor.darkGray
        identifierLabel.backgroundColor
= UIColor.lightGray
}
```

3.6 The initNotificationSetupCheck() function

This method is a sanity check when the app is first started up. It is only ever used the first time the user is opening that app to ask permission to access the user's Notification Center on their phone. If the permission Boolean has not been set, a promote will come up asking for permission. However, if the Boolean is already true, nothing will happen.

3.7 The extension UIImage() function

This method was tested but never actually used due to a Swift API issue.

The purpose of this was to support screenshotting the screen with a tap of the finger on the screen. However, this was not possible due to a property of AVCaptureVideoPreviewLayer() that did not allow the camera view finder displayed on the screen to be included in the sub layers.

This issue was figured out by reading the Swift documentation and bug reports.

3.8 The VGG16 Pre-trained model

A little about the VGG16 model is that it takes the AVCaptureOutput() collected from the camera, and converts the image into a three-dimensional array that. This array contains values for pixel locations and they are used to determine what the object is based on the information it has from being taught before. Therefore, the model is not looking at the image on a visual level, but rather a pixel level.

4 Conclusion

A Smart Camera application is introduced and designed to be "smart" and helpful. It can identify dominate objects with a high degree of accuracy. A confidence label was included to show the percent likely that object is what is says it is. With knowledge of Machine Learning, swift programming language, and app design, this application is produced to assist people with identifying everyday objects. Overall, this application can be useful for the daily user as well as people with learning challenges.

5 References

[1] GAREWAL, JAZ. "Can Core ML in IOS Really Do Hot Dog Detection Without Server-Side Processing?" Savvy Apps, 17 June 2017, savvyapps.com/blog/core-ml-ios-hot-dog-detection-no-server.

[2] Inc., Apple. "AVFoundation." AVFoundation | Apple Developer Documentation, developer.apple.com/documentation/avfoundation/.

[3] Inc., Apple. "Build More Intelligent Apps with Machine Learning." Machine Learning - Apple Developer, developer.apple.com/machine-learning/.Stack Overflow. Stack Exchange Inc. Web. 27 Mar. 2016. <http://stackoverflow.com/>.

[4] *Inc., Apple. "Swift Resources." Apple Developer, Sept. 2017, developer.apple.com/swift/resources/.*

[5] Simonyan, Karen, and Andrew Zisserman. Very Deep Convolutional Networks for Large-Scale Image Recognition. Cornell University Libriary, 10 Apr. 2015, arxiv.org/abs/1409.1556

Video Action Recognition Performance and Amelioration of HMM-PSO On Large Data Set

Haiyi Zhang

Jodrey School of Computer Science

Acadia University,

Wolfville, NS, Canada

Haiyi.zhang@acadiau.ca

Hansheng Zhang

Jodrey School of Computer Science

Acadia University,

Wolfville, NS, Canada

132579z@acadiau.ca

Abstract--
A new existing algorithm which substitutes original Particle Swarm Optimization in the previous research is introduced in this paper. By going through the same training and testing data sets, the original Hidden Markov Model combined with a recently found Nature-Inspired Algorithms optimization works. And the advantages and disadvantages are described through a chain of comparisons between not only the algorithms mentioned above, but also multiple other similar optimizations, such as Ant Colony Optimization, Particle Swarm Optimization, Bat Algorithm, and Firefly Algorithm, etc. Subsequently. Results of the accuracy for these models will generate visual and intuitional differences and will be provided the best one as the final model.

Index Terms: **Video Action, Nature inspired techniques, Particle Swarm Optimization, Ant Colony Optimization, Bat Algorithm, Firefly Algorithm, Harmony Search Algorithm**

I. Background Information

Discriminating human actions by eyes and acknowledging what people want to achieve through movements is an easy thing for people. However, based on the current algorithm and technology, it becomes a tough mission in the perspective of the computer. As the interaction between human and computer, such as intelligent video surveillance and multimedia information representation, grows gradually intimate, the ability for a computer to recognize human action through dynamic video is going to play an indispensable role to achieve further communication among mankind and plenty of technologies.

Video Action Recognition is a comprehensive method which assists computer spontaneously analyze and recognize what people in videos are doing. It can split videos into many pieces frame by frame, extract the features of actions hidden throughout them, and by analyzing the trajectories of action to distinguish what the action is. Through the whole procedure, it synthesizes different algorithms and data mining methods by sends outputs from the previous method to the next as inputs for an advanced target. Finally, according to the analyze among data, the prediction of what human is doing in videos will be provided as the final result. Even though such sort of technology is easily understandable, it is currently unmatured since of inadequate success rate to accurately distinguish certain behavior among millions of action events of mankind.

II. Introduction

In previous paper [10], we develop an approach HMM-PSO for video recognition. We proposed an action modeling method based on event probabilities, and meanwhile, present an approach to optimize the parameters of HMM. Benchmark data experiments, as well as large number of comparative experiments with other popular methods verify that our presented methods have lots of advantages.

We also know that, though HMM-PSO's performance is enhanced, the general *recognition rate* still has space to be improved, especially for larger scale active class problems. After academic research and lots of data experiments, we've gotten to know that there are two main reasons for HMM-PSO's deficiency for big size problems. The first reason is that we take the single Gauss density function to indicate observing probability, but we can not guarantee its efficiency when describing complex motions. The second reason is that we use the DTW method to calculate the event probability, but we are not sure whether it can correctly reflect the distance of the classes between the learning samples and the testing samples.

This is our motivation for contining this research. First, we will try to do more practical data experiments, especially on large data set problem, to evaluate our method, model and algorithm in whole scale. Secondly, we like to do some academic researches on how to improve the recognition rate. Thirdly, we will further discuss how to evaluate and enhance the recognition accuracy. And finally, we will try to apply our presented approaches in more practical applications.

The goal of this research is trying to achieve theses points mentioned above in the previous research, and explore the performance of HMM with other optimization algorithms which had not been invented at that time to enhance the method of Video Action Recognition. The main target is to try to search a better function than a single Gauss density function to help HMM indicate observing probability and build several facilitating models with HMM to extract and resolve the data structure and simple actions hidden in the data sets. Subsequently, due to differences in the principle of algorithms, the results presented different predict accuracies. By comparing and contrasting the quality of different algorithms under multiple conditions and data populations, these models will be ranked ultimately and the best one is chosen as the achievement of this research. Then In this research, we will ameliorate Video Action Recognition method especially under large scale samples and implement my method and test its recognition rate mostly under Java implementation environment.

III. The Available Methods and Approaches

The procedure of Video Action Recognition splits into three main parts in the current model.

The methodologies and tasks of this research are described as follows:

A. Collecting Large Set Data and Reconstructing HMM Model and Time Warping

At the beginning of Gather different types of samples in a large range of videos and clarify the problems our model currently faces.

A 2-D motion trajectory of certain target object will be extracted from video, and two main features of many, such as directions, velocities, and positions, will be analyzed to explore motion trajectory. The first one is shaped, namely the geometry derived from the pattern of the motion and the direction. The second feature is velocity, which describes the dynamics of the object's trajectory.

We Evaluate different method based on HMM, the performance of event probability to model the behavior and we take HMM-PSO with large set data and mine out the semantic event probability from the original trajectory.

The method in the previous research will remain the same, DTW (Dynamic Time Warping) is used to match the model and finally get the recognition results. We will analyze whether it can correctly reflect the distance of the classes between the learning samples and the testing samples and dig out the reason.

B. Construct Optimization Models with Nature-Inspired Algorithms (Current Process)

After building several advanced models, we will analyze the reason why it fits better than before on more complex data problems and concludes the advantages and disadvantages of it.

IV. Comparison and Analysis Between Models with different Algorithms

The considering algorithms are all optimizations generated as nature inspiring. (Iztok , Yang, Iztok , Janez , & Dušan)

A. Particle Swarm Optimization

Particle swarm optimization is a swarming derivative algorithm from swarming intelligence [7].

As the previous research mentioned, the HMM-PSO are efficient even if there exists a tremendous trajectory differences for the same sort of action. And such efficiency guarantees the decent accuracy for predicting the same behavior with different situations in videos. (Zhang, 2012)

B. Ant Colony Optimization

The Ant Colony Optimization algorithm dedicates to imitate how ants behave in nature to search for solutions from the choice of the path to be followed until the process of updating the pheromone trail. And what we mainly used in ACO as the principles are based on the behavior of ants in real world and the communication among the ants. This algorithm mimics a sequence of local optimal movement to find the global shortest way. [1,3]

The advantage for Ant Colony Algorithm is that the accuracy for local prediction for given trajectory is high, but and it may not overfit when large set of situations occur and still keep a high predict rate.

C. Firefly Algorithm

This algorithm [4,5] is proposed from nature behavior of a firefly's flash. Firefly is a luminous insect which can act as a signal system to attract other fireflies. It is depicted in three parts:

- If All fireflies are unisexual, so that any individual firefly will be attracted to all other fireflies;
- Attractiveness is proportional to their brightness, and for any two fireflies, the less bright one will be attracted by (and thus move towards) the brighter one; however, the intensity (apparent brightness) decrease as their mutual distance increases;
- If there are no fireflies brighter than a given firefly, it will move randomly.

D. Bat Algorithm

Inspired from how microbats utilize echo to locate preys and objects, the Bat algorithm is focusing on global optimization. [8, 9].

V. Conclusion

This is on going research, we are just doing the tests now following what we planning to do. Hopfully in the near future we have some results.

References

[1] D. A., & Vybihal, J. An ant colony optimization algorithm to improve software quality prediction. *Information and Software Technology*, 2010.

[2] Alam, M. N. (n.d.). *Particle Swarm Optimization: Algorithm and its Codes in MATLAB.*

[3] Al-Ani, A. Ant Colony Optimization for Feature Subset. *World Academy of Science, Engineering and Technology, 2007.*

[4] Hassan, R., Cohanim, B., Weck, O., & Venter, G. (n.d.). A Comparison of Particle Swarm Optimization and the Genetic Algorithm. *46th AIAA/ASME/ASCE/AHS/ASC Structures, Structural Dynamics and Materials Conference, Structures, Structural Dynamics, and Materials and Co-located Conferences*, 2005.

[5] Iztok , F. J., Yang, X.-S., Iztok , F., Janez , B., & Dušan , F. (n.d.). A Brief Review of Nature-Inspired Algorithms for Optimization.

[6] Kaveh, A., & Talatahari, S. A HYBRID PARTICLE SWARM AND ANT COLONY.,. Retrieved from ASIAN JOURNAL OF CIVIL ENGINEERING,2008, p329-p348.

[7] Parsopolos, K. E., & Vrahatis, M. N. Particle swarm optimization method for constrained optimization problems. In *Intelligent Technologies: Theory and Applications : New Trends, 2002,p* 214-p220.

[8] Rodrigues, D., Nakamura, R., Costa, K., & Yang, X.-S. A wrapper approach for feature selection based on Bat Algorithm and Optimum-Path Forest. In *Expert Systems with Applications, 2014,p* 2250-p2258.

[9] Yang, X. A New Metaheuristic Bat-Inspired Algorithm, in: Nature Inspired Cooperative Strategies for Optimization. *Studies in Computational Intelligence*, 2010, p65–p74.

[10] Zhang, H. VIDEO ACTION RECOGNITION BASED ON. *IADIS International Journal on Computer Science and Information Systems*,2012, 1-17 .

SESSION

INTERNATIONAL WORKSHOP ON ELECTRONICS & INFORMATION TECHNOLOGY; IWEIT-2019

Chair(s)

Prof. Cheng-Ying Yang
University of Taipei
Taiwan

Realization of Intelligent Management Platform for Cyber-Physical Systems

Nai-Wei Lo[1], Meng-Hsuan Tsai[2], Jing-Lun Lin[3], Meng-Hsuan Lai[4], Yen-Ju Chen[5]
Department of Information Management
National Taiwan University of Science and Technology
Taipei, Taiwan
nwlo@cs.ntust.edu.tw[1]
{d10709101[2], m10509121[3], m10609110[4], m10709114[5]}@mail.ntust.edu.tw

***Abstract*—Since the concept of Industry 4.0 was proposed in 2011, smart manufacturing has gradually become a central issue for industries in terms of competition strength. To establish a computerized and information-driven manufacturing industry, it is necessary to design and construct an intelligent system platform with data analysis and management functions for decision making on manufacturing and business goals. In this paper, we present an intelligent management platform prototype based on the cyber-physical systems formed through manufacturing assembly lines in the experimental factory of National Taiwan University of Science and Technology to share our experience on realizing a useful analysis and management platform for manufacturing industry.**

Keywords—Cyber-Physical System; Industry 4.0; Industrial Internet of Things; Big Data Analytics; Smart Manufacturing

I. INTRODUCTION

In recent years more sensors and corresponding applications, systems, and services are invented, created, and deployed in the world than ever before. Internet of Things technologies have profound impact on almost every perspective of human society. Therefore, industries also feel the heat and have to response with the challenges. In consequence, technologies for Industrial Internet of Things (IIoT) are derived and cyber-physical systems are generated to integrate operation technology (OT) with information technology (IT) such that industries can raise their competition strength from manufacturing side. To take advantage of IIoT, collecting the huge amount of sensed data from corresponding sensors and performing data analysis on those big data are the key to success. Therefore, it is necessary for industries to build an information-oriented and data-driven platform supporting data analyses and management functions to fulfill smart manufacturing.

To gain the biggest benefits of technology integration between OT and IT, cloud computing and services along with adoption of open source programs are quickly become good practices to foster manufacturing digitalization [1]. In 2018, Jirkovsky et al. [2] presented an implementation work of cloud-based cyber-physical system based on OPC UA, the popular industrial interoperability standard [3]. In 2019, Damjanovic-Behrendt and Behrendt [4] introduced an open source approach to design and implement micro-services for smart manufacturing. The importance of utilizing big data analytical technology on IIoT was discussed through frameworks analyses and case studies in [5]. Ruan et al. in [6] had demonstrated a realization of monitoring system on tire production process by adopting cyber-physical systems. In [7], Bassey et al. implemented a real-time control system for cyber-physical power system test bed. In addition, Skrada et al. [8] investigated how to design and develop educational platform for students to play and experience cyber-physical systems in IIoT. Recently, intelligent container concept was introduced in industry 4.0 scenarios [9]. As an intelligent container can identify smart components, sense experiences (events), create notifications and make decisions, in the future a cyber-physical system composed by multiple intelligent containers will become an autonomous and fault tolerant platform. In this paper, the design and implementation of intelligent management platform for cyber-physical systems is presented. The target cyber-physical systems for the prototype implementation are constructed on top of manufacturing assembly lines located at the experimental factory in National Taiwan University of Science and Technology.

The remainder of this paper is as follows. Section II introduces the proposed prototype of intelligent management platform. Section III gives our concluding remarks.

II. THE PROPOSED INTELLIGENT MANAGEMENT PLATFORM

The design of system architecture for the proposed intelligent management platform is shown in Fig. 1. For machines in each manufacturing assembly line, various add-on sensors are attached to them to collect sensed datasets. These real-time collected data are directly sent to Supervisory Control And Data Acquisition (SCADA) server and Manufacturing Execution System (MES) server. SCADA server can use these sensed data to monitor production status at assembly lines and response urgent events by sending control commands to corresponding machines in real time. In addition, MES server usually is responsible to store all the sensed data for later usage such as log audit, data analysis, and production processes reports. To utilize cloud-based intelligent management platform for business management through big data analytics and decision making functions, sensed data will be periodically transmitted from MES server or SCADA server to the cloud platform. Depending on the types of sensed data, SQL database and NoSQL database are both utilized to store received sensed datasets at the cloud platform. To speed up data analysis, Hadoop framework is adopted within the cloud platform to enable parallel computing capability on data analysis programs writing in various programming languages such as R or Python. In this platform, user-friendly GUI is also developed to support statistical diagrams and display details of analyzed datasets.

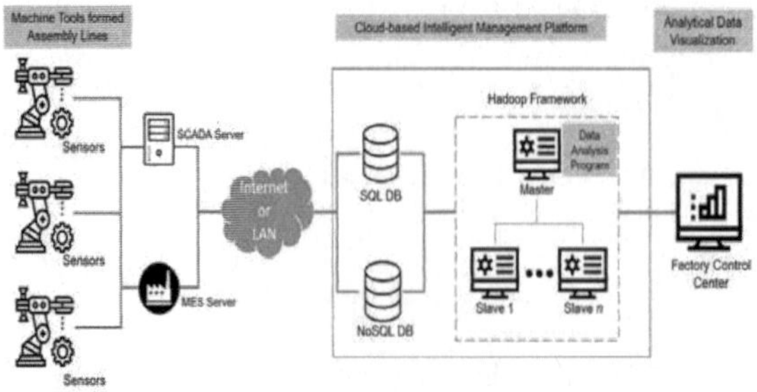

Fig. 1. The system architecture of cloud-based intelligent management platform.

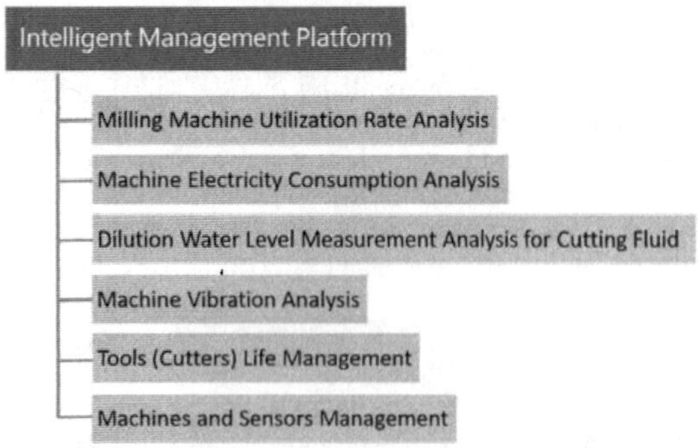

Fig. 2. Six major functionalities of implemented platform prototype in Taiwan Tech Industry 4.0 Implementation Center.

The prototype of intelligent management platform implemented at the experimental factory of Taiwan Tech Industry 4.0 Implementation Center has six major functionalities as shown in Fig. 2. There are two management functions: tools life management and machines and sensors management. Tools life management function stores detailed profile for each cutter type and records usage status of individual cutter to manage the life time of each cutter (tool). Machines and sensors management function records the usage status of each machine and the status of its corresponding sensors. If there is abnormal status occurred in a machine or a sensor, the management function will notify factory engineers. There are other four analysis functions in this prototype. Milling machine utilization rate analysis is to show the utilization rate of a target milling machine in selected period of time. The time unit is usually by day. The utilization rate of a machine can be derived from the sensed data of machine electricity usage. Machine electricity consumption analysis gives factory managers detailed electricity usage profile of each machine in the factory. Dilution water level measurement analysis for cutting fluid is used to monitor the dilution water level of cutting fluid with sensors as a part of preventive maintenance mechanism. Machine vibration analysis function utilizes sensors to monitor the amplitude and frequency of machine vibration, and detect anomaly signals.

The prototype uses Microsoft SQL server and Mongo DB to collect and store received sensed data. Table I shows the total number of received data records in million, the total amount of data in GB, the average transmission rate in Kbits/sec and records/sec, and the average record size in byte.

TABLE I. THE PROFILE OF SENSED DATA STORED IN SQL AND NOSQL DATABASES

	Microsoft SQL Server	Mongo DB
Total Number of Records	1044 Million	1611 Million
Total Amount of Data	35.946 GB	20.309 GB
Average Transmission Rate	558.79 Kbits/sec (1981 records/sec)	5431.6 Kbits/sec (51200 records/sec)
Average Record Size	36.106 Bytes	13.579 Bytes

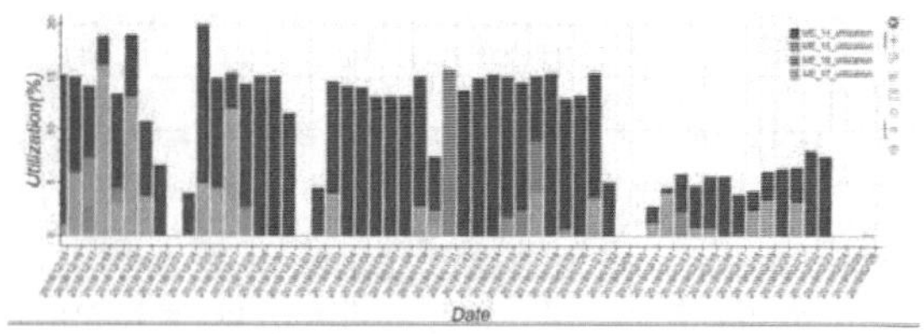

Fig. 3. The statistical diagram of milling machine utilization rate by date.

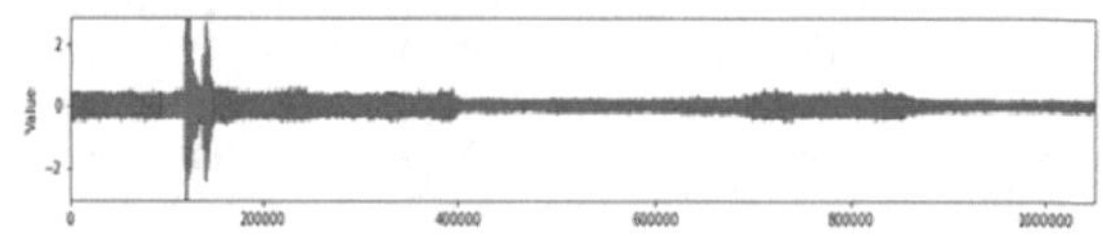

Fig. 4. The anomalies of machine vibration in amplitude.

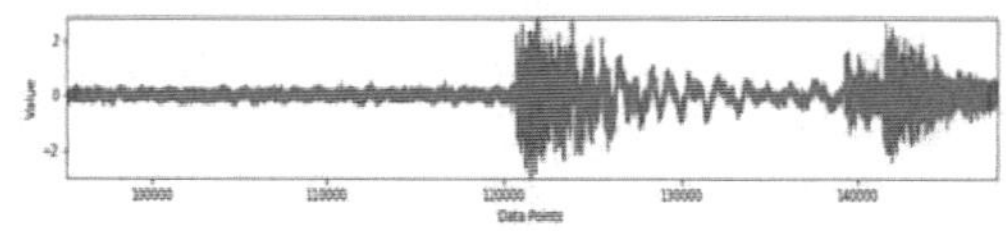

Fig. 5. The enlarged anomaly signals of machine vibration in Fig. 4.

Fig. 3 shows the GUI display of the analysis function result of the milling machine utilization rate in the platform prototype. Fig. 4 depicts the GUI display of anomaly signals of machine vibration in amplitude. Fig. 5 shows the enlarged details of the anomaly signals of machine vibration in Fig. 4.

III. CONCLUSION

In this paper a prototype of intelligent management platform for cyber-physical systems is introduced. This prototype demonstrates a general system architecture for intelligent analysis and smart management platform in manufacturing factories, which devote to build smart manufacturing by adopting and deploying cyber-physical systems within their working fields. Based on the experience learned from this prototype, we think the revolution of industry 4.0 is at its infancy. The current analysis and management platform for IIoT environment or cyber-physical systems can only achieve several useful functions such as analyzing the average life time of specific cutters or monitoring the status of sensors. More data from different dimensions with precision are required to make an intelligent management platform more capable to support complicated analyses and corresponding management such as business forecast and real-time supply chain management.

ACKNOWLEDGMENT

The authors gratefully acknowledge the support from TWISC and Ministry of Science and Technology, Taiwan, under the Grant Numbers MOST 105-2221-E-011-080-MY3, MOST 105-2221-E-011-070-MY3, and MOST 107-2218-E-011-002.

REFERENCES

[1] T. Borangiu, D. Trentesaux, A. Thomas, P. Leitao, and J. Barata, "Digital transformation of manufacturing through cloud services and resource virtualization," *Computers in Industry*, vol. 108, pp. 150-162, June 2019.

[2] V. Jirkovsky, P. Kadera, and M. Obitko, "OPC UA realization of cloud cyber-physical system," in 2018 IEEE 16th International Conference on Industrial Informatics, 2018, pp. 115-120.

[3] OPC Fundation, https://opcfoundation.org. [Accessed: 10-May-2019]

[4] V. Damjanovic-Behrendt and W. Behrendt, "An open source approach to the design and implementation of Digital Twins for Smart Manufacturing," *International Journal of Computer Integrated Manufacturing*, 2019, DOI: 10.1080/0951192X.2019.1599436.

[5] M. H. ur Rehman, I. Yaqoob, K. Salah, M. Imran, P. P. Jayaraman, and C. Perera, "The role of big data analytics in industrial Internet of Things," *Future Generation Computer Systems*, vol. 99, pp. 247-259, Oct. 2019.

[6] J. Ruan, W. Yu, Y. Yang, and J. Hu, "Design and realize of tire production process monitoring system based on cyber-physical systems," in 2015 International Conference on Computer Science and Mechanical Automation, 2015, pp. 175-179.

[7] O. Bassey, B. Chen, K. L. Butler-Purry, and A. Goulart, "Implementation of wide area control in a real-time cyber-physical power system test bed," in 2017 North American Power Symposium, 2017, pp. 1-6.

[8] A. Skraba, A. Kolozvari, D. Kofjac, B. Vavtar, R. Stojanovic, V. Stanovov, and E. Semenkin, "Development of educational cyber-physical Internet of Things platform - study of the PID controller," in 2018 7th Mediterranean Conference on Embedded Computing, 2018, pp. 1-4.

[9] A. D. Neal, R. G. Sharpe, P. P. Conway, and A. A. West, "smaRTI - a cyber-physical intelligent container for industry 4.0 manufacturing," *Journal of Manufacturing Systems*, vol. 52, part A, pp. 63-75, July 2019.

Introversion, Extraversion and Online Social Support among Facebook and LINE users

Jih-Hsin Tang

Department of Information Management
National Taipei University of Business

Tapei, Taiwan, R.O.C.
jefftang@ntub.edu.tw

Tsai-Yuan Chung
Center for Teacher Education and Career Development

University of Taipei
Tapei, Taiwan, R.O.C.
tchung@utaipei.edu.tw

Ming-Chun Chen
Department of Psychology and Counseling
University of Taipei
Taipei, Taiwan, R.O.C.
cmcchen@utaipei.edu.tw

Yi-Lun Wu

Department of Psychology and Counseling

University of Taipei

Taipei, Taiwan, R.O.C.

naomi1067@hotmail.com

***Abstract*—the purpose of the study aims at investigating the relationship between personality traits (Introversion and Extraversion) and online social support among Facebook and LINE users. Nine hundred and eight college students participated this research. The main findings were: (1) the primary purposes of using Facebook and LINE are different; Facebook is used to get updates of others, whereas LINE is to chat interactively; (2) No gender difference is shown on social support perceived or provided on Facebook; however, female subjects perceived and provided more social support than males ; (3) the higher the extraversion (both positive and negative) the subject is, the more support he or she provided or is perceived on both Facebook and LINE; (4) the higher the negative introversion the subject is, the less support he or she provided or received on social networking platforms.**

Keywords—Introversion, Extraversion, Online Social Support

I. INTRODUCTION

The social networking sites or social media such as Facebook, Twitter and LINE have permeated the everyday life. According to a survey, Facebook had a 2.32 billion active users monthly[1]. Individuals have spent considerable time to browse friends' updates, press LIKEs button, commenting on posts, update personal profiles and play games. However, why people are so addicted to the use of social networking sites is still unclear.

The possible causes of using social media so frequently is to get connected to friends, families and colleagues, and update personal information timely[2]. If this is the case, the personality traits might be a crucial factor driving these behaviors. Besides, the reason of getting friends' update is important. To exchange information, resources and emotional support is the driving forces to adopt social media. Finally, individuals use more than one social networking sites. For example, over 80% of the population use Facebook and LINE every day in Taiwan. What is the difference between the use and usage of Facebook and LINE? What is the social support they provided? What is the relationship between personality traits, the social support they provided or perceived among Facebook and LINE?

The main purpose of this study is to investigate the relationship between personality traits (introversion and extraversion), social support among Facebook and LINE users.

II LITERATURE REVIEW

Personality traits

Personal traits are the traits that an individual possess, and define the person you are. For example, a person might be described as an honest and outgoing, yet the other might be discreet and humble. Personality traits might be related to real behaviors such as aggression, bully and stress, and online behaviors such as smartphone addiction and Facebook use[2-4]. Personality traits have been shown to affect the use of social networking sites such as Facebook, twitter, Instagram etc.

One dimension of personality traits, extraversion and introversion, have been shown a critical factor on the individual's use of social networking sites[4, 5]. An individual high in extraversion is outgoing and enthusiastic, and enjoys engaging with the external world. An extravert is active both in online and offline world; that is, an individual high in extraversion tends to express more himself or herself both online and offline and interact with others more frequently. One the other hand, an individual low in extraversion, or called introversion, involves less in social activities.

Extroverts are more involved in the social activities, therefore, it is easy for them to give and receive social support from the social networking sites. Introverts are less involved in the social activities, therefore, it is less easy for them to give and receive social support from their online friends, families and colleagues.

Although extroversion and introversion are related to both online and offline behavior, the empirical studies are not consistent[4, 5]. It is quite consistent that high in extroversion might give and receive social support online [4, 6, 7], some research showed that high in introversion might also provide social support online[8]. If this is the case, there might be other intervening factor(s) behind the dimension of extraversion.
Chou (2013) proposed a new taxonomy of extraversion and introversion[9]. She added a positive/negative dimension on extraversion/introversion dimension and empirically evaluated with fair validity and reliability. The four sub-scales of Chou's scale are: positive extraversion, negative extraversion, positive introversion and negative introversion. Positive extraversion refers to the bright side of extraversion, and include sociability, influence, activation and change. Negative extraversion refers to the dark side of extraversion which covers social desirability, dominance, impulsivity. As to the positive introversion include solitude, reserve, self-orientation, thoughtfulness, and sense of organization.

Online social support
Many studies showed that use of the Internet could enhance interpersonal relationship, maintain friendship and enhance positive feelings and uplift personal satisfaction. For example, Ilich (2002) showed that people get more social support from the Internet to adjust themselves[10]. Wellman and Gulia (2002) pointed out online communities could provide sense of company, information, belongingness and social support[11]. Olson et al. (2012) showed that the more time spent on Facebook, the more informational, instrumental and emotional support received[12].

Based on the literature, the following hypotheses were proposed.
Hypotheses:
1. Personality traits (extraversion/introversion) are associated with online social support significantly.
2. Online social support is related to the use of Facebook and LINE significantly.

III RESEARCH METHOD

A. *Measures*

The instrument
Social Networking Services (Facebook and LINE) survey: this part asked about subjects' SNS use (daily use, number of friends), purposes of use, and functions used.
Introversion/Extroversion Scale: the measurement were developed by Chou (2013)[9] with four dimensions: Positive Introversion (20 items)/Negative Introversion (15 items); Positive Extraversion (22 items) /Negative Extraversion (12 items). The measure is adopted because its fair validity and reliability (Cronbach'sα =.92). All items were measured by Likert 6 points.
Online social support scale: the 10-item measurement was designed by Wu (2004) [13], and the theory is based on social support theory[14] . The sample question is like: someone shows his/her concerns on my Facebook/LINE (perceived social support). I will show my concern on other's Facebook/LINE (provide social support). All items were measured by Likert-type 5 points and showed high reliability coefficients (Cronbach'α > 0.9).

The survey
The sample was drawn from 22 colleges and university in Taiwan, and finally 908 valid sample was returned. 540 were female, 556 from National university and college. 40% of the sample were sophomore, 24% freshmen, 13% juniors, 12% graduates, 4.7% junior college.

IV RESEARCH RESULT

Table 1 Time spent on Facebook and LINE daily

Time Spent (hours)	Facebook		LINE	
	number	Percentage	number	percentage
<= 0.5 hr	160	17.6%	131	14.4%
0.5 ~ 1 hr	253	27.9%	183	20.2%
1 ~ 3 hr	326	35.9%	302	33.3%
3 ~ 5 hr	104	11.5%	142	15.6%
5 ~ 8 hr	41	4.5%	90	9.9%

>= 8 hr	24	2.6%	60	6.6%
	908	100.0%	908	100.0%

As shown in Table 1, most students spent one to three hours to use Facebook and LINE every day. However, there is slight difference between Facebook and LINE. LINE users might spent longer time then Facebook users. For example, approximately 10 percent of the subjects spent 5 hours to 8 hours a day, and 6.6% of subjects spent more than 8 hours a day.

Table 2 Number of Friends of Facebook and LINE

No. of	Facebook		LINE	
Friends	number	percentage	number	Percentage
<= 50	30	3.3%	104	11.5%
51~100	52	5.7%	222	24.4%
101~200	140	15.4%	347	38.2%
201~300	281	30.9%	190	20.9%
301~400	122	13.4%	24	2.6%
>=401	283	31.2%	21	2.3%
	908	100.0%	908	100.0%

As we analyzed the numbers of friends, the results were shown in Table 2. Most students kept more than 400 friends on Facebook; however, keep less than 200 friends on LINE. We further analyzed the functions most often used; LINE users more often chatted (50.2%), sent/got stickers (48%), sent/received photos and videos (31.9%), group chatted (29%) and talk (voice and video) (15.9%). Facebook users participated more activities on browsing through friends' updates (always, 26%) tagging, Likes and comments (17.2%), group discussions (11.6%). That is to say, college students use Facebook to get up dates of friends, whereas use LINE is to chat interactively. That is the reason why students keep more FB friends than LINE friends.

Why do these students spend so much time on FB and LINE? One of the reasons is to provide and receive online social support. As shown in Table 3, there exists no gender difference between FB uses. However, female users seems to provide and receive significantly more social support from LINE friends. Female students chose to use LINE (72%) rather than FB (23.9%); however, male students chose to use LINE (55.7%) rather than FB (39.7%).

Table 3 Gender Difference of Online Social Support

Gender	Facebook		LINE	
	Perceived Support	Provide Support	Perceived Support	Provide Support
Male (n=358)	27.3 (6.41)	27.4 (6.13)	28.1 (7.55)	28.45 (7.61)
Female (n=540)	27.0 (6.55)	27.7 (6.49)	31.8 (6.46)	31.68 (6.24)
t-test	0.66	-0.07	-7.62***	-6.73***

*** p < .001

Personality traits and online social support

As shown in Table 4, there exist positive relationship between extroversion and online social support. All the Pearson correlation coefficients between extraversion and perceived/provide support (both Facebook and LINE) were significant. No matter positive or negative, the higher extroversion is, the more support received and provide on FB and LINE. That is to say, extroverts might actively provide social support online both on FB and LINE, and they might receive mutual social support in return.

As to the introversion, the findings are interesting. For the positive introversion, the higher the introversion, the higher they provide support on FB and LINE. However, they perceived less support in return. For the negative introversion, the higher the introversion, the lower they provide and receive support on both FB and LINE respectively.

Our findings showed that introversion might be classified as positive and negative as Chou proposed (2013). Positive introverts might be willing to provide online social support as extraverts; however, negative introverts might not be willing to provide and receive online social support.

Table 4 Relationship between Introversion, Extroversion and Online Social Support

	Facebook		LINE	
	Perceived support	Provide support	Perceived support	Provide support
Positive Extroversion	0.33***	0.33***	0.25***	0.26***
Negative Extroversion	0.27***	0.20***	0.22***	0.22***
Positive Introversion	0.03	0.09**	0.08*	0.13***
Negative Introversion	-0.08*	-0.11**	-0.08**	-0.08**

*p< .05; **p<.01; ***p<.001

V Discussions

Individuals spend a lot of time on social networking sites and even addict to them. Many scholars would like to investigate the motivating factors of the use of social networking sites. This research confirmed that personality traits have an impact on the use of social networking sites. Online social support might be a moderating factor between personality traits and the use of social networking sites.

Furthermore, this research found that positive relationship between extraversion (both positive and negative) and online social support. Only the negative introversion showed negative association with online social support. This finding is interesting because introversion might be a complex construct, and might produce mixed results.

Finally, the research confirmed Hypothesis I and II, and showed individuals might use multiple social networking sites with different purposes. Facebook was used to get updates of friends, and LINE to interact directly. The major motivation behind might be online social support, both give and receive.

REFERENCES

[1].Most popular social networks worldwide as of January 2019, ranked by number of active users (in millions). 2019; Available from: https://www.statista.com/statistics/272014/global-social-networks-ranked-by-number-of-users/.

[2].Wang, J.-L., et al., Predicting Social Networking Site (SNS) use: Personality, attitudes, motivation and Internet self-efficacy. Personality and Individual Differences, 2015. 80: p. 119-124.

[3].Sulaiman, A., N.I. Jaafar, and A. Tamjidyamcholo, Influence of personality traits on Facebook engagement and their effects on socialization behavior and satisfaction with university life. Information, Communication & Society, 2018. 21(10): p. 1506-1521.

[4].Lee, E., J. Ahn, and Y.J. Kim, Personality traits and self-presentation at Facebook. Personality and Individual Differences, 2014. 69: p. 162-167.

[5].Shchebetenko, S., Do personality characteristics explain the associations between self-esteem and online social networking behaviour? Computers in Human Behavior, 2019. 91: p. 17-23.

[6]Van Zalk, M.H.W., et al., Who Benefits From Chatting, and Why?: The Roles of Extraversion and Supportiveness in Online Chatting and Emotional Adjustment. Personality and Social Psychology Bulletin, 2011. 37(9): p. 1202-1215.

[7].Swickert, R.J., et al., Extraversion, social support processes, and stress. Personality and Individual Differences, 2002. 32(5): p. 877-891.

[8].Mitchell, M.E., et al., Internet use, happiness, social support and introversion: A more fine grained analysis of person variables and internet activity. Computers in Human Behavior, 2011. 27(5): p. 1857-1861.

[9].Chou, Y.-C., Is Introversion Merely the Opposite of Extraversion? - The Development and Validation of Multi-dimensional Inventory of Introversion-Extraversion, in Education Department. 2013, National Cheng-Chi University.

[10].Ilich, M.O., The use of the Internet as a coping resource. 2002, California State University, Long Beach.

[11].Wellman, B. and M. Gulia, Net-surfers don't ride alone, in Social networks: critical concepts in sociology, Scott, Editor. 2002, Routledge: NY.

[12].Olson, D.A., J. Liu, and K.S. Shultz, the influence of Facebook usage on perceptions of social support, personal efficacy, and life satisfaction. Journal of Organization Psychology, 2012. 12(3/4): p. 133-144.

[13].Wu, C.-H., The Role of Social Support on Internet Addiction. the Journal of Information Society, 2004. 7: p. 173-189.

[14].Sheldon, C. and S.L. Syme, Social support and Health. 1985, New York: Academic Press.

Algorithms for the p-centdian problem

Yen Hung Chen[1]
[1]Department of Computer Science, University of Taipei, Taipei, Taiwan
Email:yhchen@utaipei.edu.tw

Abstract— *Given an undirected graph $G = (V, E, l)$ with a nonnegative edge length function l, and two integers p, λ, $0 < p < |V|$, $0 \leq \lambda \leq 1$, let V' be a subset of V with $|V'| = p$. For each vertex $v \in V$, we let $d(v, V')$ denote the shortest distance from v to V'. An eccentricity $\pounds_C(V')$ of V' denotes the maximum distance of $d(v, V')$ for all $v \in V$. A median-distance $\pounds_M(V')$ of V' denotes the total distance of $d(v, V')$ for all $v \in V$. The p-centdian problem is to find a vertex set V' of V with $|V'| = p$, such that $\lambda\pounds_C(V') + (1 - \lambda)\pounds_M(V')$ is minimized. The vertex set V' is called as the centdian set and $\lambda\pounds_C(V') + (1 - \lambda)\pounds_M(V')$ is called as the centdian-distance. The purpose of the p-centdian problem is to find p open facilities which satisfy the quality-of-service of the minimum total delay (median-distance) and maximum delay (eccentricity) to their service clients, simultaneously. In this paper, we prove the p-centdian problem is NP-Complete even when the centdian-distance is $\pounds_C(V') + \pounds_M(V')$. Then we design the first non-trivial brute force exact algorithm. Finally, we design a heuristic algorithm for the pDP, and then claim the performance ratio is $(1 + \epsilon)$ and the cardinality of the centdian set is less than or equal to $O((1 + 1/\epsilon)p \times ln|V|)$, in which $\epsilon > 0$.*

Keywords: combinatorial optimization, computational complexity, approximation algorithm, heuristic algorithm, NP-Complete, p-centdian problem

1. Introduction

Let $G = (V, E, \ell)$ be a undirected graph with $\ell : E \to R^+$ on the edges. Given a vertex set $V' \subset V$, for each vertex $v \in V$, we let $d(v, V')$ denote the shortest distance from v to V'. The *eccentricity* of a vertex set V' is defined the maximum distance of $d(v, V')$ for all vertices v in V, denoted by $\pounds_C(V')$ (i.e., $\pounds_C(V') = max_{v \in V} d(v, V')$). A *median-distance* $\pounds_M(V')$ of V' denotes the total distance of $d(v, V')$ for all vertices v in V (i.e., $\pounds_M(V') = \sum_{v \in V} d(v, V')$). Given a undirected complete graph $G = (V, E, \ell)$ with a nonnegative edge length function ℓ and an integer p, $0 < p < |V|$, the *p-center problem* (pCP) (respectively, *p-median problem* (pMP)) is to find a vertex set V' in V, $|V'| = p$, such that the *eccentricity* (respectively, *median-distance*) of V' is minimized [1], [2], [3], [4]. These problems had been shown to be NP-Complete [2], [3], [5] and many approximation algorithms [6], [7], [8], [9], [10], [11] and approximation complexities [11], [12], [13], [14] had been proposed. It had been shown these problems had many important applications in the operations research of facility location models [1], [2], [3], [4], [9], [15], [16], [17], [18], [19], [20], [21], [22], [23] and the selected influential person of social network [24], [25].

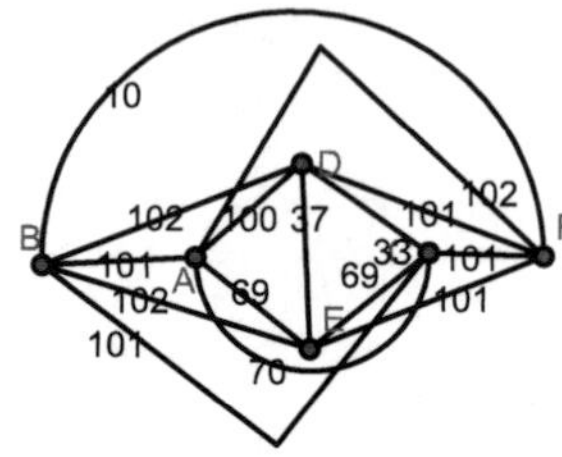

Fig. 1

AN INSTANCE: COMPLETE GRAPH $G = (V, E, \ell)$, $p = 2$, AND $\lambda = 0.5$.

Motivated by the application of finding p open facilities which satisfy the quality-of-service of the minimum total delay (*median-distance*) and maximum delay (*eccentricity*) to their service clients, simultaneously [26], [27], [28], Hooker [28] studied the *p-centdian problem*. Given a undirected complete graph $G = (V, E, \ell)$ with a nonnegative edge length function ℓ, a real number λ, $0 \leq \lambda \leq 1$, and an integer p, $0 < p < |V|$, the *p-centdian problem* (pDP) is to find a vertex set V' in V, $|V'| = p$, such that the $\lambda\pounds_C(V') + (1 - \lambda)\pounds_M(V')$ is minimized [28]. The vertex set V' is called as the *centdian set*. and $\lambda\pounds_C(V') + (1 - \lambda)\pounds_M(V')$ is called as the *centdian-distance*. If $\lambda = 0$, this problem is equal to the pMP, and however $\lambda = 1$ this problem is equal to the pCP. Hence, it is not hard to see that the pDP is NP-Complete. The following example illustrates the pDP. Consider the instance shown in Fig. 1, in which the graph $G = (V, E, \ell)$, an integer $p = 2$, and a real number $\lambda = 0.5$. An optimal solution of G for the pDP is shown in Fig. 2, in which the *centdian-distance* is 126.

In this paper, we focus on a special case of the *centdian-distance* for the pDP : $\pounds_C(V') + \pounds_M(V')$ and discuss the complexity, the non-trivial brute force exact algorithm, and a heuristic algorithm for the pDP. First, we prove that the pDP is NP-Complete even when the *centdian-distance* is $\pounds_C(V') + \pounds_M(V')$. Then we present the first non-trivial brute force exact algorithm for the pDP. Finally, we design a heuristic algorithm for the pDP, and then claim that the performance ratio is $(1 + \epsilon)$ and the cardinality of the

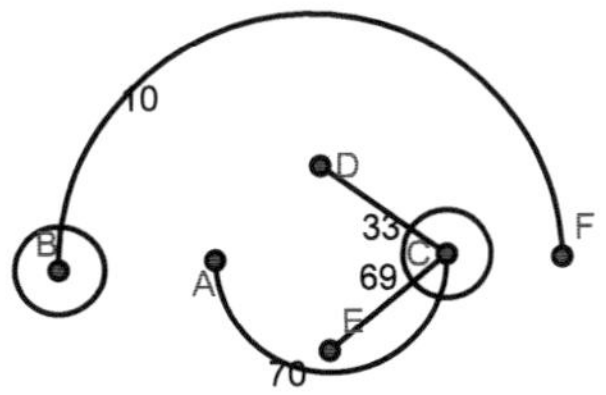

Fig. 2
THE OPTIMAL SOLUTION $\{B, C\}$ FOR THE 2DP. (NOTE THAT $0.5 \times \pounds_C(\{B, C\}) + 0.5 \times \pounds_M(\{B, C\}) = 126$)

centdian set is less than or equal to $O((1 + 1/\epsilon)p \times ln|V|)$, in which $\epsilon > 0$.

The rest of this paper is organized as follows.

In Section 2, we prove that the pDP is NP-Complete even when the *centdian-distance* is $\pounds_C(V') + \pounds_M(V')$. In Section 3, we present a non-trivial brute force exact algorithm for the pDP. In Section 4, we design a heuristic algorithm for the pDP and claim that the performance ratio is $(1 + \epsilon)$ and the cardinality of the *centdian set* is less than or equal to $O((1 + 1/\epsilon)p \times ln|V|)$, in which $\epsilon > 0$. Finally, we make a conclusion in Section 5.

2. Hardness Result for the pDP

In this section, we prove that the pDP is NP-Complete even when the *centdian-distance* is $\pounds_C(V') + \pounds_M(V')$. We *reduce* the *dominating set problem* (DSP) [29], [30], [31], [32] to the pDP. Hence, we review the definition of the *dominating set problem.* A *dominating set* of G, denoted by $\mathcal{Z}$, is a subset of V such that every vertex in $V \setminus \mathcal{Z}$ is *adjacent* to a vertex in $\mathcal{Z}$ [29], [30], [31], [32].

DSP (dominating set problem) [29], [30], [31], [32]
Instance: A connected, undirected graph $G = (V, E)$.
Question: Find a *dominating set* $\mathcal{Z}'$ with minimum cardinality.

Note that the DSP had been shown to be NP-Complete [5].

In order to prove that the pDP is NP-Complete, we also need to define pDP and DSP decision problems.

pDP Decision Problem
Instance: A connected, undirected complete graph $G = (V, E, \ell)$ and two integers $p > 0$ and $U > 0$.
Question: Does there exist a vertex set V', $|V'| = p$, such that $\pounds_C(V') + \pounds_M(V') \leq U$.

DSP Decision Problem
Instance: A connected, undirected graph $G = (V, E)$, and a positive integer κ.
Question: Does there exist a dominated set $\mathcal{Z}$ such that $|\mathcal{Z}|$ is less than or equal to κ?

Theorem 1: The pDP decision problem is NP-Complete.

Proof: First, it is easy to see that the pDP decision problem is in NP. Then we show the *reduction*: the transformation from the DSP decision problem to the pDP decision problem.

Let a graph $G = (V, E)$ and a positive integer κ be an instance of the DSP decision problem. We transform it into an instance of the pDP decision problem, say $\overline{G} = (\overline{V}, \overline{E}, \ell)$ and two positive integers p and U, as follows.

$\overline{V} = V$.
$\overline{E} = E$.
For each edge $(u, v) \in \overline{E}$,

$$\ell(u, v) = \begin{cases} 1, & \text{if } (u, v) \in E \\ d(u, v), & \text{otherwise.} \end{cases} \quad (1)$$

$U = |V| - \kappa + 1$ and $p = \kappa$.

Now, we show that there is a dominating set $\mathcal{Z}$ such that $|\mathcal{Z}|$ is κ if and only if there is a vertex set $\overline{V'}$ in $\overline{G}$ such that the $|\overline{V'}|$ is p and $\pounds_C(\overline{V'}) + \pounds_M(\overline{V'})$ is U.

(Only if) If there exists a dominating set $\mathcal{Z}$ for G and the cardinality of $\mathcal{Z}$ is κ, then we let $\overline{V'}$ for $\overline{G}$ be the corresponding vertex set of $\mathcal{Z}$ for G. Hence, we have $\pounds_C(\overline{V'}) = 1$, $\pounds_M(\overline{V'}) = |V| - \kappa$ and $|\overline{V'}| = \kappa$. (If) If there exists a vertex set $\overline{V'}$ of $\overline{G}$ such that $|\overline{V'}|$ is p and $\pounds_C(\overline{V'}) + \pounds_M(\overline{V'})$ is U. Clearly, each vertex v in $V \setminus \overline{V'}$, $d(v, \overline{V'}) = 1$, otherwise $\pounds_C(\overline{V'}) + \pounds_M(\overline{V'}) > U = |V| - \kappa + 1$. Hence, the corresponding vertex set of G is a dominating set of G and the cardinality is p, for the vertex set $\overline{V'}$ of $\overline{G}$. ■

3. An Exact Algorithm for the pDP

In this section, we show an integer programming to solve the pDP. We combine the integer programmings for the pMP and pCP by [16]. Given a undirected complete graph $G = (V, E, \ell)$ with a nonnegative edge length function ℓ, the pDP can be formulated as an integer programming (I) as follows.

$$\text{minimize} \quad \sum_{i \in V} \sum_{j \in V} d(i, j) x_{i,j} + C \quad (2)$$

$$\text{subject to}$$

$$\sum_{j \in V} x_{i,j} = 1, \forall i \in V \quad (3)$$

$$\sum_{j \in V} y_j = p \quad (4)$$

$$x_{i,j} \leq y_j, \forall i, j \in V \quad (5)$$

$$\sum_{j \in V} d(i, j) x_{i,j} \leq C, \forall i \in V \quad (6)$$

$$x_{i,j}, y_j \subset \{0, 1\} \quad (7)$$

$$C \geq 0, \quad (8)$$

where y_j, $x_{i,j}$ and C are variables of the integer programming (I), for each i and j, $i, j \in V$. The variable $y_j = 1$ if and only if vertex j is chosen as a centdian, and the variable $x_{i,j} = 1$ if and only if $y_j = 1$ and vertex i is assigned to vertex j, and C is a feasible *eccentricity*. For completeness, we list the exact algorithm for the pDP problem as follows.

Algorithm OPT-pDP

Input: A connected, undirected complete graph $G = (V, E, \ell)$ with a nonnegative length function ℓ on edges and an integer $p > 0$.

Output: A vertex set P_{opt} with $|P_{opt}| = p$.

1. Use the integer programming (I) to find all $y_j = 1$ and put the corresponding vertex j of y_j to P_{opt}.
2. Return P_{opt}.

It is easy to show that Algorithm OPT-pDP is an exact algorithm for the pDP. However, the integer programming is NP-Complete [5], [33]. Hence, next section we design a heuristic algorithm for the pDP, and then claim that the performance ratio is $(1 + \epsilon)$ and the cardinality of the *centdian set* is less than or equal to $O((1 + 1/\epsilon)p \times ln|V|)$, in which $\epsilon > 0$.

4. A Heuristic Algorithm for the pDP

In this section, we design a heuristic algorithm for the pDP, and then claim that the performance ratio is $(1 + \epsilon)$ and the cardinality of the *centdian set* is less than or equal to $O((1 + 1/\epsilon)p \times ln|V|)$, in which $\epsilon > 0$. First, we relax the integer programming (I) for the pDP to the linear programming (I_L) to solve the pDP called as the fractional pDP as follows.

$$\text{minimize} \quad \sum_{i \in V}\sum_{j \in V} d(i,j)x_{i,j} + C \qquad (9)$$

subject to

$$\sum_{j \in V} x_{i,j} = 1, \forall i \in V \qquad (10)$$

$$\sum_{j \in V} y_j = p \qquad (11)$$

$$x_{i,j} \leq y_j, \forall i,j \in V \qquad (12)$$

$$\sum_{j \in V} d(i,j)x_{i,j} \leq C, \forall i \in V \qquad (13)$$

$$0 \leq x_{i,j}, y_j \leq 1 \qquad (14)$$

$$C \geq 0 \qquad (15)$$

The main difference between I_L and I is that variables y_j and $x_{i,j}$ can take rational values between 0 and 1 for I_L. Let $\tilde{y}$ and $\tilde{x}$ be the output values of the linear programming I_L. Then it is clear that the *centdian-distance* of the optimal solution for the fractional pDP is a lower bound on the *centdian-distance* of the optimal solution for the pDP. Moreover, the linear programming can be solved in polynomial time [34], [35].

Given a fractional solution $\tilde{x}_{i,j}$, for each $i \in V$, let $\tilde{D}(i) = \sum_{j \in V} d(i,j)\tilde{x}_{i,j}$ be the distance of assigning vertex i to its fractional centdian. Given $\epsilon > 0$, we also let the neighborhood set $N(i)$ of vertex i be $N(i) = \{j \in V | d(i,j) \leq (1+\epsilon)\tilde{D}(i)\}$.

The following Lemma is similar to the previous algorithm for the pMP [36]. We state the result.

Lemma 2: [36] For each $i \in V$ and $\epsilon > 0$, we have $\sum_{j \in N(i)} \tilde{y}_j \geq \sum_{j \in N(i)} \tilde{x}_{i,j} > \epsilon/(1+\epsilon)$.

Then we transform the pDP to the *set cover problem* [37], [38], [39]. Given a finite set $\mathcal{U}$ of elements and a collection $\mathcal{S}$ of (non-empty) subsets of $\mathcal{U}$. A *set cover* [37], [38], [39] is to find a subset $\mathcal{S}' \subseteq \mathcal{S}$ such that every element in $\mathcal{U}$ belongs to at least one element of $\mathcal{S}'$. Given a finite set $\mathcal{U}$ of elements, a collection $\mathcal{S}$ of (non-empty) subsets of $\mathcal{U}$, the *set cover problem* (SCP) [37], [38], [39] is to find a *set cover* $\mathcal{S}''$ such that the number of sets in $\mathcal{S}''$ is minimized. An instance of SCP contains a finite set $\mathcal{U}$ of elements, a collection $\mathcal{S}$ of (non-empty) subsets of $\mathcal{U}$. We let each vertex $i \in V$ correspond to each element in $\mathcal{U}$, and each vertex $j \in V$ with $\tilde{y}_j > 0$ correspond to each set in $\mathcal{S}$, respectively. Then for each vertex $i \in V$, if $j \in N(i)$, then the corresponding element of i in $\mathcal{U}$ belongs to the corresponding set of j in $\mathcal{S}$. Then we use the greedy approximation algorithm for the SCP whose performance ratio is $(\ln |\mathcal{U}| + 1)$ [37], [38], [39] to find a set cover of $\mathcal{U}$ and $\mathcal{S}$. Finally, output the corresponding vertex set for the output set of the greedy approximation algorithm for the SCP.

The result of this section is summarized in the following claim. The main idea is similar to the previous algorithm for the pMP [36], but the proof is omitted.

Claim 3: There is a $(1 + \epsilon)$-approximation algorithm for the pDP satisfying the cardinality of the *centdian set* is less than or equal to $O((1 + 1/\epsilon)p \times ln|V|)$, in which $\epsilon > 0$.

5. Conclusion

In this paper, we have investigated the pDP and proved that the problem is NP-Complete even when the *centdian-distance* is $\pounds_C(V') + \pounds_M(V')$. Then we have designed the first non-trivial brute force exact algorithm for the pDP. Finally, we have designed a heuristic algorithm for the pDP, and then claim the performance ratio is $(1 + \epsilon)$ and the cardinality of the centdian set is less than or equal to $O((1 + 1/\epsilon)p \times ln|V|)$, in which $\epsilon > 0$. It would be interesting to find approximation complexities for the pDP. Another direction for future research is whether the pDP has a polynomial time exact algorithm for some special graphs.

References

[1] S.L. Hakimi, "Optimal distribution of switching centers in a communication network and some related theoretic graph theoretic problems," *Operations Research*, vol. 13, pp. 462–475, 1965.

[2] O. Kariv and S.L. Hakimi, "An algorithmic approach to network location problems I: the p-centers," *SIAM Journal of Applied Mathematics*, vol. 37, pp. 514–538, 1979.

[3] O. Kariv and S.L. Hakimi, "An algorithmic approach to network location problems II: the p-medians," *SIAM Journal of Applied Mathematics*, vol. 37, pp. 539–560, 1979.
[4] B.C. Tansel, R.L. Francis, and T.J. Lowe, "Location on networks: a survey. Part I: the p-center and p-median problems," *Management Science*, vol. 29, pp. 482–497, 1983.
[5] M.R. Garey and D.S. Johnson, *"Computers and Intractability: A Guide to the Theory of NP-Completeness."* W.H. Freeman and Company, San Francisco, 1979.
[6] V. Arya, N. Garg, R. Khandekar, A. Meyerson, K. Munagala, and V. Pandit, "Local search heuristics for k-median and facility location problems," *SIAM Journal on Computing*, vol. 33, pp. 544–562, 2004.
[7] T.F. Gonzalez, "Clustering to minimize the maximum intercluster distance," *Theoretical Computer Science*, vol. 38, pp. 293–306, 1985.
[8] A. Gupta, K. Tangwongsan, "Simpler analyses of local search algorithms for facility location," *CoRR abs/0809.2554*, 2008.
[9] D.S. Hochbaum and D.B. Shmoys, "A unified approach to approximation algorithms for bottleneck problems," *Journal of the ACM*, vol. 33, pp. 533–550, 1986.
[10] J. Plesnik, "A heuristic for the p-center problem in graphs," *Discrete Applied Mathematics*, vol. 17, pp. 263–268, 1987.
[11] V.V. Vazirani, *"Approximation Algorithms."* Berlin, Germany:Springer-Verlag, 2001.
[12] D.S. Hochbaum, *Various notions of approximations: good, better, best, and more,* in "Approximation Algorithms for NP-hard Problems," D.S. Hochbaum Ed. PWS Publishing Company, Boston, pp. 346–398, 1997.
[13] W.L. Hsu and G.L. Nemhauser, "Easy and hard bottleneck location problems," *Discrete Applied Mathematicsm* vol. 1, pp. 209–216, 1979.
[14] K. Jain, M. Mahdian, E. Markakis, A. Saberi, and V.V. Vazirani, "Greedy facility location algorithms analyzed using dual fitting with factor-revealing LP," *Journal of the ACM*, vol. 50, pp. 795–824, 2003.
[15] SK. Abu Nayeem and M. PAL, "Genetic algorithm to solve the p-centre and p-radius problem on a network," *International Journal of Computer Mathematics*, vol. 82, pp. 541–550, 2005.
[16] M.S. Daskin, *"Network and Discrete Location: Models Algorithms and Applications."* Wiley, New York, 1995.
[17] M.S. Daskin, "What you should know about location modeling," *Naval Research Logistics*, vol. 55, pp. 283–294, 2008.
[18] Z. Drezner and H.W. Hamacher, *"Facility Location Applications and Theory,"* 2nd edition. Springer, 2004.
[19] D.S. Hochbaum and A. Pathria, "Generalized p-center problems: complexity results and approximation algorithms," *European Journal of Operational Research*, vol. 100, pp. 594–607, 1997.
[20] J. Mihelic and B. Robic, "Facility location and covering problems," in *Proceedings of the 7th International Multiconference Information Society*, vol. D–Theoretical Computer Science, Ljubljana, Slovenia, 2004.
[21] C.S. ReVelle and H.A. Eiselt, "Location analysis: a synthesis and survey," *European Journal of Operational Research*, vol. 165, pp. 1–19, 2005.
[22] C.S. ReVelle, H.A. Eiselt, and M.S. Daskin, "A bibliography for some fundamental problem categories in discrete location science," *European Journal of Operational Research*, vol. 184, pp. 817–848, 2008.
[23] A. Tamir, "Improved complexity bounds for center location problems on networks by using dynamic data structures," *SIAM Journal of Discrete Mathematics*, vol. 1, pp. 377–396, 1988.
[24] A. Chaudhury, P. Basuchowdhuri, and S. Majumder, "Spread of information in a social network using influential nodes," in *Advances in Knowledge Discovery and Data Mining (PAKDD' 12)*, 2012, Malaysia, P.-N. Tan, S. Chawla, C.H. Ho, J. Bailey, Eds. Lecture Notes in Computer Science, vol. 7302, pp. 121–132, 2012.
[25] T. Takaoka, "Effcient algorithms for the 2-center problems," in *Proceedings of the 13th International Conference on Computational Science and Applications (ICCSA' 10)*, 2010, Vietnam, D. Taniar, O. Gervasi, B. Murgante, E. Pardede, B.O. Apduhan, Eds. Lecture Notes in Computer Science, vol. 6017, pp. 519–532, 2010.
[26] J. Halpern, "The location of a center-median convex combination on an undirected tree," *Journal of Regional Science*, vol. 16, pp. 237–245, 1976.
[27] J. Halpern, "Finding minimal center-median convex combination (cent-dian) of a graph," *Management Science*, vol. 24, pp. 535–544, 1978.
[28] J.N. Hooker, R.S. Garfinkel, and C.K. Chen, "Finite dominating sets for network location problems," *Operation Research*, vol. 39, pp. 100–118, 1991.
[29] C. Berge, *"Theory and Graphs and its Applications."* Methuen, London, 1962.
[30] E.J. Cockayne and S.T. Hedetniemi, "Towards a theory of domination in graph," *Networks*, vol. 7, pp. 247–261, 1977.
[31] O. Ore, *"Theory of Graphs."* American Mathematical Society Colloquium Publications, 1962.
[32] D.B. West, *"Introduction to Graph Theory."* Prentice Hall, USA, 2001.
[33] T.H. Cormen, C.E. Leiserson, R.L. Rivest, and C. Stein, *"Introduction to Algorithm."* 3rd ed.. MIT Press, Cambridge, 2009.
[34] N. Karmarkar, "A new polynomial-time algorithm for linear programming," *Combinatorica*, vol. 4, pp. 373–395, 1984.
[35] L.G. Khachiyan, "A polynomial algorithm in linear programming (in Russian)," *Doklady Akademii Nauk SSSR*, vol. 244, pp. 1093–1096, 1979 (English translation: *Soviet Mathematics Doklady*, vol. 20, pp. 191–194, 1979).
[36] J.-H. Lin and J.S. Vitter, "ϵ-approximations with minimum packing constraint violation (extended abstract)," in *Proceedings of the 24th annual ACM Symposium on Theory of Computing (STOC 92)*, 1992, pp. 771–782.
[37] V. Chvatal, "A greedy heuristic for the set-covering problem," *Mathematics of Operations Research*, vol. 4, pp. 233–235, 1979.
[38] D.S. Johnson, "Approximation algorithms for combinatorial problems," *Journal of Computer and System Sciences*, vol. 9, pp. 256–278, 1974.
[39] L. Lovasz, "The ratio of optimal integral and fractional covers," *Discrete Mathematics*, vol. 13, pp. 383–390, 1975.

Greedy Algorithm Applied Secrecy Rate Analysis in the Cooperative Communication

Jong-Shin Chen[1], Shu-Chen Chang[2], Pin-Yen Huang[3] and Cheng-Ying Yang[4,*]
[1] Dept. of Information and Communication Engineering, Chaoyang University of Technology, Taiwan
[2] Department of Business Administration, National Formosa University, Taiwan
[3] Department of Computer Science, National Chengchi University, Taipei, Taiwan
[4] Department of Computer Science, University of Taipei, Taipei, Taiwan

Abstract - *Cooperative communication is the future tendency because of low cost. Three fundamental schemes including Amplify-and-Forward (AF) mode, Decode-and-Forward (DF) mode and Compress and Forward (CF) mode could be employed. In the system, relays play the role to transmit the delivered signal to the destination. However, there might be the eavesdroppers pretend the relay to snip the message. Currently, privacy and security are highly requested in the communication. Hence, the secrecy protection becomes important. Traditionally, the complex encryption scheme would be applied but it is not practical to apply to the equipment with low computing resources. According to Shannon Theory, positive secrecy rate could support secure communications. Maximum secrecy rate is the initial step to analyze the possible secure communication in the cooperative system. The exhaustive method to find the extreme secrecy rate in the system could be realized. However, time efficiency is not considerable. In order to reduce the computational complexity, a greedy algorithm might provide an acceptable solution to approach the purpose of analysis. In this work, the DF mode cooperative mode is adopted for analysis with a greedy algorithm. The result shows the effects of eavesdropper are not significant if the destination station select the strong signal from legitimate stations.*

Keywords: secrecy rate, encryption, greedy algorithm, Cooperative communication, DF mode

1 Introduction

Wireless networks provide a variable multimedia service. The throughput was 96 EB very month in 2016. It could be expected to increase to 278 EB in 2021. Also, mobile communication could occupy 63% of the throughput on the internet [1]. Hence, wireless networks play an important role in future communication. To access the wireless services is convenient for mobile users, but the degradation characteristics of signal fading, multipath transmission, signal inferences, bandwidth limitation and so on degrade the system performance. Under the limitation of transmission bandwidth, to improve system performance in the wireless systems becomes important. Employing spatial diversity could be the solution to improve system performance [2]-[3].

To combat the fading, with the spatial diversity, Multiple-Input Multiple-Output (MIMO) improving the system capacity, transmission speed and system performance have been an effective scheme. However, because of high-cost consideration, using multiple antennas at the transmitter and the receiver, MIMO could not be easily implemented [4]. Similar to MIMO, cooperative communication with diversity gain is a solution to increase the system performance [5]. In the cooperative communication systems, the relay plays with a character of spatial diversity. Not only forwarding the transmitted data but also processing the received data, the relay provides a high throughput performance. The destination station could receive data with spatial diversity. Although the destination station has no multiple antennas, it increases the transmission data rate and provides a reliable channel capacity [6].

For the transmission, there are Amplify-and-Forward (AF) mode, Decode-and-Forward (DF) mode and Compress and Forward (CF) mode in the cooperative communication system [7]. AF mode provides low complicated hardware and is easy to be implemented. In DF mode, the relay decodes and demodulates the received signal, and then recodes and modulates the signal to retransmit to the destination. DF mode could have benefits on the coding gain. The relay station does not have to decode the compressed signal in CF mode. The transmission mode uses the coding schemes to compress the received signal and transfer the signal to the destination station.

However, wireless communication is not a secure environment. Privacy and security have become increasingly important. The purpose of secure communications is to enable the authentic destination could successfully receive the information from the source station without any information leaking. Traditionally, the security depends on the cryptographic encryption at the application layer. The complex and difficult cryptography is practical. For example, RSA based asymmetric encryption and X.509 certifications were proposed for a two-way authentication security scheme [8]. Cryptographic encryption converts meaningful information to be the apparent nonsense to avoid the eavesdroppers to release the transmitted information.

However, the encryption algorithms assume the limited computational capability at the eavesdroppers and there are perfectly secret key management and the distribution scheme. For the real-time wireless application, it is not practical. For the accessing internet, the authentication protocol within the networking could be the limitation because of less computing resource. For secure communication, physical layer security is proposed [9].

In the cooperative communication system, the transmitted information is unwrapped in the environment with eavesdroppers. The information could be snooped from the source station or from the relay which the source station adopts. Also, the relay might be the eavesdropper. Hence, the relay selection strategy could be a critical scheme. It depends not only on the mutual information between the source station and the destination station but also on the secrecy rate between the source station and the destination station. To approach the secure cooperative communication between the source station and the destination station, the relay selection algorithm should base on the analysis of the positive secrecy rate [4][10]. Based on the maximum secrecy rate, the analysis of cooperative communication system is proposed. In the following, the cooperative communication system model is described with a theoretical performance evaluation. In section 3, the maximum secrecy rate is analyzed under the condition of the wiretap channel model. In Section 4, the numerical results show the secrecy evaluation for the cooperative system. The conclusion is given in the final.

2 Cooperative Communication System

The cooperative communication system could be illustrated in Fig. 1.

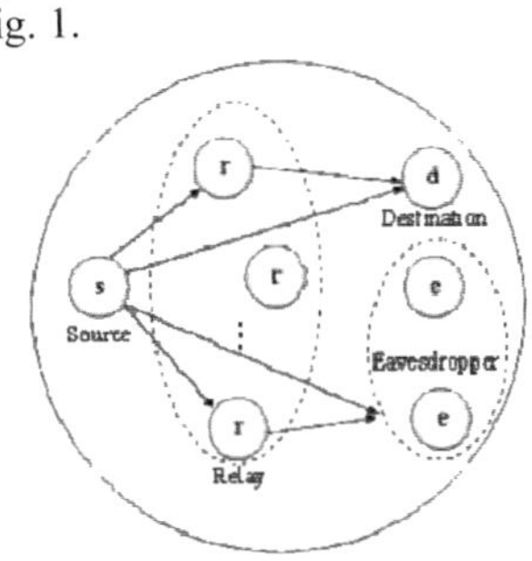

Fig. 1 The cooperative communication system

The system includes source stations, a relay group, an eavesdropper group and a destination station. In the system, the source station transmits the information. The information could be delivered directly to the destination through the transmission link between the source station and the destination. Also, the information might be transmitted to the relay station and, then, delivered to the destination station with the help of the relay. Consider a single user environment, as shown in Fig. 2. $h_{s,d}$ is denoted as the channel response between the source station to destination station. $h_{s,r}$ and $h_{r,d}$ are denoted as the channel response between source station to the relay and the channel response between the relay to the destination station, respectively.

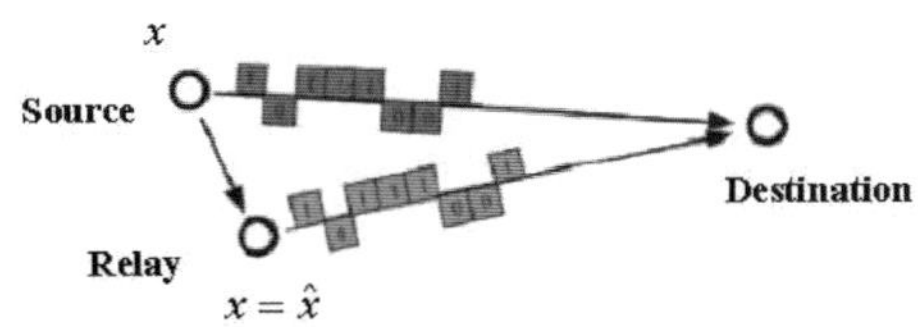

Fig. 2 DF mode transmission model

In DF mode, after receiving the transmitted signal from the source station, the relay begins to decode the signal and, then, re-transmit it to the destination station [4][11]. In Fig. 2, the source station transmits the coded signal x at the first time. The relay station decodes the signal to be $\hat{x}$ and, then, recode and transmit the signal at the second time. The mathematical analysis is given below.

$$y_{s,r} = \sqrt{P_s} h_{s,r} x + n_{s,r} \qquad (1)$$

$$y_{s,d} = \sqrt{P_s} h_{s,d} x + n_{s,d} \qquad (2)$$

where P_s is the signal power from the source station, x is the transmitted coded signal from the source station, and $n_{s,r}$ and $n_{s,d}$ are AWGN with the variance N_0. The relay retransmits the coded signal to the destination station. At the second time, the received signal, from the relay station, at the destination station is

$$y_{r,d} = \sqrt{p_s} h_{r,d} \hat{x} + n_{r,d} \qquad (3)$$

where $\hat{x}$ is the decoded signal and $n_{r,d}$ is AWGN with the variance N_0. The decoded signal x should be the same as the one transmitted from the source station. Or, it will cause a catastrophic error. Hence, eq. (3) could be written as

$$y_{r,d} = \sqrt{p_s} h_{r,d} x + n_{r,d} \qquad (4)$$

In a normalized channel, the mutual information between the source station and the destination station could be evaluated by

$$I_{s,d} = \frac{1}{2}\log_2\left(1 + \frac{P_s}{N_0}\left|h_{s,d}\right|^2\right) \qquad (5)$$

Also, the mutual information between the relay and the destination station could be evaluated by

$$I_{r,d} = \frac{1}{2}\log_2\left(1 + \frac{P_s}{N_0}\left|h_{r,d}\right|^2\right) \qquad (6)$$

if the signal power transmitted at the relay is kept as P_s. Hence, for the single user, the minimum mutual information between the source station and the destination station could be

$$I_{DF} = \min(I_{s,d}, I_{r,d}) \quad (7)$$

Similarly, the scenario of the information transmitted to the eavesdropper could be held in this wireless environment as shown in Fig. 1. The leaked information to the eavesdropper under AWGN is

$$I_{s,e} = \frac{1}{2}\log_2\left(1+\frac{P_s}{N_0}\left|h_{s,e}\right|^2\right) \quad (8)$$

3 Secrecy Rate Analysis

In the cryptanalysis, it assumes the eavesdropper could access the complete message from the source, i.e. the received message at the destination is the same as that received at eavesdropper. However, the wire- tap channel model [12] depicts an entire communication system from the source to the destination. The message sent from the source through the main channel to the destination. On the other hand, the transmitted message is received by the eavesdropper via the wiretap channel, as shown in Fig. 3. For the physical-layer security, the wiretap channel model could be modified with coding scheme. In the cryptanalysis, the encrypted message is known by the eavesdropper. However, in the wiretap channel model, the error-free encrypted message known by the eavesdropper is a special case of the consideration because the physical-layer security is gained by the channel characteristics, such as noise.

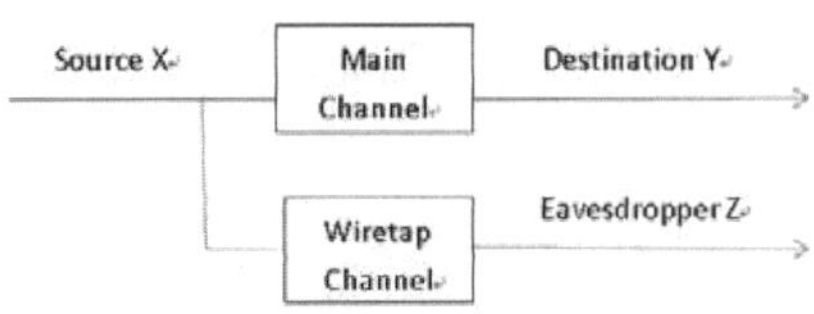

Fig. 3 Wiretap channel model for the communication

According to Shannon theorem [13], a secure communication achieves not only an arbitrarily low error probability but also security against the attackers. Hence, in the wiretap channel model, the secrecy rate is defined based on the previous two purposes [14].

$$C_S = \max_{p(x)} I(X;Y\,|\,Z) = \max_{p(x)}\big(I(X;Y) - I(X;Z)\big)$$
$$\geq \max_{p(x)} I(X;Y) - \max_{p(x)} I(X;Z) \quad (9)$$

This equation provides a valuable point for secure communication, i.e. the positive secrecy capacity could have security against the eavesdropper. It might be held because of the quality of the main channel.

In eq. (9), secrecy rate C_s should be positive for secure communication. It means that the channel capacity between the source to the destination must be larger than that between the source to the eavesdropper.

$$C_d = \max_{p(x)} I(X;Y) = \max(I_{DF}) \quad (10)$$

and

$$C_e = \max_{p(x)} I(X;Z) = I_{s,e} \quad (11)$$

For simplification, in this work, the relay could connect at most one destination station only. Also, the eavesdropper is assumed as the relay at the end of the communication. AWGN channel is assumed in both the main channel and the wiretap channel,

$$I_{s,e} = I_{s,r} = \frac{1}{2}\log_2\left(1+\frac{P_s}{N_0}\left|h_{s,r}\right|^2\right) \quad (12)$$

Under the above situation, considering each destination station received the signal from one relay station only, this work intends to find the pairs to match these N destination stations and the corresponding M relay stations. Hence, the total secrecy rate becomes

$$C_{s,total} = \max_{\rho_{ij},\forall i,\forall j} \sum_{i=1}^{M}\sum_{j=1}^{N} \rho_{ij}\cdot C_{s,ij} \quad (13)$$

under the conditions

$$\sum_{i=1}^{M} \rho_{ij} = 1 \;, \forall\, j = 1,2,..., N \quad (14)$$

and

$$\sum_{j=1}^{N} \rho_{ij} \leq 1 \;, \forall\, i = 1,2,..., M \quad (15)$$

$\rho_{i,j}$ is defined as the connection between relay station i to destination station j.

4 Numerical Results

With the exhaustive search method, the algorithm should begin to calculate eq. (13).

First, for each relay station, calculate eq. (10) and eq. (12), respectively.

Second, calculate $C_{s,ij}$ and recode in an MxN array such as

i \ j	d_1	d_2	…	d_N
r_1	$C_{s,11}$	$C_{s,12}$	…	$C_{s,1N}$
r_2	$C_{s,21}$	$C_{s,22}$	…	$C_{s,2N}$
⋮	⋮	⋮	⋱	⋮
r_M	$C_{s,M1}$	$C_{s,M2}$	…	$C_{s,MN}$

Third, iterative calculate the (i, j) combination for maximum value in the eq. (13) under the limitation of eq. (14) and eq. (15). The optimal mapping for the relay station and destination station could be found with calculation within combinations.

The computation is with high complicated computing to implement if there are large M and N. Especially, the computing complexity is high for the burst traffic arriving. In order to reduce the computational complexity, a greedy algorithm could be applied. The benefit of greedy algorithm is that the solutions can be straightforward and easy to understand [15]. The applied greedy algorithm could be modified from the exhaustive search method.

Step 1, calculate C_d and C_e for all relay stations.

Step 2, create an MxN array, calculate $C_{s,ij}$ and recode in the array.

Step 3, according to the created array, assign the maximum value of $C_{s,ij}$ to the pair of relay station i and destination station j. Randomly, choose one of maximum value to assign if there more than one maximum value appeared. Record the pair (i,j) to represent the ith relay station is assigned to sever the jth destination station. At the meantime, corresponding to the chosen cell, delete all other row cells in the array. It means the chosen relay station could not serve for other destination stations. Similarly, corresponding to the chosen cell, delete all other column cells in the array. It means the chosen destination is served by one relay station only. Then, a new reduced matrix is created.

Step 4, Repeat step 3 till finishing the assignment work.

Step 5, according to the pair assignment, calculate the total secrecy rate $C_{s,total}$.

In the numerical experiment, the symbol (N,M,E) shown in Fig. 4 represents that there are N source stations, M relays and E eavesdroppers. In this result, it is clear to illustrate in DF mode cooperative communication, the effects of relay assistance to forward the transmitted signal could not be significant. The communication between the source and the destination could still be connected with the legitimate stations.

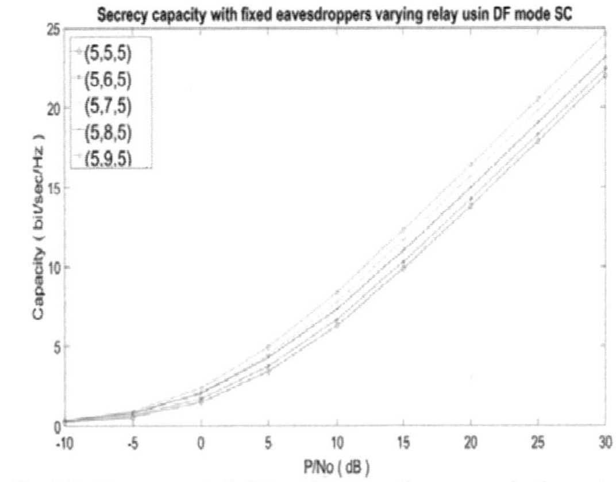

Fig. 4 Total secrecy rate in DF mode cooperative communication system

5 Conclusions

The cooperative system is a tendency for the future wireless communications because of low cost. In this work, the solution for a secret DF mode cooperative communication has been proposed. According to Shannon theory, the physical layer could provide a secure transmission if there exists a positive secrecy rate. Hence, secrecy rate computation is a major concern in this work. The maximum secrecy rate is highly complicated. To develop an efficient algorithm to find a positive secrecy rate could be a research issue. This work adopts greedy algorithm for search the relay mapping. In the numerical results, the effects of eavesdropper is not serious in the cooperative system. The other issue on the power control at the relay station might be considered in the next research. While the eavesdropper has been detected, how to control the transmission power might be another feasible solution for the secret communication.

Acknowledgment

This research was partially supported by the Ministry Of Science and Technology, Taiwan (ROC), under contract no.: MOST 107-2221-E-845 -002 -MY3 and MOST 107-2221-E-845 -001 -MY3.

References

[1] Cisco Co., "Systems Cisco. Cisco visual networking index: Forecast and methodology, 2016-2021." White Paper, 2017

[2] L. Li, X. Zhou, H. Xu, G. Y. Li, D. Wang, and A. Soong, "Simplified relay selection and power allocation in cooperative cognitive radio systems," IEEE Trans. on Wireless Communications, Vol. 10(1), pp. 33-36, Jan. 2011

[3] H. C. Lu and W. Liao, "Cooperative strategies in wireless relay networks," IEEE Journal on Selected Areas in Communications, Vol. 30(2), pp. 323-330, 2012

[4] X. Chen, L. Lei, H. Zhang and C. Yuen, "Large-scale MIMO relaying techniques for physical layer security: AF or DF?," IEEE Trans. on Wireless Communications, Vol. 14(9), pp. 5135-5146, 2015

[5] A. Nosratinia, T. E. Hunter and A. Hedayat, "Cooperative communication in wireless networks," IEEE Communications Magazine, Vol. 42(10), pp. 74-80, 2004

[6] Y. Wang and G. Noubir, "Distributed cooperation and diversity for hybrid wireless networks," IEEE Trans. on Mobile Computing, Vol. 12(3), pp. 596-608, 2013

[7] J. P. Hong, B. Hong, T. W. Ban and W. Choi, "On the cooperative diversity gain in underlay cognitive radio systems," IEEE Trans. on Communications, Vol. 60(1), pp. 209-219, 2012

[8] P. Porambage, C. Schmitt, P. Kumar, A. Gurtov, M. Ylianttila, "Two-phase Authentication Protocol for Wireless Sensor Networks in Distributed IoT Applications," Proceedings of the 2014 IEEE Wireless Communications and Networking Conference (WCNC), pp. 2728-2733, 2014

[9] Y. Zou, J. Zhu, X. Wang and V. Leung, Improving physical-layer security in wireless communications using diversity techniques, IEEE Network, Vol. 29(1), pp. 42-48, 2015

[10] L. Wang, N. Yang, M. Elkashlan, P.L. Yeoh and J. Yuan, "Physical layer security of maximal ratio combining in two-wave with diffuse power fading channels," IEEE Trans. on Information Forensics and Security, Vol. 9, Issue 2, pp. 247-258, 2014

[11] Xiaowen Gong, S.A. Vorobyov and C. Tellambura, "Admission Control-Based Joint Bandwidth and Power Allocation in Multi-User DF Relay Networks," Proceedings of Forty Fourth Asilomar Conference on Signals, Systems and Computers (ASILOMAR 2010), pp. 1723 - 1727, 2010

[12] A.D. Wyner, "The wire- tap channel," Bell system technical journal, Vol. 54(8), pp. 1355-1387, 1975

[13] C.E. Shannon, "Communication theory of secrecy systems," Bell Syst. Tech. Journal, Vol. 29, pp. 656–715, 1949

[14] Y. Chou, J. Zhu, X. Wang and V.C. Leung, "Improving physical-layer security in wireless communications using diversity techniques," IEEE Network, Vol. 29(1), pp. 42-48, 2015

[15] A. Trongratsameethong and J.L. Mitrpanont, "Exhaustive Greedy Algorithm for Optimizing Intermediate Result Sizes of Join Queries," Proceedings of IEEE/ACIS ICIS 2009, pp. 643-648, June 2009

LSTM Neural Network for Electricity Consumption Forecast

Ying-Chin Lin[1,*], Yu-Min Zhang[2], Yen Hung Chen[3], and Wei-Kuang Wang[4]
[1,*]Department of Applied Mathematics, Feng Chia University, Taichung, Taiwan, R.O.C.
E-mail: yichlin@fcu.edu.tw
[2]Department of Applied Mathematics, Feng Chia University, Taichung, Taiwan, R.O.C.
E-mail: k12501599501@gmail.com
[3]Department of Computer Science, University of Taipei, Taipei, Taiwan, R.O.C.
E-mail: yhchen@utaipei.edu.tw
[4]Department of Environmental Engineering and Science, Feng Chia University, Taichung, Taiwan, R.O.C.
E-mail: wkwang@fcu.edu.tw

Abstract - *With the increasing of energy demand year by year, we suffered both the high construction cost of electric equipment and slow progression of renewable energy sources, which reduces the operating reserve of electricity. Without more electricity generated, how to save electric power becomes increasingly important, where a crucial step is to install the advanced electric meter, i.e., smart meter, that enables energy data collection with a massive scale. Smart meters have been deployed in many countries across the world since early 2000s, while many academic works are proposed. This paper studies the classification and forecast of the electric consumption. We perform the consumer classification based on the feature of peak of electric consumption, and according to the classification result, a deep learning model of LSTM (Long Short-Term Memory) is used to forecast the electric consumption for each classified group. Moreover, several experiments are conducted to evaluate the performance of our work, which takes the MAPE and R^2 as the measurement. Experimental result exhibits the good forecasting performance by our LSTM model compared to the traditional regression methods. Accordingly, our work is capable of being the reference for the decision-making of related departments to issue the alert for electric supply, propagate the knowledge for saving power, and so on.*

Keywords: Smart meter; Consumer classification; LSTM; Deep learning

1 Introduction

Nowadays, the efficient management for supply and consume energy is a critical issue. Taiwan Power Company points out that the typical household contributes 51% of the electricity consumption in their 2016 investigation report [1], and hence, the household is growing into an important group for saving power. The current trend drives our government to hasten the deployment of smart meter, and Executive Yuan of Taiwan expects 3 million installations by the end of 2024 [2].

With the increasing deployment of smart electric meters across 35 countries, the amount of smart meters grew by over two times in 2013 than the previous year [3]. There are more and more works related to the smart meter, including the analysis of real-time data for the electricity usage, consumption classification, loading prediction, abnormal electricity energy consumption, real-time demand response potential evaluation [4][5]. Also, many studies focus on the analysis of domestic electricity smart metering data [6][7]. Niu et al. proposed a loading prediction model by analyzing 7,200 historical records of electricity consumption [8]. Iyengar et al. analyzed 14,836 records of advanced electric and gas meters for the whole and individual consumer, and pointed out the group of inefficient electricity usage [9]. In the works of loading profile, the conventional methods are k-means [9][10][11], Artificial Neural Network [12][15], Hidden Markov Model [13][14], Self-Organizing Map [14] as well as time series analysis [14][15].

On the other hand, the deep learning uses the network of deep but simpler structure to fit complicated non-linear functions. The deep learning can be regarded as a subset of machine learning, while its neural network has some characteristics compared to the conventional one, such as simpler features, adaption of high-dimensional data, greater dataset and computing power [16]. LSTM (Long Short-Term Memory) based on the basic RNN (Recurrent Neural Network) in the deep learning is an improved neural network [17], where the major improvement is the vanishing gradient issue that the RNN would suffer when dealing with long data sequences. Also, LSTM has additional designs of input and output gates compared to the RNN. Many studies try to optimize LSTM and the famous one is the improvement of Gers et al. [18], which adds the forget gate (Figure 1) and has become the mainstream model [19].

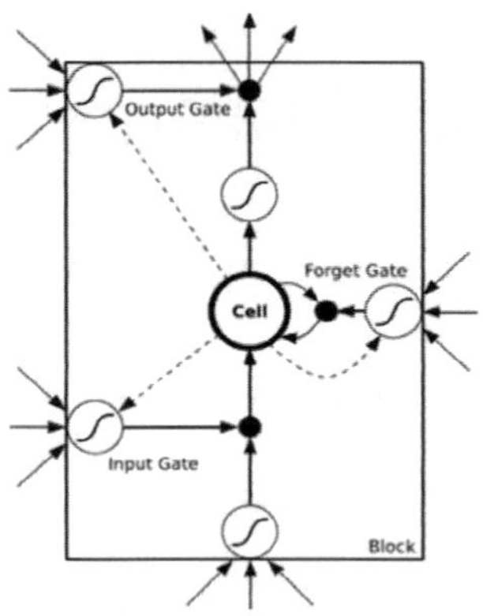

Figure 1: Three gates of LSTM neural network

LSTM, similar to RNN, is good at processing the time series problem. Since the electricity consumption of each user is itself a kind of time series and the excellence of LSTM to harness sequences [20], we use LSTM to predict the electricity consumption of peak, half-peak and off-peak hours for each group given by the consumption classification. This work can be the decision reference for the related line units.

The rest of this paper is organized as follows. Processing flow and details of each component are described in Section 2. Section 3 presents the experimental results, while Section 4 gives concluding remarks of this work.

2 Material and method

There are two types of the dataset in this work. One is the temperature data in 2016, coming from the Taipei side at CODiS (CWB Observation Data Inquire System) of Central Weather Bureau of Taiwan, R.O.C. [21], and every one hour has a temperature record. The other is the electricity consumption of smart meters at Taipei and New Taipei Cities in 2016, totally 7,827 households, coming from the contest [22] and every 15 minutes generates a record for a household. For the consistency of time unit, we merge the four values into one and leave the value missing if one of the four values is missing.

2.1 Missing value imputation

Since the missing value could influence the follow-up analysis, it needs to impute the missing value first. Several works proposed the periodicity of electricity consumption [23][24] and based on these works, we develop a method called *n-order imputation*. The procedure is to scan data one by one from the beginning, while the imputation is performed once a missing value occurs. Assume that the t-th value is missing and $n = 1$. Then, the n-order Imputation is to find a candidate set S_{mv} and computes its average for imputing the t-th value. The candidate set consists of four values, including the (t–1)-th, (t+1)-th, (t–1 week)-th and (t+1 week)-th values. Note that the (t+1)-th and (t+1 week)-th values could also be missing and at this time we ignore them. Therefore, the t-th missing value can be imputed by the value $value(t)$=average(S_{mv}), where $S_{mv}=\{value(t-1), value(t+1)\} \cup \{value(t \pm c) \mid c = 24 \times 7 \times a, a=1, 2, \cdots, n\}$.

2.2 Time segmentation

This work is to forecast the electricity consumption of peak, half-peak and off-peak hours every week. At first, we integrate the imputed data, 24 records a day, into several segments. With the reference to three-stage pricing of Taiwan Power Company (Figure 2(a)) and the completeness of a day, we take the 00:00 as the separation of two days and finally obtain 7 records a day (Figure 2(b)).

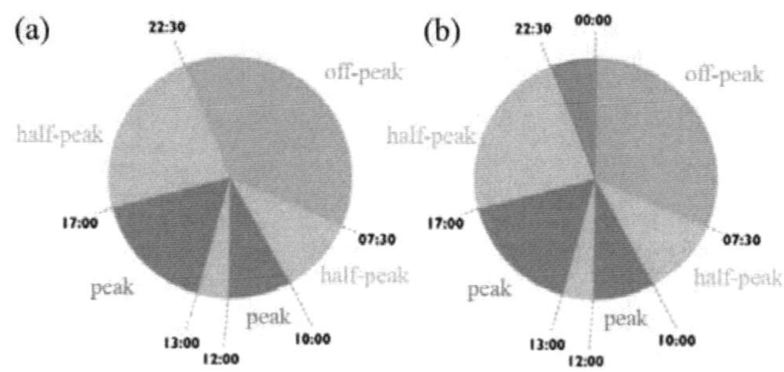

Figure 2: (a) 6 segments a day of Taiwan Power Company; (b) 7 segments in this work

2.3 Consumption classification

The consumption classification is a hot research topic in studying the smart meter [4], and before the classification procedure we have to select consumer features, such as residence, the curve or type of the electricity consumption. This study investigates the behavior of the electricity consumption in the 7 segments, where each segment is reduced to its average consumption. Next, the averages to the 7 segments are standardized between 0 and 1, because we care the behavior instead of the numeric value of electricity consumption.

We then use the classical k-means algorithm to the classification. Given a parameter k, the algorithm picks k centers and distributes each point to the nearest center by the Euclidean distance, next computing the new center of each group, and iterate the procedure until the centers are unchanged [25]. Finally, the consumers are classified into 5 groups, named class_0, class_1, class_2, class_3 and class_4. Figure 3 is the percentages of five group, and the behavior of electricity consumption for each group is illustrated in Figure 4. The different behaviors in five groups show that the classification here is reasonable.

2.4 LSTM model

We like to forecast the electricity consumptions of five time segments for five groups, and the LSTM model together with its parameters needs to be constructed firstly. A conventional LSTM is as Figure 5, where there are four neurons at the input layer, two neurons at the hidden layer and five neurons at the output layer.

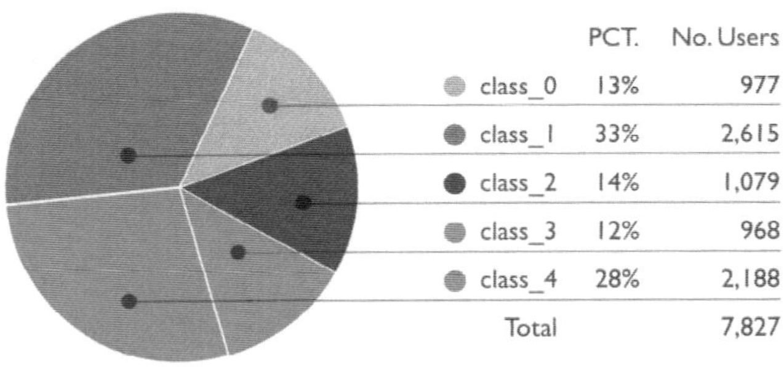

Figure 3: Percentages of five classified groups

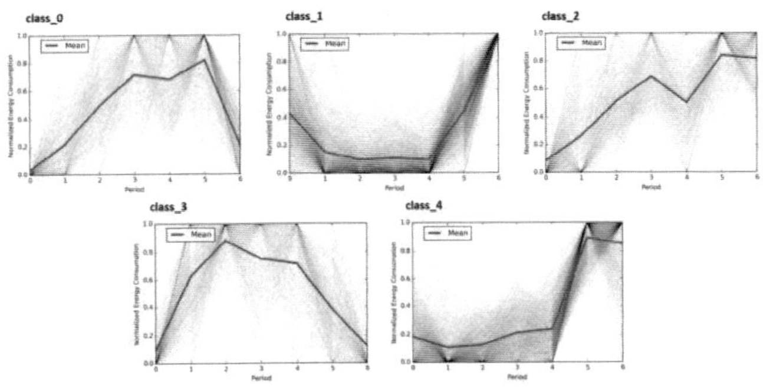

Figure 4: Behaviors of electricity consumption for five groups

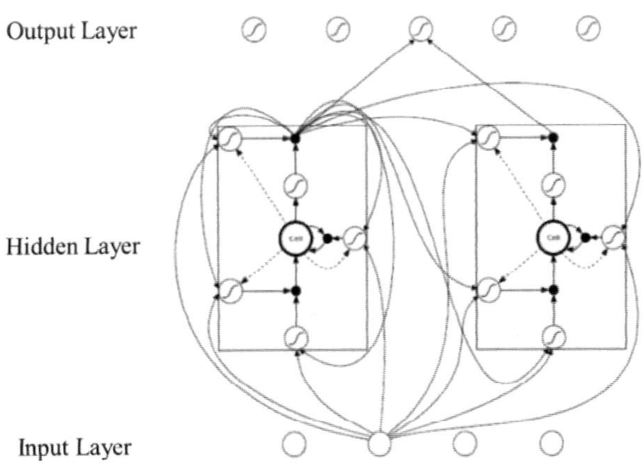

Figure 5: LSTM model

There is no conclusion to the number of neurons or layers, but depending on the environmental attributes, such as the size of training set, the amount of data features, computing performance. In general, the number of layers is inversely proportional to the number of neurons, while a larger amount of layers could suffer issues like gradient vanishing and overfitting. There is no standard procedure to decide these parameters. We use the basic LSTM model with the following structure to fit our requirement: Since each record has electricity consumptions of seven segments and the highest temperature, there are eight neurons at the input layer. Considering the computing performance, our LSTM has 250 neurons, and there are seven neurons at the output layer because of the prediction of power consumptions for seven segments.

In the neural network, the activation function is critical to guide the network through the fitting process of training set. The activation function simply has two categories, linear and non-linear functions, where the latter is common used. Traditional activation functions in LSTM are sigmoid and tanh functions, which are also adapted in our model. There is recently the ReLu function with the fast convergence and good performance [26], and hence it is adapted in the output layer.

In addition, the effect of the cost function in machine learning is to evaluate the gap between real and forecasting values during the training phase, and modifies the neurons and weights of the neural chains using the back propagation method. The back propagation uses the gradient descent, which computes the partial derivative to derive the slope, and revise the weights. The most common cost functions are mean square error and cross entropy, applying to the regression and classification problems respectively. The time series forecast studied in this work is a regression problem, and thus we adapt the mean square error as the cost function of model.

There is a strong correlation between the learning rate and the gradient descent. The learning rate can determine the step each time when performing the gradient descent. A high learning rate could never appropriate the optimal solution, whereas a small one would lead to a long training time. Therefore, the parameter of learning rate is important in the machine learning. In our model, the learning rate is initially set to the traditional value of 0.1 [27], and iterated by decreasing 10% each round to obtain a better error value. Through our experiment, the learning rate in our model is set to 0.001, which will be clear in the next section.

On the other hand, the overfitting problem is common in machine learning, which is briefly getting more and more error of the verification set as the error of the training set is less and less. Several methods are proposed to improve the effect of overfitting learning, and there are two common methods: One is the straightforward way, early stop, which stops training procedure before the obvious difference between the training and validation sets. The other is recently famous method, dropout [26], trying to overcome the fitting problem from the algorithmic view.

2.5 Training model

The input is the historical records of electricity consumption every week of five classified groups, whereas the output is the record of next week. There are total 51 records with this combination, where each record begins at Friday and ends at Thursday of next week (Figure 6). Subsequently, we randomly pick a week for each month as the following validation set, and finally the training and testing sets have 39 and 12 records respectively.

Input	Fri.	Sat.	Sun.	Mon.	Tues.	Wed.	Thur.
	1/1	1/2	1/3	1/4	1/5	1/6	1/7

Output	Fri.	Sat.	Sun.	Mon.	Tues.	Wed.	Thur.
	1/8	1/9	1/10	1/11	1/12	1/13	1/14

Figure 6: Example of each record

There are eight standardized records in every day, which are the electricity consumptions of seven segments and the highest temperature in that day. Moreover, the batch size is the number of records in the training dataset used to the back propagation in every training round. Sutskever suggested that the division of the number of training records and the batch size should be less than 15 [27]. There are 39 training records in this work and accordingly the batch size is set to 3 (39/3 < 15). In addition, there are two types, stateful and stateless, in the LSTM of keras package [28], where we adapt the stateless type because the time in our records is discontinuous (we randomly take out one week).

We visualize the testing result of validation set to see the variation of errors during the training process. Illustrated by Figure 7, the curve is smooth and consistent, indicating no overfitting problem. Besides, the error does not decrease significantly, and thus the number of training does no longer increases.

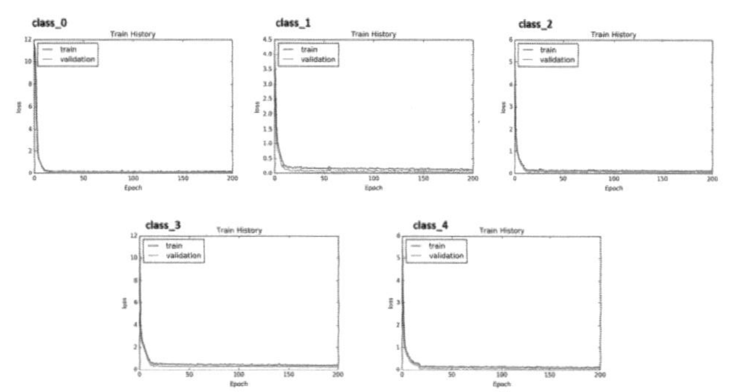

Figure 7: Errors of five groups

3 Experimental result and discussion

We use the classical LSTM as the forecasting model, where there are 8 neurons in the input layer, 250 LSTM neurons in the hidden layer as well as 7 neurons in the output layer. Five LSTM models are trained corresponding to the five groups, and evaluating the test set by the measures of MAPE and R^2. Furthermore, we compare with the linear and polynomial regressions.

3.1 MAPE

MPAE is one of indices used to assess the forecasting performance of time series, and its formula is as follows, where A_t and F_t are the real and forecasting values, respectively. MAPE is a relative value and not be affected by the units of measure and forecast. The forecasting result would be better if the MAPE approaches to 0.

$$MPAE = \frac{100}{n} \sum_{t=1}^{n} \left| \frac{A_t - F_t}{A_t} \right| \quad (1)$$

3.2 Determination coefficient

The *determination coefficient* is often represented as R^2, which measures confound goodness of fit and explanatory power of the model in statistics. The R^2 value is between 0 and 1, while a larger value indicates a better explanatory power of the model. Its model is as follows, where y_i and f_i are real and forecasting values, respectively:

$$R^2 = 1 - \frac{SS_{reg}}{SS_{tot}}$$
$$SS_{reg} = \sum_i (f_i - \bar{y})^2, SS_{tot} = \sum_i (y_i - \bar{y})^2 \quad (2)$$

3.3 Experimental result

We use there forecasting methods, multiple linear regression, multiple quadratic regression and LSTM, to draw five forecasting figures for each group. Figure 8, Figure 9 and Figure 10 are the illustrations, where the *x*-axis is the time and *y*-axis is the average electricity consumption. In these figures, the real and forecasting values of the testing sets are represented by the blue and red lines, respectively. Note that these figures are bar charts, whose *x*-axis contains 588 (= 12 × 7 × 7) scales, and help to visualize whether the forecasting values fit the real values.

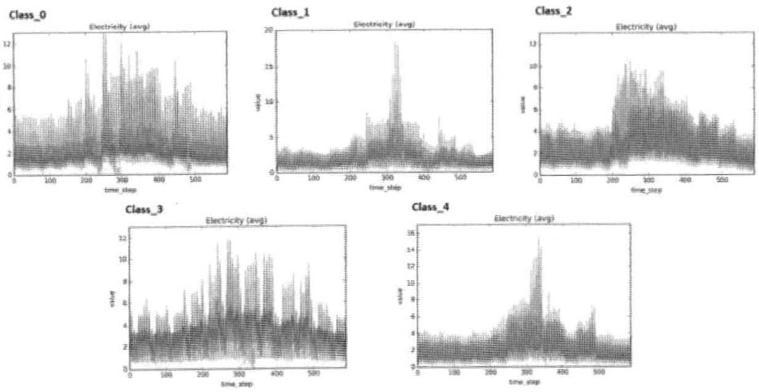

Figure 8: The real (blue lines) and forecasting (red lines) values of multiple linear regression

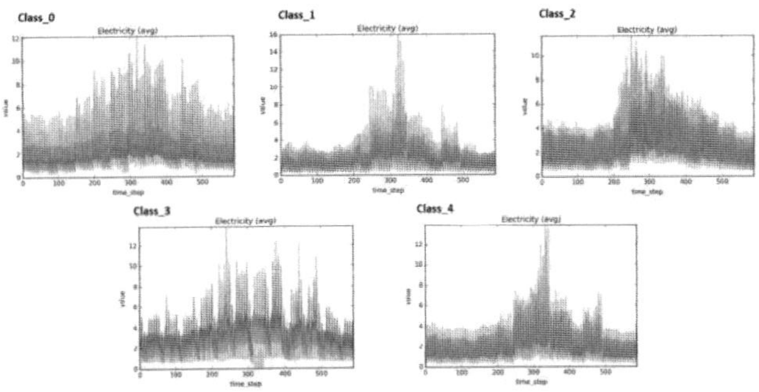

Figure 9: The real (blue lines) and forecasting (red lines) values of multiple quadratic regression

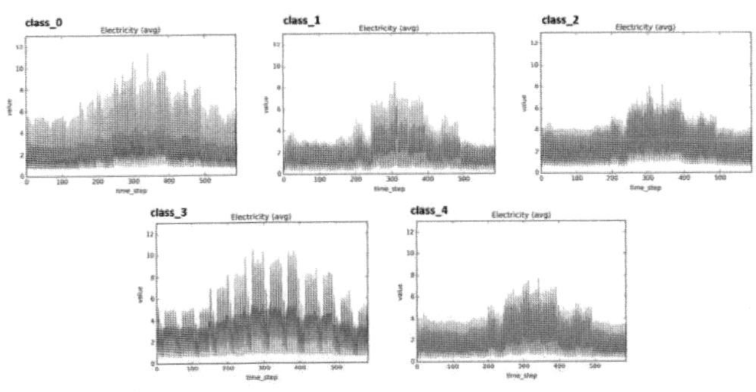

Figure 10: The real (blue lines) and forecasting (red lines) values of LSTM

From these figures, we can see that the forecasting result is roughly consistent to the real situation. Table 1 is the MAPE and R^2 for five groups and these are of high accuracy, indicating the good forecasting result and explanatory power of the model.

Table 1: MAPE and R^2 of five LTSM models

Class ID	0	1	2	3	4
MAPE	8.36%	8.29%	7.46%	9.07%	7.71%
R^2	0.954	0.967	0.964	0.933	0.969

The forecasting results of three compared methods are listed in Table 2 and Table 3. These results show the outstanding performance of our LSTM model.

Table 2: MAPE of three forecasting methods

Class ID	Multiple Linear Regression	Multiple quadratic Regression	LSTM
0	21.52%	16.30%	8.36%
1	24.98%	21.25%	8.29%
2	26.58%	23.97%	7.46%
3	16.47%	19.06%	9.07%
4	19.71%	17.18%	7.71%

Table 3: R^2 of three forecasting methods

Class ID	Multiple Linear Regression	Multiple quadratic Regression	LSTM
0	0.598	0.844	0.954
1	0.388	0.542	0.967
2	0.540	0.538	0.964
3	0.706	0.203	0.933
4	0.599	0.708	0.969

4 Conclusions

This work studies the electricity consumption of smart meters at Taipei and New Taipei Cities in 2016. According to the behavior of electricity consumption, we classify the users into seven groups and visualize the trends of behavior for each group. Moreover, the LSTM neural network model in deep learning is used to forecast the electricity consumption for each group. With the measures of MAPE and R^2, this is a good forecasting performance by our LSTM model compared to the traditional multiple linear and quadratic regressions. As a result, our work is capable of being the reference for the decision-making of related departments to issue the alert for electric supply, propagate the knowledge for saving power, and so on.

5 Acknowledgement

This work is partially supported by the Ministry of Science and Technology under the contract number MOST 107-2115-M-845-001. The dataset of electricity consumption is collected from the contest held by the Industrial Technology Research Institute of Taiwan, R.O.C and Bureau of Energy, Ministry of Economic Affairs, R.O.C.

6 References

[1] Taiwan Power Company, Retrieved from http://www.taipower.com.tw/

[2] Executive Yuan R.O.C. (Taiwan), *Low-voltage smart meters promote energy conservation*, https://english.ey.gov.tw/

[3] D. Alahakoon and X. Yu, "Advanced analytics for harnessing the power of smart meter big data," in *Proc. IEEE Int. Workshop Intell. Energy Syst. (IWIES'13)*, Nov. 2013, pp. 40–45.

[4] A.M. Tureczek and P.S. Nielsen, "Structured literature review of electricity consumption classification using smart meter data," *Energies*, Vol. 10, No. 5, 2017.

[5] D. Alahakoon and X. Yu, "Smart electricity meter data intelligence for future energy systems: a survey," *IEEE Transactions on Industrial Informatics*, Vol. 12, No. 1, pp. 425–436, 2016.

[6] Y. Wang, et al., "Clustering of electricity consumption behavior dynamics toward big data applications," *IEEE Transactions on Smart Grid*, Vol. 7, No. 5, 2016.

[7] L. Jin, et al., "Clustering of electricity consumption behavior dynamics toward big data applications," *AAAI Workshops*, 2017.

[8] D. Niu, H. Shi and D. Wu, "Short-term load forecasting using Bayesian neural networks learned by hybrid Monte Carlo algorithm," *Applied Soft Computing*, Vol. 12, No. 6, pp. 1822–1827, 2012.

[9] S. Iyengar, et al., "Analyzing energy usage on a city-scale using utility smart meters," in *Proc. ACM Int. Conference Syst. Energy-Efficient Bui. Env. (BuildSys'16)*, Nov. 2016, pp. 51–60.

[10] J. Kwac, J. Flora and R. Rajagopal, "Household energy consumption segmentation using hourly data," *IEEE Transactions on Smart Grid*, Vol. 5, No. 1, pp. 420–430, 2014.

[11] A. Al-Wakeela and J. Wua, "K-means based cluster analysis of residential smart meter measurements," *Energy Procedia*, Vol. 88, pp. 754–760, 2016.

[12] S.M. Sulaiman, P.A. Jeyanthy and D. Devaraj, "Artificial neural network based day ahead load forecasting using Smart Meter data," *Biennial International Conference on Power and Energy Systems: Towards Sustainable Energy (PESTSE'16)*, Jan. 2016.

[13] A. Albert and R. Rajagopal, "Smart meter driven segmentation: what your consumption says about you," *IEEE Transactions on Power System*, Vol. 28, No. 4, pp. 4019–4030, 2013.

[14] H. Liu, et al., "Electricity consumption time series profiling: a data mining application in energy industry," *Industrial Conference on Data Mining* (*ICDM*), July 2012, pp. 52–66.

[15] I. Khan, et al., "Segmentation of factories on electricity consumption behaviors using load profile data," *IEEE Access*, Vol. 4, pp. 8394–8406, 2016.

[16] L. Yann, Y. Bengio and G. Hinton, "Deep learning," *Nature*, 2015.

[17] Hochreiter and Schmidhuber, "Long short-term memory," *Neural Computation*, 1997.

[18] F.A. Gers, J. Schmidhuber and F. Cummins, "Learning to forget: continual prediction with LSTM," *Neural Computation*, 2000.

[19] K. Greff et al., "LSTM: A search space odyssey," *IEEE Transactions on Neural Networks and Learning Systems*, Vol. 28, No. 10, pp. 2222–2232, 2017.

[20] F.A. Gers and J. Schmidhuber, "LSTM recurrent networks learn simple context free and context sensitive languages," *IEEE Transactions on Neural Networks*, Vol. 12, No. 6, pp. 1333–1340, 2001.

[21] CWB Observation Data Inquire System, Retrieved from http://e-service.cwb.gov.tw/HistoryDataQuery/

[22] Industrial Technology Research Institute of Taiwan, R.O.C and Bureau of Energy, Ministry of Economic Affairs, R.O.C., Low-Voltage Advanced Meter Infrastructure (LVAMI) contest, Retrieved from http://www.smartgrid.org.tw/LVAMI

[23] M. Espinoza, et al., "Short-term load forecasting, profile identification and customer segmentation: A methodology based on periodic time series," *IEEE Transactions on Power System*, Vol. 20, pp. 1622–1630, 2005.

[24] C. Bennett, R.A. Stewart and J. Lu, "Autoregressive with exogenous variables and neural network short-term load forecast models for residential low voltage distribution networks," *Energies*, Vol. 7, pp. 2938–2960, 2014.

[25] S.P. Lloyd, "Least squares quantization in PCM," *IEEE Transactions on Information Theory*, Vol. 28, No. 2, pp. 129–137, 1982.

[26] A. Krizhevsky, I. Sutskever, and G. Hinton, "ImageNet classification with deep convolutional neural networks," *Advances in Neural Information Processing Systems (NIPS)*, pp. 1106–1114, 2012.

[27] I. Sutskever, A Brief Overview of Deep Learning, Retrieved from http://yyue.blogspot.tw/2015/01/a-brief-overview-of-deep-learning.html

[28] Keras: The Python Deep Learning Library, Retrieved from https://keras.io/

SESSION

POSTER PAPERS AND EXTENDED ABSTRACTS

Chair(s)

TBA

Knowledge-Based Neural Net for Electronic Modeling

L. Zhang[1,2], and Q.J. Zhang[2]
[1]Colonel By Secondary School, Ottawa, Ontario, Canada
[2]Department of Electronics, Carleton University, Ottawa, Ontario, Canada

Abstract – *A knowledge-based neural net is presented for electronic device modeling. The proposed model includes a neural network accurately representing device behavior within the training range, and a knowledge equation providing reliable tendencies of electronic behavior outside the training range. A correctional neural network is also proposed to map the knowledge equations onto the boundary data through training. The proposed method is more robust than the neural net alone because of improved extrapolation ability, and more accurate than the knowledge equations alone because of the neural net's ability to learn non-ideal relationships inherent in the practical data. The method is demonstrated by applying it to a practical high-frequency, high-power transistor called a HEMT (High-Electron Mobility Transistor) used in wireless transmitters.*

Keywords: Neural network, electronic modeling, knowledge-based model.

1 Introduction

Artificial neural networks are useful for interpolating within a dataset and can be used to learn and represent non-linear relations between inputs and outputs of electronic devices [1]. Such a neural net representation is especially efficient when existing analytical equations cannot accurately represent the practical, non-ideal behavior of new types of electronic devices. Neural nets are reasonably accurate within the region of learning, however they are not reliable at extrapolation outside the data range. Mathematically-based extrapolation methods have been used to help neural nets to improve extrapolation quality [2]. Building on the concept of knowledge-based neural networks [3], a more efficient method is proposed in this abstract exploiting available knowledge about electronic devices.

2 Proposed Knowledge-Based Model

Knowledge about electronic devices is typically available in many engineering designs. More specifically, knowledge in the form of predefined analytical equations can give better tendencies for the values of electronic devices outside of the dataset. The proposed overall model includes a neural network accurately representing device behavior within the training range, and a knowledge equation providing reliable tendencies of electronic behavior outside the training range.

To create a smooth transition between the neural network and equation predictions, the equation parameters are optimized towards the values at the boundary of the training range as closely as possible. Knowledge equations typically reflect general physics / empirical relationships within the device, while the training data reflect device reality where the actual relationships are non-ideal. Thus, the knowledge equations may not precisely match the data at the boundaries; subsequently a gap will appear between the neural net interpolation model and the knowledge equation extrapolation model. To solve this problem, a correctional neural network is proposed to map the knowledge equations to the boundary values through training. Finally, the neural net interpolation model and the neural-net mapped knowledge equation are combined using sigmoid-based gating functions which blend the two parts smoothly according to the boundary values. Figure 1 shows the overall proposed structure. This combined model is a knowledge-based neural net model.

As a further step for the use of the proposed model for electronic design, the derivatives of the proposed model are derived as:

$$\frac{dy_{total}}{dx_i} = \sigma_1 \frac{dy_{nn}}{dx_i} + \sigma_2 \frac{dy_{nnc}}{dy_k}\frac{dy_k}{dx_i} + y_{nn}\frac{d\sigma_1}{dx_i} + y_{nnc}\frac{d\sigma_2}{dx_i}, i=1,2 \quad (1)$$

where y_{total} is the final output of the combined model, y_{nn} is the output of the neural network trained on the data, y_{nnc} is the output of the correctional neural network, and y_k is the output of the knowledge equation, as shown in Figure 1. σ_1 and σ_2 are sigmoid-based gating functions. The values of dy_{nn}/dx_i and dy_{nnc}/dy_k can be obtained using adjoint neural networks [4] which have the same synaptic weights as the original neural nets y_{nn} and y_{nnc}. The expression for dy_k/dx_i is derived from the knowledge equation.

3 Application to Electronic Modeling

This method is demonstrated by applying it to a practical high-frequency, high-power transistor called a HEMT (High Electron Mobility Transistor) used in wireless transmitters [5]. The purpose is to accurately model the output current (I_d) as a function of voltage at the gate (V_{gs}) and drain (V_{ds}) terminals given a bounded dataset.

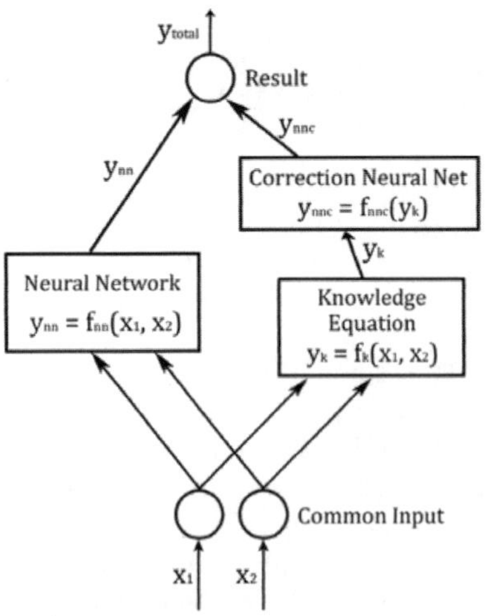

Figure 1. Structure of the proposed knowledge-based neural network.

The training data for the device contains 166 samples in the training range $V_{gs} \in \{-4, 0.5\}$, $V_{ds} \in \{0, 15\}$ in volts as shown in Figure 2. First, a neural network is trained on the data, using backpropagation or second-order methods such as quasi-Newton methods. The neural net is accurate within the dataset but diverges outside the dataset range at larger values of V_{ds}. A popularly recognized equation for the high-frequency transistor, namely the Statz IV equation, is used as the knowledge equation. To create a smooth transition between the two methods, the three parameters of the equation are optimized towards the 10 boundary samples (at V_{ds} = 15V) as closely as possible. A second neural net is trained using the 10 approximate boundary values provided by the equation as input, and the 10 boundary values of the dataset as target. The final model combining neural net and the neural-net mapped knowledge equations from the Statz model can accurately predict values both within and outside the dataset. The derivatives from Equation (1) represent the transconductance (for $i = 1$) and the inverse of drain-source resistance (for $i = 2$) of the device. The proposed method is more robust than the neural net alone because of improved extrapolation ability, and more accurate than the Statz equations alone because of the neural net's ability to learn non-ideal relationships inherent in the practical data. Ongoing work is to expand this method to handle more input variables for the model, and to incorporate different knowledge equations. In addition, this method will be applied to high-power transistor modeling including additional temperature variables to the proposed model to represent variation of transistor voltage and current due to heating effects.

4 Conclusions

By combining a neural network with knowledge equations of electronic devices, a knowledge-based neural net has been developed for device modeling. The proposed method is more robust than the neural net alone, and more accurate than the knowledge equations alone. The method has been demonstrated by the high-frequency, high-power transistor example, and can be extended to handle more inputs and different knowledge equations.

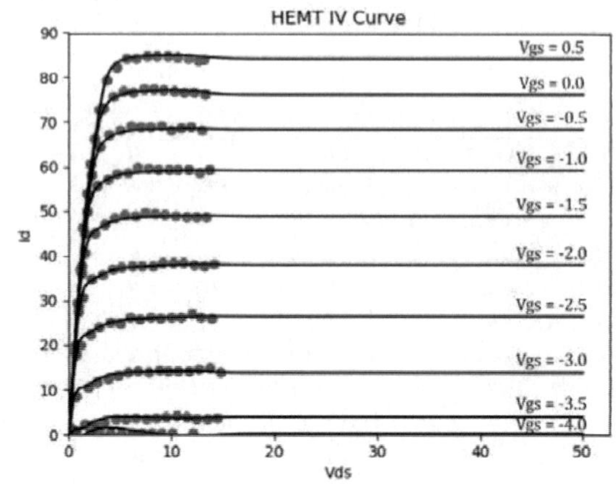

Figure 2. HEMT IV curve from the proposed knowledge-based neural model. Within the region where training data (represented by the points •) is available, the model is described by the neural network; outside the training region it maintains correct tendencies due to the knowledge equations.

5 References

[1] Q.J. Zhang, K.C. Gupta and V.K. Devabhaktuni, "Artificial neural networks for RF and microwave design: from theory to practice," *IEEE Transactions Microwave Theory Tech.*, vol. 51, no. 4, pp. 1339-1350, April 2003.

[2] W.C. Na, W.Y. Liu, L. Zhu, F. Feng, J.G. Ma and Q.J. Zhang, "Advanced extrapolation technique for neural-based microwave modeling and design," *IEEE Transactions Microwave Theory Tech.*, vol. 66, no. 10, pp. 4397-4418, October 2018.

[3] Q. Liu, M. Gao, Q.J. Zhang, "Knowledge-based neural network model for FPGA logical architecture development," *IEEE Transactions Very Large Scale Integration Systems*, vol. 24, no. 2, pp. 664-677, February 2016.

[4] S.A. Sadrossadat, Y. Cao and Q.J. Zhang, "Parametric modeling of microwave passive components using sensitivity-analysis-based adjoint neural network technique", *IEEE Transactions Microwave Theory Tech.*, vol. 61, no. 5, pp. 1733-1747, May 2013.

[5] A. Prasad, M. Thorsell, H. Zirath and C. Fager, "Accurate modeling of GaN HEMT RF behavior using an effective trapping potential," *IEEE Transactions Microwave Theory Tech.*, vol. 66, no. 2, pp. 845-857, Feb. 2018.

CASANDRA - Informatic Tool for the Insurgence of Relevant Information in the Study of Structural Vulnerability in the Municipality of La Florida, Nariño, Colombia, in Volcanic Events

Jurado G[1], Córdoba G[1], Hernández G[1].

[1] **Universidad de Nariño, Colombia.** gan0191@gmail.com, gcordobaguerrero@gmail.com, gonzalohernandez@udenar.edu.co

ABSTRACT

Development of an Android Application that serves as a tool in the process of gathering information about the physical characteristics of homes located in the Municipality of La Florida (Nariño) - Colombia. This information enables the study of the structural vulnerability of these houses in the face of volcanic-type events in order to measure the risk that this population faces in its proximity to the Galeras Volcano.

Keywords: Vulnerability, Risk, Volcanic Hazards, Mobile Application

Type of the submission: Extended Abstract/Poster Paper

INTRODUCTION

The study of vulnerability to volcanic-type threats is a fundamental process that must be carried out by each region located in the areas that are vulnerable to possible volcanic eruptions. The results of this study will result in the prevention of economic and human tragedy.

The municipality of La Florida (Nariño) - Colombia, has a population of 11,423 people, of which 1,876 are located in the main town (Dane, 2005). This municipality is located in the Zone of High Volcanic Affectation (ZAVA) near the volcano Galeras, as stipulated in Decree 4106 of 2005. The study of vulnerability and risk estimation must be contemplated in the Territorial Ordinance Scheme of the Municipality in order to mitigate possible losses in the event of a natural disaster.

Historically, the gathering of the information necessary for an appropriate vulnerability study has been carried out manually, resulting in long processing times of the information accumulated. Software engineering offers considerable help in optimizing this process, providing a computer tool that improves the mechanism for obtaining data, and in turn processing and delivering a database that is easy to interpret and benefits studies conducted.

METHODOLOGY

Definition of Volcanic Hazards

Threats that affect the population should be defined according to the historical facts and the geographical location in order to carry out the vulnerability study. This information will serve as a filter to focus the resources and efforts to high priority tasks, allowing for decisions to be made based on the panorama found.

Phenomena such as: Shock Wave, Burying, Lahars and Falling Ash are those that would have more impact on this region and on the population in general. Once the threats have been defined, the Exposed Elements that will be studied are identified, located, and characterized. This will provide a solid knowledge base for the development of the software tool and the subsequent study of vulnerability and risk mitigation that these threats entail.

Development of the Cassandra software tool

Once the functional requirements that must be taken into account for software development are defined, three work modules are established that will focus on providing and covering the different options that the end user will use to perform the task of gathering information from the homes assigned.

The modules that make up the Casandra tool are:

- Design and development of the forms for the volcanic threats Shock Wave, Burial, Lahar and Falling Ash.
- Georeference of the houses and validation of the information of the forms.
- Design, development, and management of the database.

Design and development of Forms

The design of the forms takes into account that the end users are students of the schools of the municipality of Florida. Its interface is therefore characterized by being very intuitive. This process was supported by Civil Engineers who were in charge of defining the characterization of the Exposed Elements, thus adding the elements according to the requested requirements to the interface of the tool.

Georeferencing and information validation

During the implementation of this work module, efforts were focused on verifying the accuracy of the coordinates provided by the program, in order to obtain information with a minimum margin of error. To do so, Google's mapping libraries were used, which give the coordinates and in turn assign extra information to the location. In addition, these libraries allow for the dynamic handling of the visual markers on the map, giving real-time verification of the information stored with the help of the forms.

Design, development, and managing of the database

This module is of vital importance to the storage of information that is collected with the forms and the map, which allows a simple but understandable export of the data for its use in the study of structural vulnerability of the dwellings. This study uses each element found and its respective characterization to generate vulnerability maps for each volcanic type threat.

While using the tool, it is evident that the response times both in the application and the characterizations of the different threats, as well as the subsequent handling of said information, decrease considerably, allowing for the realization of a census of the entire population, and not only sampling as it was done previously.

PRODUCT

This application can be found in: http://192.68.185.32/casandra/

SESSION

LATE BREAKING PAPERS: INFORMATION EXTRACTION AND APPLICATIONS

Chair(s)

TBA

Serendipity-Aware Noise Detection System for Recommender Systems

Wissam Al Jurdi
Department of Computer Science
Notre Dame University
Deir el Qamar, Lebanon
wsjurdi@ndu.edu.lb

Miriam El Khoury Badran
Department of Computer Science
Notre Dame University
Zook Mosbeh, Lebanon
mabadran@ndu.edu.lb

Chady Abou Jaoude
Ticket Lab., Faculty of Engineering
Antonine University
Baabda, Lebanon
chady.aboujaoude@ua.edu.lb

Jacques Bou Abdo
Department of Computer Science
Notre Dame University
Deir el Qamar, Lebanon
jbouabdo@ndu.edu.lb

Jacques Demerjian
LaRRIS, Faculty of Sciences
Lebanese University
Fanar, Lebanon
jacques.demerjian@ul.edu.lb

Abdallah Makhoul
FEMTO-ST Institute, UMR 6174 CNRS
Universite de Bourgogne
Franche-Comté, Belfort, France
abdallah.makhoul@univ-fcomte.fr

***Abstract*—In the modern age, recommender systems are becoming a prominent and essential solution to the information overload problem, however, they are immensely susceptible to two significant types of noise: malicious noise that is caused by attacks and natural noise that is due to the human error. Many detection algorithms attempt to solve the noise problems, but since natural noise and serendipity overlap in their definition, removing noise results in eliminating serendipity. Serendipity is the happy surprise of unexpectedly finding something relevant, and is important for the issue of over-personalization caused by most recommender systems. The aim of this study is to implement a serendipity-aware noise detection algorithm that will serve as a pre-processing phase to a recommender system application and protects the user's trust without leaving him in a "filter bubble". Finally, to measure the effectiveness of the proposed algorithm, a new metric called top-N adjusted is used.**

***Index Terms*—Recommender systems, Noise detection, Serendipity**

I. Introduction

In the current era of information, the massive quantities of data render the users unable to apprehend what's presented to them. This problem was dubbed as "The Information Overload Problem" [1]. There are many solutions that try to tackle this problem depending on its type, but mainly all solutions are based on machine learning procedures and the most famous of which are recommender systems. Like many machine learning techniques, a recommender system makes predictions based on users' historical behaviors [2]. Specifically, it's to predict user preference for a set of items based on past experience. In order to reduce the consumer's cognitive efforts and increase the quality of his/her decisions (and consequently, his/her satisfaction), decision-support systems (DSS) are implemented in the shape of recommendations. A recommender system aims at filtering, rating and ranking the huge chunks of information to try to predict the user's tastes and eventually support him in efficient decision making [3]. To build a recommender system, the two most popular approaches are Content-based and Collaborative Filtering. All the various techniques adapted to enhance the capabilities of said systems have one goal in common, to gain the user's trust, however, this trust is at risk in many cases since the datasets are highly susceptible to noise.

There are two types of noise in recommender systems datasets, shilling noise (aka profile injection attacks) [4] and natural noise. The former is usually caused deliberately by the attacker in order to have a certain degree of prediction advantage of some products for example, while the latter is basically associated with the unintentional human behavior when rating or giving reviews online usually due to fast decisions etc.

As a solution to this problem that generally affects most datasets in any online system, many detection algorithms were proposed with one aim in mind, to remove the noise completely from the system. Certainly, removing the noise from a dataset can lead to better accuracy results and prediction performance of a recommender system, however, this approach completely eliminates the possibility of serendipitous ratings. Serendipity in recommender systems is an area that lacks decent investigation and its definition is rather ambiguous as there is not a consensus on it [5]. In general, serendipity can be summarized as the happy coincidence of finding a relevant item (product, article, video, etc.). This is a precisely valuable, and quite often overlooked, aspect of a recommender algorithm that serves very well in helping maintain the prime aim of a recommender system. It protects the user from an over-personalized profile that eventually causes him to lose interest in a system that is predicting nothing but items that he/she is already familiar with.

In general, building recommender systems is more of an art since this involves understanding user's tastes and trying to predict what they might like or dislike. Therefore, accuracy, noise, serendipity and the user's trust must all be delicately handled in the system.

The aim of our study is to create an algorithm that takes into consideration serendipity while dealing with noise in the dataset. It is an extension of our previous work that showed how serendipity increases the user's satisfaction in a recommender system [6]. The algorithm is built with two main modules, the first detects and deals with the possible noise in a given dataset, and the seconds extends the code's architecture and functions as a filter that discerns between noise and serendipity, creating the ultimate balance for better predictions. Furthermore, in order to measure the effectiveness of the top-n predicted ratings offline, we propose a new technique that focuses on their quality and significance for a each target user.

The rest of the work is organized as follows: Section two explains the state-of-the-art about noise in its two forms and serendipity. Section three describes the proposed algorithm, shedding light on the constructed modules and the new metric that is used in our method, section four contains the experiment details and the simulation results, and section five concludes this work.

II. Literature Review

A. Noise

Natural noise in a dataset is basically the collection of ratings that the user does unintentionally [7], so they are not accurate and do not reflect the user's correct preferences and biases. Natural noise is related to the methods by which the system infers the user preferences or collects them. There are two types of ratings used by recommender systems depending on the type of the recommender engine, explicit ratings where the user is asked to rate items, and implicit ratings, where the user preferences are induced from his actions on the web. Both types are prone to behavioural errors that eventually transform into noise in a dataset causing the quality of predictions to decrease gradually [8], however, the implicit rating mechanism is much highly susceptible to natural noise [7]. Pham et al. [9] and Amatriain et al. [10] summarize the phenomenon of natural noise in datasets as:

- Alteration in user preference over a period of time.
- Impact of several factors on a user like personal conditions, social media influence, emotional states and context.

There are many different types of proposed algorithms that attempt to detect and remove natural noise. Amatriain et al. [12] propose a novel algorithm based on having many repetitions of user ratings, i.e. re-rating items. The job of the algorithm is to compare the different ratings of the same user for the same item and based on some possible conditions, give the output. This type requires extra input and effort from the user's end which might be its biggest flaw. O'Mahony et al. [11] proposed a method based on a threshold comparison. They define what they call the consistency of a rating as the MAE (Mean Absolute Value) between the actual and the predicted ratings. As long as it is within a predefined threshold, it is accurate, free of noise. If it exceeds this threshold it will be considered as noise. Yera et al. [13] proposed a method that only requires the ratings matrix; it does not require any additional information and solely relies on the ratings in the usual user-item matrices. Our proposed algorithm is based on this study so the details of this technique will be provided in the next section.

B. Serendipity

Serendipity in recommender systems is an area that is still ambiguous and hard to measure. In general, it can be summarized as the happy coincidence of finding relevant items (product, article, video, etc.) and this can be a very important aspect of a recommender engine that serves very well in helping maintain the prime aim of a recommender system, which is mainly to predict the best items to a certain user [14]. The components of serendipity are: relevance, novelty and unexpectedness (Fig. 1), and to better understand serendipity, one has to understand its components [15].

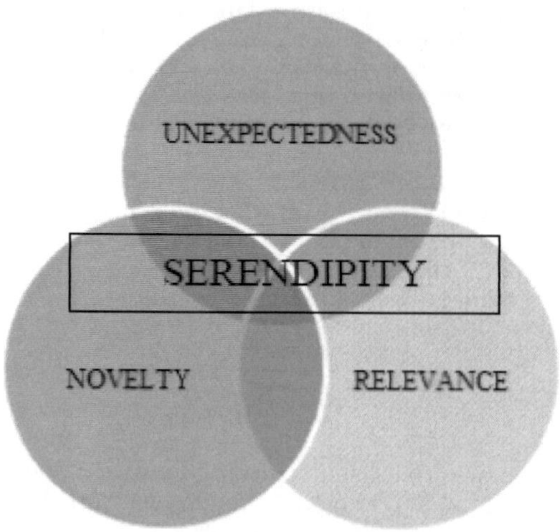

Fig. 1. Components of Serendipity

In their re-ranking serendipity-oriented algorithm, Adamopoulos et al. [16] assign overall scores to items based on two metrics, unexpectedness and quality. With the goal of creating a recommender system that respects diversity, novelty and serendipity, Zhang et al. [17] propose an algorithm called Full Auralist. It is composed of three algorithms that individually return a ranked list of items that will be integrated together using linear combination to produce the final output. Jenders et al. [18] proposed a recommender system for newspapers based on the concept of serendipity. Moreover, Kawamae [19], proposed an algorithm that is based on the estimated search time. The work explains how the probability of an item being serendipitous varies proportionally to the difficulty to find this item, the easier it is to find it, the less serendipitous it is. Iaquinta et al. [9] a strategy called anomalies and exceptions to introduce serendipity. They create a hybrid recommender system that joins both, the content-based algorithm and the serendipitous heuristics, providing serendipitous recommendations alongside classical ones. The TANGENT algorithm was proposed by Onuma et al. [20] to broaden user tastes while retaining the accuracy of recommendations. TANGENT detects groups of users that are like-minded and suggests items to users from different groups. The algorithm proposed by De Gemmis et al. [21] uses an item similarity graph with uncommon similarity measure. designations.

III. Proposed Algorithm

A. Detection Module

In order to detect possible noise in a dataset, we built on top of the algorithm proposed by Toledo et al. [13]. Their algorithm allows the detection of both, natural noise and shilling attacks. The classification of the ratings is based on a combination of items, users, and ratings of users on items *r(u,i)*. First, the classification thresholds are set, and three categories are proposed for each separate group, users, items and their ratings; every category has its own unique classification thresholds:

1) User
   - Weak-average user-dependent threshold *ku*
   - Strong-average user-dependent threshold *vu*
2) Item
   - Weak-average item-dependent threshold *ki*
   - Strong-average item-dependent threshold *vi*
3) Rating
   - Weak-average threshold *k*
   - Strong-average threshold *v*

In order to categorize the users and items in the dataset, all the ratings are compared to the threshold values and grouped based on the above divisions.

The resulting groups would be as follows:

1) User
   - Weak: $r(u,i) < ku$
   - Average: $ku <= r(u,i) < vu$
   - Strong: $r(u,i) >= vu$
2) Item
   - Weak: $r(u,i) < ki$
   - Average: $ki <= r(u,i) < vi$
   - Strong: $r(u,i) >= vi$

Afterwards, the categorized ratings matrix is used in order to label users and items based on the number of occurrences of the user or the item in a certain category (Weak, Average or Strong). For example, if the sum of occurrences of a user as weak, average or strong was higher than the sum of his occurrences in different categories, than said user will be labeled as critical, average or benevolent respectively. Let W, A and S be the sets that represent the total number of occurrences of a user as weak, average or strong:

1) If $W > A+S$, the user is considered a critical user
2) If $A > W+S$, the user is considered an average user
3) If $S > W+A$, the user is considered a benevolent user

The same logic is applied for items in our dataset:

1) If $W > A+S$, the item is weakly-preferred
2) If $A > W+S$, the item is averagely- preferred
3) If $S > W+A$, the item if strongly preferred

Labeling ratings as possible noise lies in the combination of the previous classifications of users and items with the values of the ratings themselves. If the three are not synchronized, then the rating is characterized as possible noise. For instance, if a benevolent user is rating a strongly preferred item the rating should be considerably high; if this is not the case, this rating is a possible noise. Table I shows the combinations that are marked as possible noise:

TABLE I
Possible noise based on the user/item category

User/Item	WP	AP	SP
Critical	$r(u,i)>=k$		
Average		$r(u,i)<k$ or $r(u,i)>=v$	
Benevolent			$r(u,i)<v$

WP: weakly-preferred, AP:averagely-preferred, SP:strongly-preferred

This proposal relies heavily on the values chosen for the weak-average parameters (k, ku, ki) and the average-strong parameters (v, vu, vi). These parameters are highly domain-dependent, therefore, having their optimal value predetermined is not straightforward. Nevertheless, a strategy can be defined to assign acceptable initial values. A global perspective approach is used for the initialization: different studies have come to the conclusion that this method for calculating the parameters is the best. Due to the fact that three possible classes are considered, the thresholds should be picked in a way that divides the ratings into three cases approximately. Parameter choices:

- $ku=ki=k= minR + rnd\ (1/3*(maxR - minR)) = 2$
- $vu=vi=v= maxR - rnd\ (1/3*(maxR - minR)) = 4$
- serendipityThreshold = 2
- n = 5 (in top-n ratings for every user in the test set)

Serendipity intersects noise in the possible arrangements: In these cases (see Table II), a differentiation should be made between natural noise and serendipity.

B. Serendipity Module

The serendipity module of the algorithm is responsible for filtering out the records that might be relevant to the

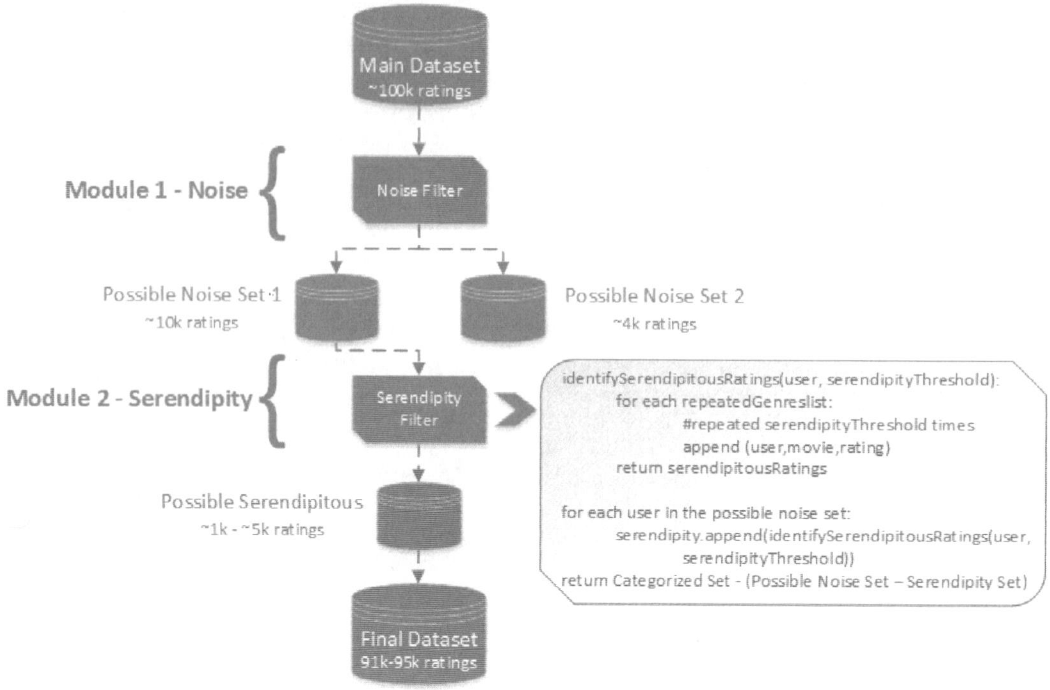

Fig. 2. Algorithm flow with a brief about the serendipity module

TABLE II
INTERSECTION OF NATURAL NOISE AND SERENDIPITY

User/Item	WP	AP	SP
Critical	r(u, i) >= k		
Average		r(u, i) >= v	
Benevolent			

user. In order to accomplish this task, we use the pipe-delimited genres field that is provided in the Movielens datasets' raw data. For each user rating record in the possible noise dataset (the output of the first module of the algorithm), the unique genres list is counted in order to check the number of repetitions. Based on this, we can identify the taste of the user in the possible noise data and filter out the records that might lead to serendipitous predictions. Figure 2 depicts the two modules of the algorithm and shows a brief about the second module. The flow of the module runs as follows:

1) For every user in the noise set:
   - Retrieve the movie genres lists
   - Load the Genres into a data-frame in order to easily calculate the count of the duplicated genre lists
   - Take only the genres that were repeated based on the serendipityThreshold variable
2) The final dataset that contains all the serendipitous records from the previous step would be achieved by the following formula: *Categorized Set - (Possible Noise Set - Serendipity Set)*

In the below example (see Table III), a subset of possibly noisy ratings for a certain user is shown. The combination of Thriller and Horror clearly does not suit the user while Thriller alone seems to be a good option. Therefore, the serendipity module (where *serendipityThreshold >= 2* will take keep movies 2 and 3 and remove the rest from the training set.

TABLE III
SAMPLE OF POSSIBLY-NOISY ITEMS FOR USER U

MovieId	**Genre**	**Rating**
1	Thriller|Horror	3
2	Thriller	4.5
3	Thriller	4
4	Horror	2

IV. Experimental Results

A. Metrics

The traditional famous accuracy metrics such as MAE and RMSE are not suitable to evaluate the output in this case since they are accuracy-oriented. Our goal is to increase the serendipity of the top-N recommended lists for each user in our test set, and as previously discussed, this is very hard to measure offline albeit being quite simpler online through some forms of A/B tests.

In an attempt to quantify the value of the output of our algorithm, a new metric is proposed that is specifically tailored to tackle the quality of the top-N recommended lists. This metric, called top-N adjusted, measures the

TABLE IV
EXPERIMENT RESULTS

Dataset	MAE	RMSE	top-N adjusted	Dataset Size	Possible Serendipitous Records
Without Noise Detection	0.6732	0.8779	4.15635	100836	-
Noise Removed (v.1)	0.5988	0.7924	4.29859	90181	-
Noise Removed (v.2)	0.6606	0.8649	4.25477	97183	-
With Possible Serendipity (v.1)	0.6315	0.8289	4.37078	94479	4298
With Possible Serendipity (v.2)	0.616	0.8139	4.39314	92881	2700
With Possible Serendipity (v.3)	0.6165	0.8151	4.39687	92149	1968
With Possible Serendipity (v.4)	0.6166	0.8131	4.403010	91769	1588
With Possible Serendipity (v.5)	0.6102	0.8087	4.50904	91091	910

average expected ratings for every user's top-N output and then averages them all out for all users. This allows us to quantify the quality and significance of the top-N ratings recommended items for a user, items that the user has not previously seen. The proposed algorithm is expected to score a high top-N average output as there is a better ratings quality in the dataset after adding the possible ratings that might result in serendipitous predictions for all users in the test set, and removing the ratings that are considered as noise.

$$top - N\ adjusted = \frac{\sum_1^n \frac{\sum_1^N r'(u,i)}{N}}{n} \quad (1)$$

Where, N is the total number of ratings in the top-N predicted recommendations for every user, n is the total number of user in the test set and $r'(u,i)$ is the predicted rating of user u on item i.

B. Environment

In order to show the impact of the proposed algorithm, the following scenarios were applied on the recommender base code (for more details see Table IV):

1) Without noise detection, passing the dataset as it is to the recommender
2) With noise detection (noise removed v.1)
3) Ratings that are below expectations are removed keeping the ones that are higher than what they are supposed to be (noise removed v.2)
4) With serendipity filter, keeping items that might result in serendipitous ratings. Different thresholds are considered in this case:
   - Variation 1: serendipityThreshold >= 2
   - Variation 2: serendipityThreshold >= 3
   - Variation 3: serendipityThreshold >= 4
   - Variation 4: serendipityThreshold >= 5
   - Variation 5: serendipityThreshold >= 9

The proposed algorithm is applied on a Movielens dataset called ML-Latest-Small [22]. The total number of users is 609 and their ratings count is around 100k. The language used to code the algorithm is Python. The base algorithm for recommending top-N lists for every user in the test set is the SVD (Singular Value decomposition), where the split ratio of train/test is set to 0.8.

C. Results and discussions

Table IV summarizes the MAE, RMSE and top-N adjusted outputs for all the scenarios of the algorithm testing. As previously argued, the traditional metrics such as MAE and RMSE only account for the accuracy of the recommended items without taking into account the quality of the recommendations or their relevance to the user. MAE and RMSE fail to measure the nature of a top-N recommended list, so in our study which is mainly focused on trying to increase serendipity by treating the data in a dataset, we execute the top-N adjusted metric (see Equation 1). After testing the first module of the algorithm (removing noise only), we notice that there are some variations in the top-N adjusted results, but nothing significant (note that the higher the average of top-N adjusted, the better is the quality of the recommended items); however, there is significant variation in the values of MAE and RMSE, especially in (v.1) which is expected since the noise in the dataset is being completely eliminated. On the other hand, the top-N adjusted metric results start to increase after we introduce the serendipity module to reach a maximum of 4.4904 with around 9.7k noisy ratings eliminated from the set, while keeping a very considerable MAE and RMSE values of 0.6102 and 0.8087 respectively. In the case of (v.1) the algorithm showed an 11% and a 9.7% decrease in MAE and RMSE respectively, and a 5.8% increase in top-N adjusted from the raw dataset (first variation), while in the case of (v.5), the algorithm resulted in a 9.4% and a 7.9% decrease in MAE and RMSE respectively, and an **8.5%** increase in top-N adjusted. Figure 3 shows the plot of the metrics under the tested dataset variations. These results prove that the algorithm was able to discern between noisy ratings and ratings that might be of tremendous importance to the users profile in terms of serendipity, while keeping very acceptable values of MAE and RMSE. Serendipity and accuracy are completely different in their form where increasing the one results in the decrease of the other, and this is where our algorithm succeeds, by keeping the highest values possible of both metrics, with a slight edge in top-N adjusted since we want to achieve the true aim of recommender systems.

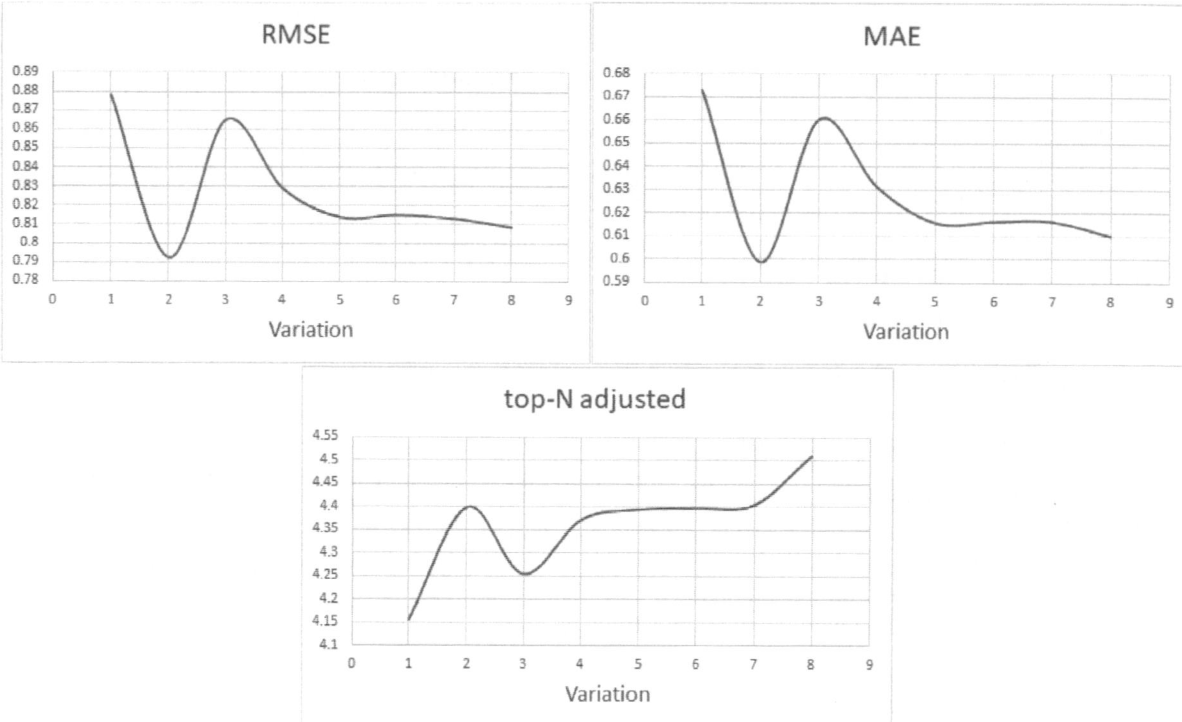

Fig. 3. Algorithm performance against MAE, RMSE and top-N adjusted. Variations 1-8 represent the scenarios in Table IV

V. Conclusion

The world faces the problem of information overload due to the huge amounts of data at the user's disposal. In many cases, the data is served to the user without being properly filtered. To overcome this issue, recommender systems aim at giving the users what is relevant and useful in hope of gaining their trust, however, this trust is endangered by the presence of noise in most datasets. This noise can be due to attacks or a result of natural noise that the user unintentionally makes. Noise detection algorithms free the systems from noise without taking into consideration that natural noise and serendipity overlap in their definition, and as a result, disregard the importance of serendipity. In general, recommender systems target accuracy, and this naturally leads to the over-personalization of the data being recommended. On the other hand, serendipity introduces the happy surprise i.e. the unexpected relevance and is often overlooked in the recommender system implementations. Our proposed algorithm removes noise yet allows serendipity to exist in the system, and the new top-N adjusted metric measures the effectiveness of the algorithm's output. The results proved that the performance was radically enhanced. This work can be further developed by conducting online A/B tests with real subjects. Moreover, the noise in the dataset can be treated instead of it being completely removed from the training set.

References

[1] P. Melinat, T. Kreuzkam, and D. Stamer, "Information Overload: A Systematic Literature Review" in Perspectives in Business Informatics Research, vol. 194, B. Johansson, B. Andersson, and N. Holmberg, Eds. Cham: Springer International Publishing, 2014, pp. 72-86.

[2] S. Luo, "Introduction to Recommender Systems, Approaches of Collaborative Filtering: Nearest Neighborhood and Matrix Factorization", towardsdatascience, 2018

[3] M. Aljukhadar, S. Senecal, and C.-E. Daoust, "Information Overload and Usage of Recommendations" vol. 612, p. 8, 2010.

[4] G. Ihsan, K. Cihan, B. Alper, P. Huseyin, "Shilling attacks against recommender systems: A comprehensive survey", Artificial Intelligence Review, 2013, 42. 10.1007/s10462-012-9364-9.

[5] D. Kotkov, "Serendipity in Recommender Systems", University of JyvÃďskylÃď, JyvÃďskylÃď Studies in Computing 281, 2018

[6] M. Badran, J. Abdo, W. Jurdi, and J. Demerjian, "Adaptive Serendipity for Recommender Systems: Let It Find You" in Proceedings of the 11th International Conference on Agents and Artificial Intelligence, Prague, Czech Republic, 2019, pp. 739-745.

[7] J. Castro, R. Yera, and L. Martinez, "An empirical study of natural noise management in group recommendation systems" Decision Support Systems, vol. 94, pp. 1-11, Feb. 2017.

[8] X. Amatriain, J. M. Pujol, and N. Oliver, "I Like It... I Like It Not: Evaluating User Ratings Noise in Recommender Systems" in User Modeling, Adaptation, and Personalization, vol. 5535, G.-J. Houben, G. McCalla, F. Pianesi, and M. Zancanaro, Eds. Berlin, Heidelberg: Springer Berlin Heidelberg, 2009, pp. 247-258.

[9] L. Iaquinta, M. de Gemmis, P. Lops, G. Semeraro, M. Filannino, and P. Molino, "Introducing Serendipity in a Content-Based Recommender System" in 2008 Eighth International Conference on Hybrid Intelligent Systems, Barcelona, Spain, 2008, pp. 168-173.

[10] H. Yamaba, M. Tanoue, K. Takatsuka, N. Okazaki, and S. Tomita, "On a Serendipity-oriented Recommender System

based on Folksonomy and its Evaluation" Procedia Computer Science, vol. 22, pp. 276-284, 2013.

[11] M. P. O'Mahony, N. J. Hurley, and G. C. M. Silvestre, "Detecting noise in recommender system databases" in Proceedings of the 11th international conference on Intelligent user interfaces - IUI '06, Sydney, Australia, 2006, p. 109.

[12] X. Amatriain, J. M. Pujol, N. Tintarev, and N. Oliver, "Rate it again: increasing recommendation accuracy by user re-rating" in Proceedings of the third ACM conference on Recommender systems - RecSys '09, New York, New York, USA, 2009, p. 173.

[13] R. Y. Toledo, Y. C. Mota, and L. Martinez, "Correcting noisy ratings in collaborative recommender systems" Knowledge-Based Systems, vol. 76, pp. 96-108, Mar. 2015.

[14] T. Sun, M. Zhang, and Q. Mei, "Unexpected Relevance: An Empirical Study of Serendipity in Retweets" p. 10.

[15] D. Kotkov, S. Wang, and J. Veijalainen, "A survey of serendipity in recommender systems" Knowledge-Based Systems, vol. 111, pp. 180-192, Nov. 2016.

[16] P. Adamopoulos and A. Tuzhilin, "On Unexpectedness in Recommender Systems: Or How to Better Expect the Unexpected" p. 50.

[17] Y. C. Zhang, D. O. Seaghdha, D. Quercia, and T. Jambor, "Auralist: introducing serendipity into music recommendation" in Proceedings of the fifth ACM international conference on Web search and data mining - WSDM '12, Seattle, Washington, USA, 2012, p. 13.

[18] M. Jenders, T. Lindhauer, G. Kasneci, R. Krestel, and F. Naumann, "A Serendipity Model for News Recommendation" in KI 2015: Advances in Artificial Intelligence, vol. 9324, S. Holldobler, R. Penaloza, and S. Rudolph, Eds. Cham: Springer International Publishing, 2015, pp. 111-123.

[19] N. Kawamae," Serendipitous recommendations via innovators", Proceedings of the 33rd International ACM Conference on Research and Development in Information Retrieval, ACM, New York, NY, USA, 2010, pp. 218-225 .

[20] K. Onuma, H. Tong , C. Faloutsos, "Tangent: a novel 'surprise me', recommendation algorithm", Proceedings of the 15th ACM International Conference on Knowledge Discovery and Data Mining, ACM, New York, NY, USA, 2009, pp. 657-666.

[21] M. de Gemmis, P. Lops, G. Semeraro, and C. Musto, "An investigation on the serendipity problem in recommender systems" Information Processing and Management, vol. 51, no. 5, pp. 695-717, Sep. 2015.

[22] F. Maxwell Harper, Joseph A. Konstan. 2015. The MovieLens Datasets: History and Context. ACM Transactions on Interactive Intelligent Systems (TiiS) 5, 4: 19:1âĂŞ19:19. https://doi.org/10.1145/2827872

Identifying Potential Mismatches Prior to Products Being Packed in Retail Industry Using Convolutional Networks

Gurpreet Singh Bawa/ Analytics Sr. Manager
Accenture Digital
Accenture Solutions Pvt. Ltd.
India
gurpreet.singh.bawa@accenture.com

Sanjay Sharma/ Managing Director
Accenture Digital
Accenture Solutions Pvt. Ltd.
India
sanjay.s.sharma@accenture.com

Kaustav Pakira/ Analytics Consultant
Accenture Digital
Accenture Solutions Pvt. Ltd.
India
kaustav.pakira@accenture.com

Tejas Wagh/ Data Science Analyst
Accenture Digital
Accenture Solutions Pvt. Ltd.
India
tejas.wagh@accenture.com

Abstract — **Artificial Intelligence is rapidly making its presence felt in the retail domain. From customer experience to product recommendation, businesses are using AI and deep learning applications to address business problems wherever possible. One such domain which is having extensive research done on is computer vision, specifically object detection. The primary idea of object detection is to find instances of real-world entities from images or video feeds using learning algorithms trained on extracted features from training data comprising of a wide range of objects. The objective behind our approach is to use this idea of object detection and recognition to identify the final purchased entities prior to being packed and tallying them with the recorded transaction in POS. The idea is to track or identify potential mismatches that might happen due to human fallacy and raise a flag in case of any such instances where items in the final bill/cheque (or record in POS) does not match with the objects put in the bag/tray.**

Convolutional Neural Network; Deep Learning; Image Recognition; Retail Monitoring

I. Introduction

Given a dataset consisting of numerous images with their correct labels, our proposition is a semi-supervised approach built on a couple of steps with the aim of predicting boxes that bind the objects in the test images. These classified entities in the bounding boxes are then compared to the POS records and any potential mismatch raises an alarm.

The first step is primarily a straightforward Fully Convolutional Network (FCN) (1) which is competent in categorizing occurrences of objects in the image. The characteristic feature of FCN is utilized where a mask for images bigger than those in training data is returned, thus enabling to obtain a principal output segmentation mask while testing by providing a transitory pyramid of image over it. The convolutional networks involved are influential graphic models yielding the feature ordering or pyramid. These networks become one of the best in the domain in semantic segmentation, when a complete end-to-end training on the complete pixels is done. The key objective of the first algorithm to construct these FCNs which takes inputs of any random length but comes up with output of corresponding size with efficiency in learning and inference.

Once the mask from the FCN output is established, further enhancement is achieved by construction of boxes that bind the output. This is obtained using a convolutional encoder decoder, our second step. This apparatus of the second step primarily contains an encoder network, a decoder network that corresponds to the encoder network and a layer which performs a pixel wise categorization. The topology of the encoder network architecture is relatively similar to the convolutional layers in a network such as the VGG16 (2). It is much smaller and can be trained with ease. On the other hand, the objective of the decoder network is charting the feature maps from the encoder (having a low resolution) to feature maps having complete resolution for making the pixel-wise categorization. The uniqueness lies is in the way in which up-sampling of its input feature maps of lower resolution is done by the decoder. Precisely, the decoder utilizes the pooling index calculated in the max-pooling stage of the relevant encoder with the aim to do the up-sampling which is non-linear in nature. This dismisses the requirement of having to 'learn' up-sampling. Summarizing, this encoder-decoder is capable of localizing entities basis a synthesized dataset consisting of output segmentation masks.

Herein lies the efficacy of this technique utilized to localize entities in the tray/bag where interpreting data for detection of objects is difficult, primarily because of the presence of multiple entities on the testing instance.

II. BUSINESS PROBLEM

Audit in retail or monitoring sections of the store using visual information is a growing field where methods involving computer vision can be utilized to create a process which is primarily automated with the aim to recognize, localize, track to further analyze the products on POS counters during check-out. This paper deals with the task of entity localization on retail counters, i.e. a certain type of object detection where the information obtained from the process if further compared against the POS data, can identify any potential mismatches between the POS records and the actual check-out tray. The task at hand is dealt using a weak supervised algorithm for detecting objects and using the prediction to compare against POS records.

Annotating the boxes that bound the objects manually across image instances - having many occurrences per image and simultaneously multiple object classes consumes a lot of time and is extremely costly as well. The annotation of the boxes which bounds the retail products in images is often infeasible because of the huge number/variety of retail products present, recurrent differences in methods of package, presence of newer items (a very high count of categories and dynamic in terms of how it looks) and the high proximity with which the items are placed in the tray (small tray size and multiple instances). Hence, this trouble of obtaining datasets with correct annotation in a way constricts the utilization of completely supervised approaches on these datasets.

Performing tasks dealing with detecting objects on these datasets requires an approach that will be using just instances of objects and at the same time is capable of recognizing the instances and localizing them as well. This paper attempts to do this task. The involved algorithm is our approach is categorized into a weak supervised technique for detecting objects since there are a few occurrences which are offered as opposed to some completely supervised method that functions on plurality of image files having objects with tags as well as boxes for bounding.

The objective is to localize objects with the help of the same network that has been trained for classifying instances of objects. A Fully Convolutional Network is used as a classifier. Each of the layers that can learn in the FCN contain convolutions. Any completely connected or dense layer is absent in the network. This property enables us in passing to the network an input instance having higher resolution and in turn obtain an equivalent output mask. Another voluntary network can be utilized to augment the FCN outputs for the task of detecting objects. A convolutional network constructed on the foundation of encoder-decoder has been used for this network. Training has been done on a synthetic dataset constructed using the instances of the objects. Ultimately, the encoder-decoder output is transformed to get the boxes that does the bounding for the task of detecting objects.

III. WEAKLY SUPERVISED APPROACH AND ARTIFICIALLY GENERATED INSTANCES

In the setting of a weak supervised learning, there is no presence of the traditional labelled training instances, instead the labelled instances exist in some different form which is beneficial. Weak supervision learning is a method where the approach is characterized by a supervision which is not direct, exact or incomplete. Weakly supervised learning is also called semi-supervised learning. Historically, previous research has been done in the domain of semi-supervised localization on popular datasets like PASCAL VOC (3). These semi-supervised techniques are generally Multiple Instance Learning (MIL) based, where instead of receiving individual labelled instances, the learner is given a set of annotated bags, each of which contains multiple instances. They can also have end-to-end CNN based architecture, which is similar to our approach. The pictorial clarification approach using deep networks via gradient based localization can also be used to do this weakly supervised object localization task but conversion of the annotation maps for creating the bounds around entities fail when plurality of small objects is kept in unison on the tray.

Conceptually, the FCN element of our approach is conceptually similar to a setting where a classifier that has been trained on instances is used for detecting objects as well. The proposed approach is relatively less complicated and constructs the boxes for bounding correctly. A slight level of dissimilarity exists between the algorithms in terms of the data on which training/testing has been done. In our case, training has been done on single annotation images of retail entities. Other algorithms are mostly trained using multi-annotation datasets such as PASCAL VOC.

The discretionary module in our approach that handles refinement is learned on an artificially generated dataset. Creation of the artificial dataset can be done in many ways. One erudite method is to keep the entities in its settings to develop an existing dataset or construct a fresh one. On the other hand, our approach places the entities on blank trays with some rational parameters for arbitrariness. The uniqueness of our method lies in the fact that the discretionary module for refinement is not directly learned on synthetic images from the artificially generated dataset, but somewhat on the output after crossing through the FCN. Additionally, the artificially generated dataset is used with the aim of improving the performance of the localization task and in a way help to minimize Type I error.

IV. Process Components

1) FULLY CONVOLUTIONAL NETWORK

a) Training:

In the course of the learning exercise, our approach attempts to classify entity instances. The FCN architecture can be described as:

- Layers of VGG11 from torchvision1 that has been trained earlier. From them, eliminate every fully convolutional layer.
- Next, a single convolutional layer is added in the end with suitable kernel dimension with the aim to obtain a Kx1x1 output, where K is the count of categories, a visualization of which is given in Fig 2.

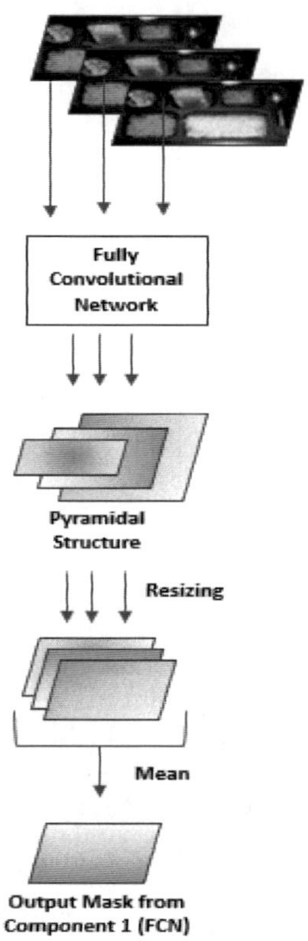

Fig 1: Entity Identification Process Flow

b) Testing:

A prime plus-point of our technique is that the fully convolutional networks do not depend on the input dimensions. A reasonable assumption is taken that the entity instances (images in train set) are relatively small in terms of dimensions in comparison to the test instances (images having plurality of entities). Thus, the fully convolutional network which had been constructed with the objective of classifying (1x1 dimensional output) will produce an equivalent output mask when an input having higher resolution is used.

During the testing phase, a pyramid of images is passed to the same network having different economized versions of the images. A factor of approximately 1.5 is used to scale down for generating the pyramid. The corresponding output masks from every level of the pyramidal structure are then resized to the actual image dimension. Next, the average of the output masks from the pyramid is taken as the final output mask as shown in Fig 1.

It is very much likely that the dataset will not be capturing the different dimensions of the entities since the network learns on discrete entity instances. This factor would have had a negative effect while testing but it is tackled appropriately using the pyramidal structure of images used while testing. The rationale behind this being that the network hence becomes capable of capturing the entity at least in one of its down-sampled level.

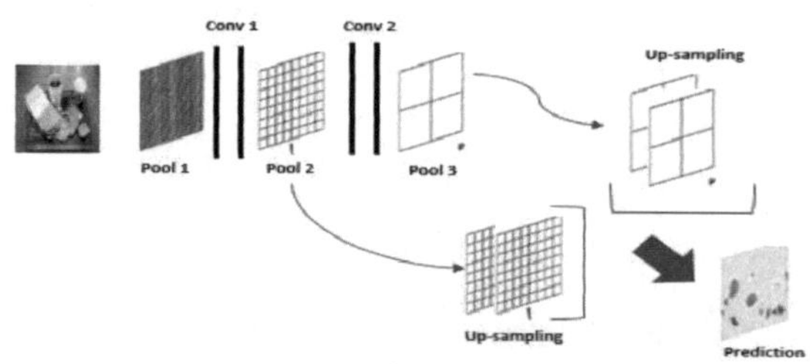

Fig 2: Fully convolutional network process

2) DISCRETIONARY REFINEMENT UNIT

This basic objective of the discretionary refinement unit is to refine the outputs obtained from the Fully Convolutional Network in the course of the task of entity detection. Though output maps from component 1 apprehends the entities, their primary emphasis is on areas having higher discriminatory power since the learning for them was done keeping classification in mind. This characteristic helps them in localizing the key discriminative features of the entities, but there is no guarantee on producing the boxes which bound and surround them. Consequently, this may produce lower Intersection over Union (IoU) scores. These networks additionally might throw Type I errors on background (because of the dearth of background training instances). Hence the Discretionary Refinement Unit (DRU) used to tackle both drawbacks. The convolutional network receives the learning for improvement on the output maps produced by component 1. It must be kept in mind that this unit is discretionary, and it does not add much value if in case component 1 or the FCN performs well alone.

a) Artificially synthesized dataset:

This task involves creation of a synthesized dataset with the help of the entity instances in the training dataset. A few images (ranging between 30-40) are selected randomly from Google with the keyword 'tray'. We place entities randomly on these empty trays in the form of a planogram having plurality of columns (for each image) and plurality of rows (across images). Scaling is also done for the entity dimensions in a random manner with factors between 0.5-1.1. As a baseline model, a black monochromatic background was also used instead of the tray images. However, a slight increment in the mean Average Precision (mAP) value while using the tray images.

b) Architecture:

The architecture for the Discretionary Refinement Units (DRU) can be conceptualized as a convolutional encoder-decoder network. This setup has a standard encoder-decoder set up with some convolution layers some layers to down-sample followed by a corresponding count of layers for deconvolution and up-sampling. Each of the conv2D and deconv2D layers have 3x3 kernel dimensions. Only the concluding deconvolution layer which has 1x1 dimension is an exception. Each of the maxpool2D layers have kernel dimensions 2x2 while all the up-sampling layers are pairwise linear and homogenous in a linear fashion having factor 2.

c) DRU Network:

While learning, the images from the synthesized dataset are processed through the Fully Convolutional Network producing the segmentation prediction. This output prediction mask from the FCN acts as the input to the convolutional encoder-decoder or the DRU network. The DRU is trained using CrossEntropyLoss and information from the synthesized dataset.

While testing, the prediction from component 1 is passed through the DRU with the aim of enhancing and easing the localizing process. The predicted segmentation mask from the DRU then gets treated to extract the boxes for bounding. First binarization of the mask is done using application of an optimum threshold value. Finally, the coordinates for the box to be used for bounding is extracted from the connected elements of the mask that had undergone binarization. The DRU architecture is shown in Figure 3.

3) MISMATCH DETECTION UNIT

Once the images have been passed through the component 1 and 2, the process predicts the entities present in the image. These output key-value pairs are the predicted objects present in the frame and the count of the same. These key-value pairs are then passed over to the Mismatch Detection Unit (MDU) which compares the predictions to the logged POS data and identifies any potential mismatch for the same prior to the items getting packed. The attached probability scores also help in categorizing the level of alarm for the mismatch – scores above 0.85 raising a serious flag.

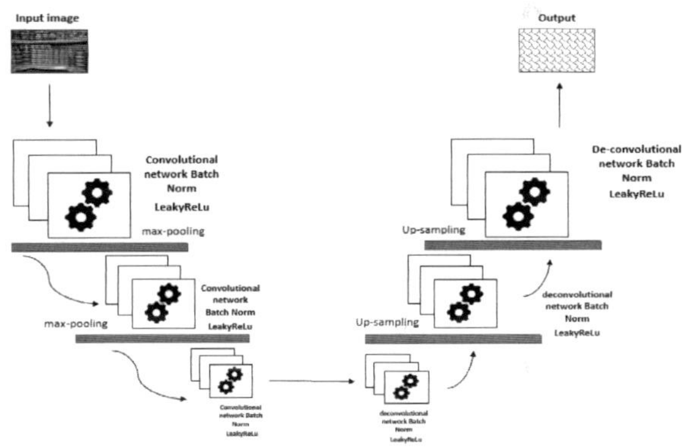

Figure 3: DRU Architecture

V. Experimental Analysis

To test the efficacy of our approach, we apply this technique on a collated dataset we created combining the MS-COCO (4) dataset with the Grocery Dataset (5). The MS-COCO dataset contains over 80 object categories and 91 stuff categories. The Grocery Dataset specifically focuses on retail items such as fruits, vegetables, cartons, edibles etc. Our objective also was to check the efficiency of the approach in identifying entities which look very similar and are kept in close proximity – whether it detects it as separate or individually.

1) Dataset Characteristics

The Grocery Dataset contains roughly 8300 training instances spanned over ~ 80 semantic object classes. These images are captured under ideal lighting and other settings. The test set consists of ~ 700 real tray images captured in various retail outlets. However, the annotations on the testing dataset consists of a collection of individual entities instead of providing the bounding boxes for each of the instances after the task of entity identification. Luckily, Tonioni and Di Stefano had performed the bounding annotations for the boxes for a small sample of 74 images belonging to the test dataset.

2) Implementation

Approaches and methods performed earlier focused mostly on recognizing the entities from the dataset, but it did not have the additional characteristics of detection and localization that our approach does. Earlier methods consisted of these high-level steps: Multi-category rank-ordering, quick-dense pixel comparison and a multi-class image classification with a modified genetic algorithm as foundation. Also, we use a sliding frame of varying scale values, aspect ratio values on the test instance and categorize the sliding frame into different categories.

For component 1 or the fully convolutional layer, the last convolutional layer kernel dimensions are set to (7,5). The input instance is of constant dimensions obtained from the mean of the dataset. The fully convolutional network is trained using Stochastic Gradient Descent with momentum 0.85 and learning rate 0.001. The weight decay used equals 0.0005 with early stopping of 40 epochs. Techniques for data augmentation and pre-processing such as scaling, flipping, rotating etc. were performed using the Python package called "imgaug". The synthesized dataset was created by setting the image length and breadth as (2400,3600) and (1500,2500) in accordance to the count of rows of entities appearing in the image instance. For component 2 or the encoder-decoder DRU network, we used the filter count for the 3 convolutional and deconvolutional blocks as 15,25,30 respectively. Finally, the DRU is trained using Stochastic Gradient Descent with momentum 0.85 and learning rate 0001, weight decay of 0.005 and early stopping of 10 epochs.

3) Experimental results

Model	**Mean Avg Precision (iou=0.3)**
Discriminating search (with FCN)	-
Sliding frame (with FCN)	0.579
Pyramidal FCN without encoder decoder	0.66
Pyramidal FCN with convolutional encoder decoder	0.79

Table 1: Results from experiment

The mean Average Precision (mAP) of the iterations are provided in Table 1. The mAP is a measure whose calculation is done basis the mean of the Average Precision metric (AP) of all categories. The AP is calculated directly from the Visual Object Classes development kit present in, Python. The VOC-07 11-point method has been used. In terms of baseline, we used 3 scale values and 5 aspect ratio values for the sliding frames. The features for each spot are established with the help of the pyramidal fully convolutional network. However, the image pyramid approach does better in comparison to the baseline sliding frame approach. The outcomes improve on addition of the DRU network to the FCN. The difference in precision can be observed in Table 1.

4) Mismatch Detection

Once the predicted objects and their counts are obtained from the above, these key-value pairs are passed to the MDU which tallies the same with the POS records and raises alarm in case of a potential mismatch.

Figure 4: Object Localization

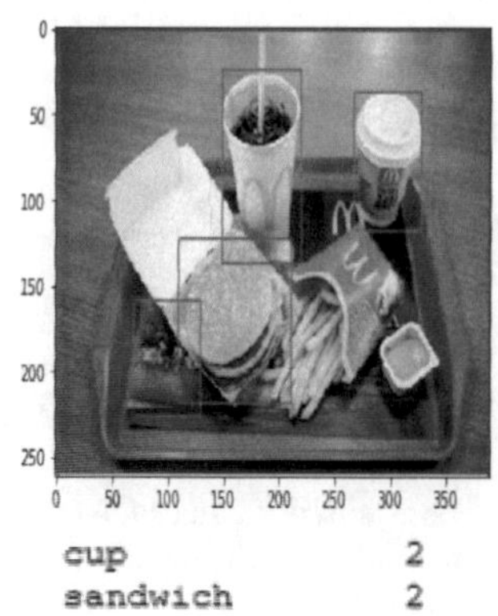

Figure 5: Identification of checkout tray

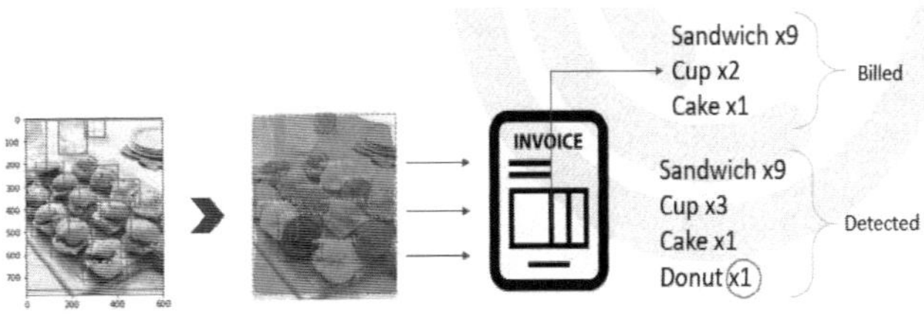

Figure 6: Mismatch identification

VI. CONCLUSIONS

In this paper, our proposition is a fresh and straightforward approach for localizing and identifying objects with the help of only the instances of the entities (classification annotations). A discretionary refinement unit has also been proposed to magnify the localization degree and reduce type I error as well. Numerically, a satisfactory outcome from the experiment on the database used vouches for the efficacy of the approach.

It must be noted that the IoU cutoff for calculation of the mAP is low (0.3). The reason behind this being - firstly, the weak supervised learning technique occasionally cannot fit the entire entity and secondly, sometimes it produces a fused bounding box in situations where boundary between similar entities is somewhat difficult to segregate. The second approach is somewhat specific to retail packing where similar entities are kept nearby. The DRU component is optional simply because it helps in improving the degree of localization task.

As next steps, focus can be given on obtaining improvement on the approach's efficacy based on greater threshold values. Additional robustness can be achieved by using training instances where the images are taken from various angles, orientations and views.

CONTACT

Gurpreet Bawa
Accenture Solutions Pvt. Ltd
E-mail: gurpreet.singh.bawa@accenture.com

Kaustav Pakira
Accenture Solutions Pvt. Ltd.
E-mail: kaustav.pakira@accenture.com

Tejas Wagh
Accenture Solutions Pvt. Ltd.
E-mail: tejas.wagh @accenture.com

REFERENCES

(1) Long, J., Shelhamer, E., Darrell, T., Fully Convolutional Networks for Semantic Segmentation, 2014.
(2) Simonyan, K., Zisserman, A., Very deep convolutional networks for large-scale image recognition, 2015
(3) Everingham, M., Gool, L., Williams, C.K.I., Winn, J., Zisserman, A., The Pascal Visual Object Classes (VOC) Challenge, International Journal of Computer Vision, 2010, Volume 88, Number 2, Page 303
(4) Lin, T.Y et al., Microsoft COCO: Common Objects in Context, 2015
(5) Klasson, M., Zhang, C., Kjellström, H., A Hierarchical Grocery Store Image Dataset with Visual and Semantic Labels, 2019

Author Index

CSREA Press
ATTN: Hamid R. Arabnia
1060 Long Creek Drive
Watkinsville, GA 30677
USA

ISBN 978-1-7138-5244-5

Eastern Snow Conference 2019

Fairlee, Vermont, USA
4-6 June 2019

Eastern Snow Conference